The Way of the House Husband

KOUSUKE OONO

5

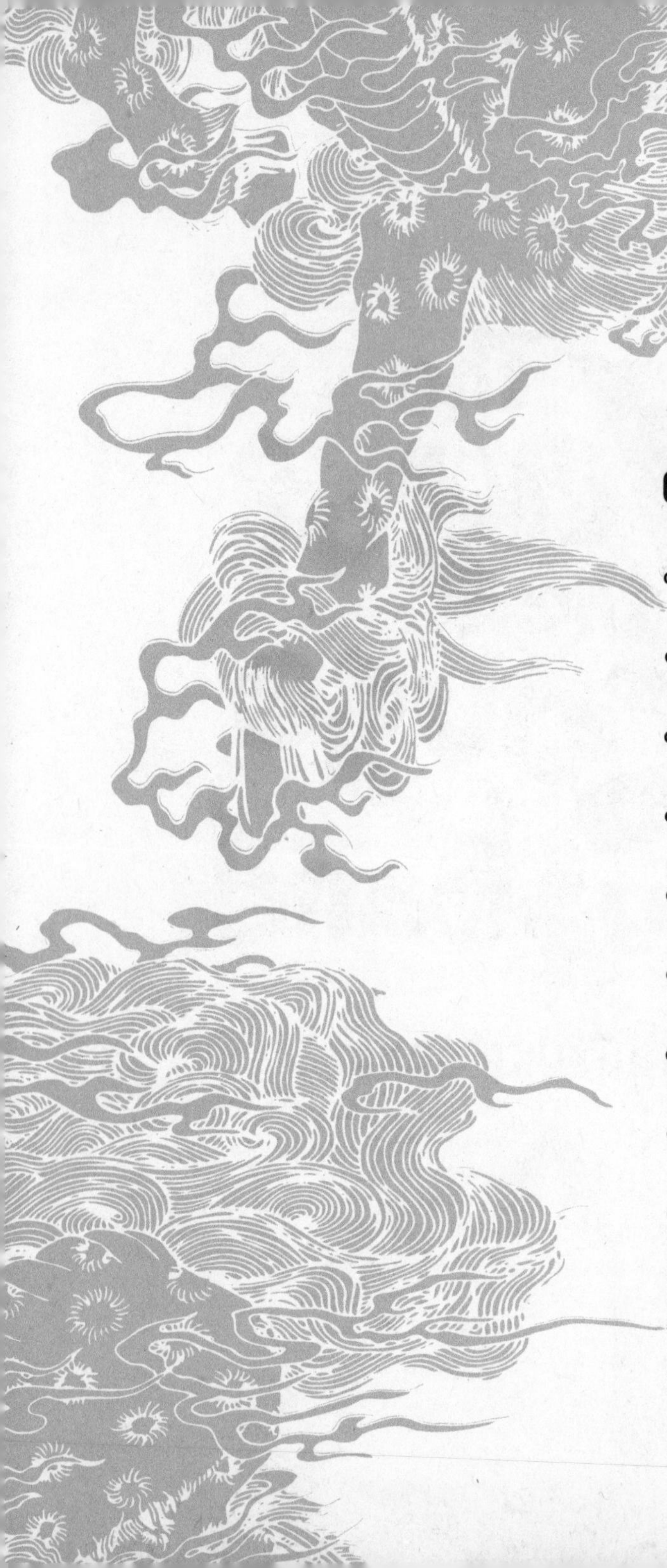

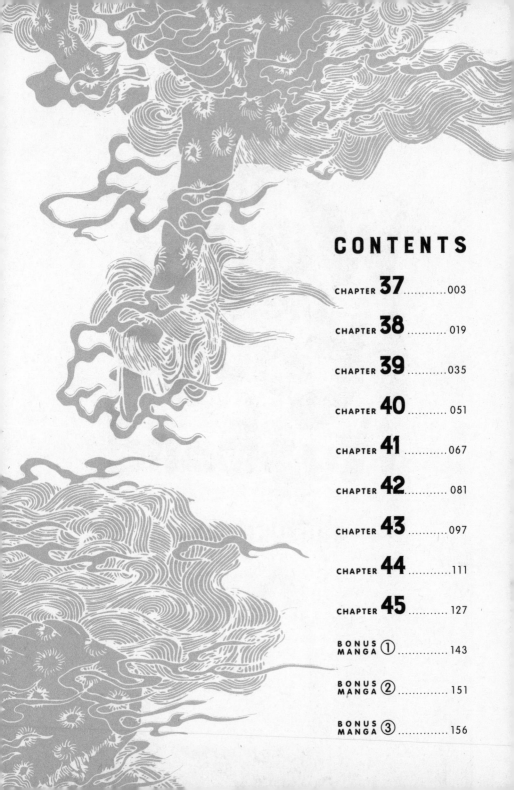

CONTENTS

CHAPTER 37

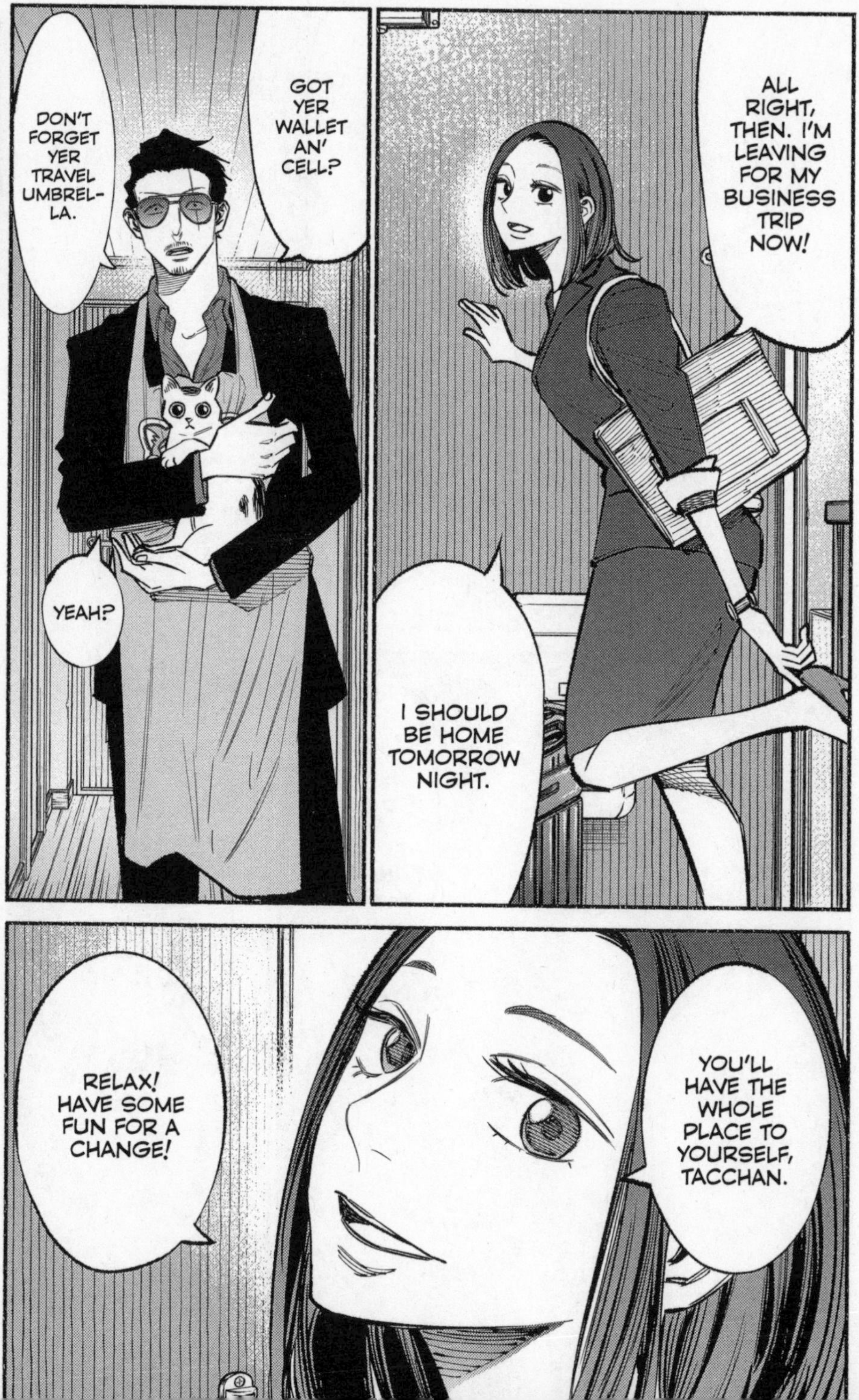
ALL RIGHT, THEN. I'M LEAVING FOR MY BUSINESS TRIP NOW!
I SHOULD BE HOME TOMORROW NIGHT.
GOT YER WALLET AN' CELL?
DON'T FORGET YER TRAVEL UMBREL-LA.
YEAH?
YOU'LL HAVE THE WHOLE PLACE TO YOURSELF, TACCHAN.
RELAX! HAVE SOME FUN FOR A CHANGE!

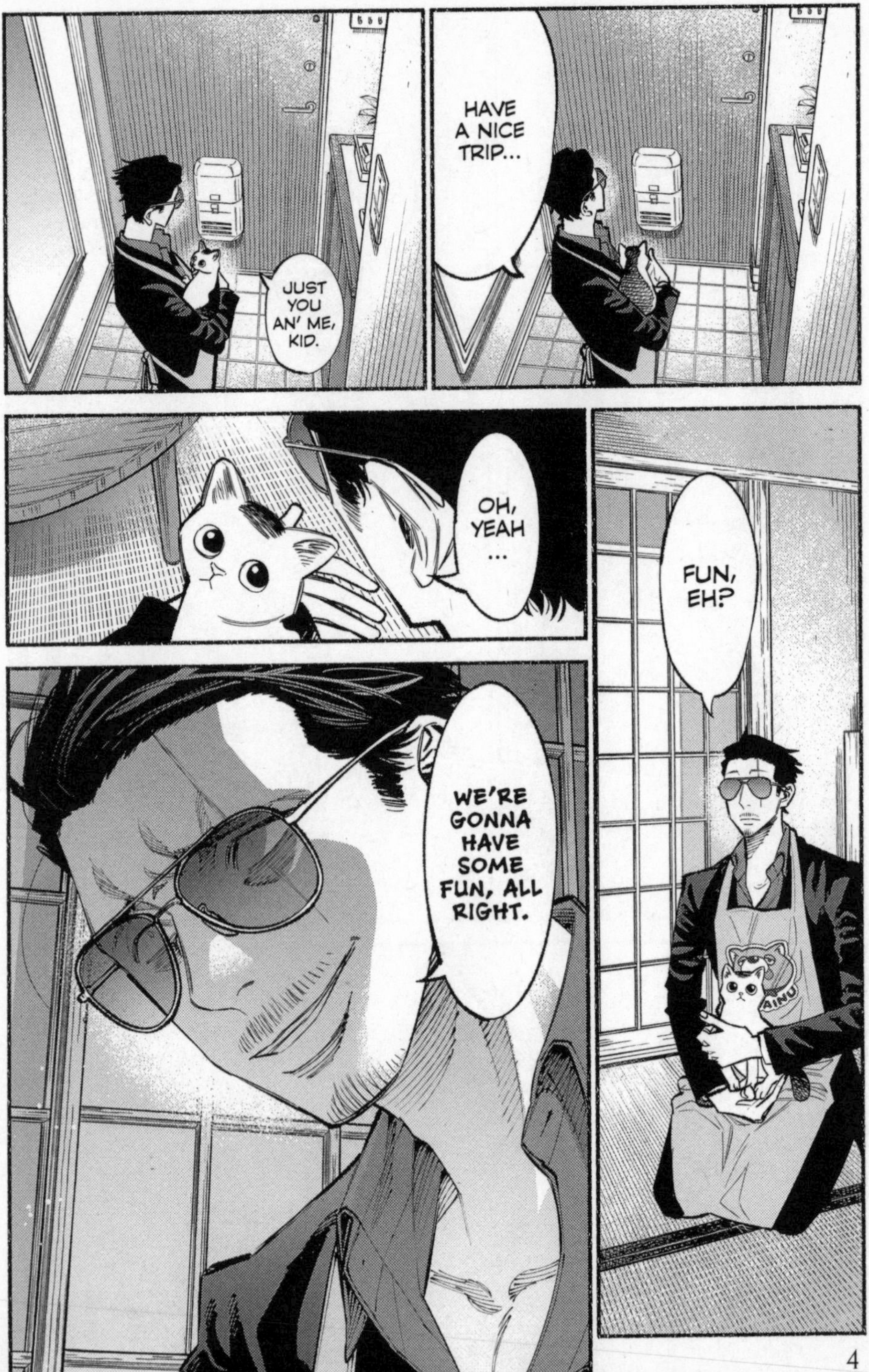
HAVE A NICE TRIP...
JUST YOU AN' ME, KID.
FUN, EH?
OH, YEAH ...
WE'RE GONNA HAVE SOME FUN, ALL RIGHT.

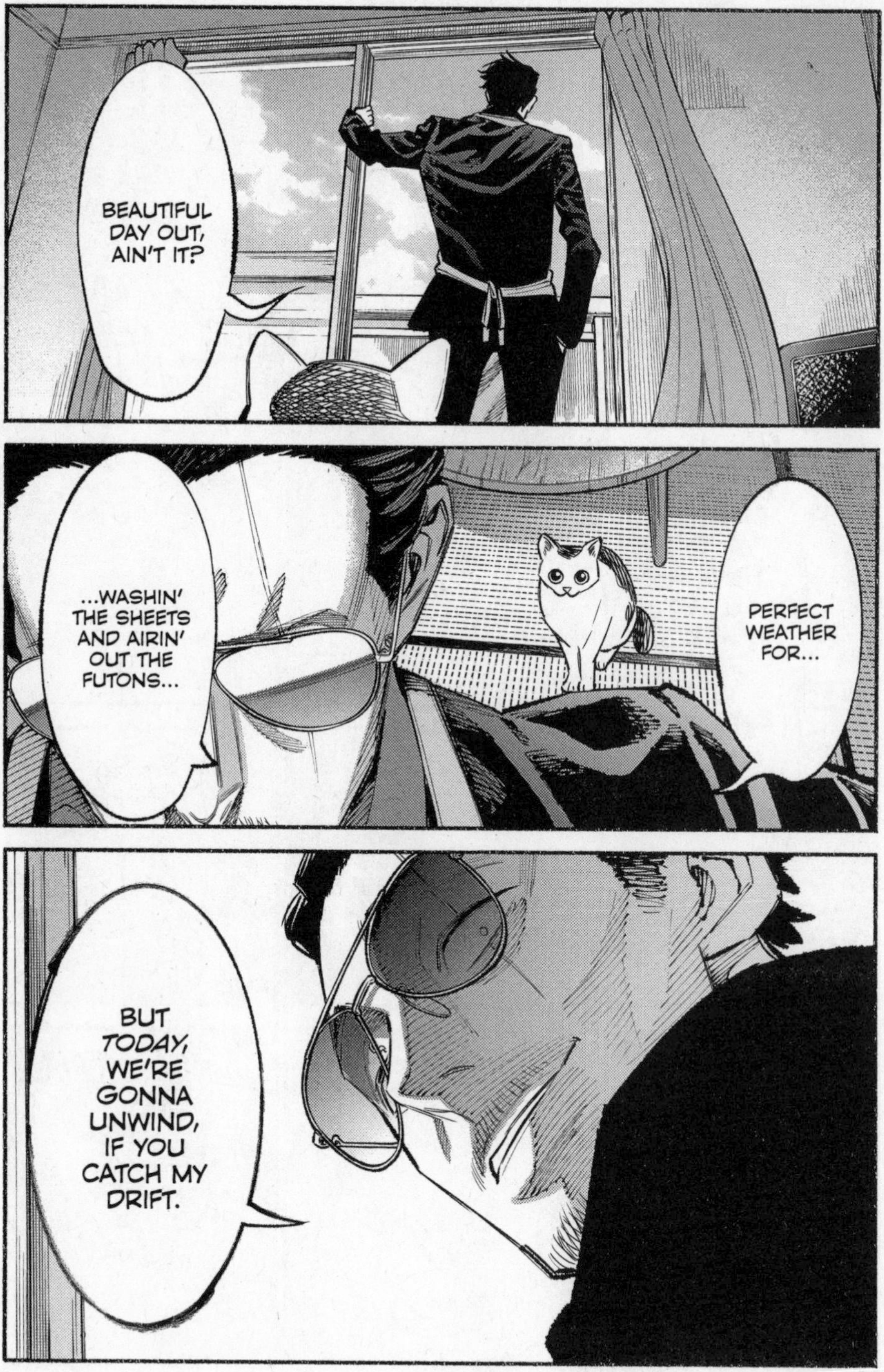
BEAUTIFUL DAY OUT, AIN'T IT?
PERFECT WEATHER FOR...
...WASHIN' THE SHEETS AND AIRIN' OUT THE FUTONS...
BUT *TODAY*, WE'RE GONNA UNWIND, IF YOU CATCH MY DRIFT.

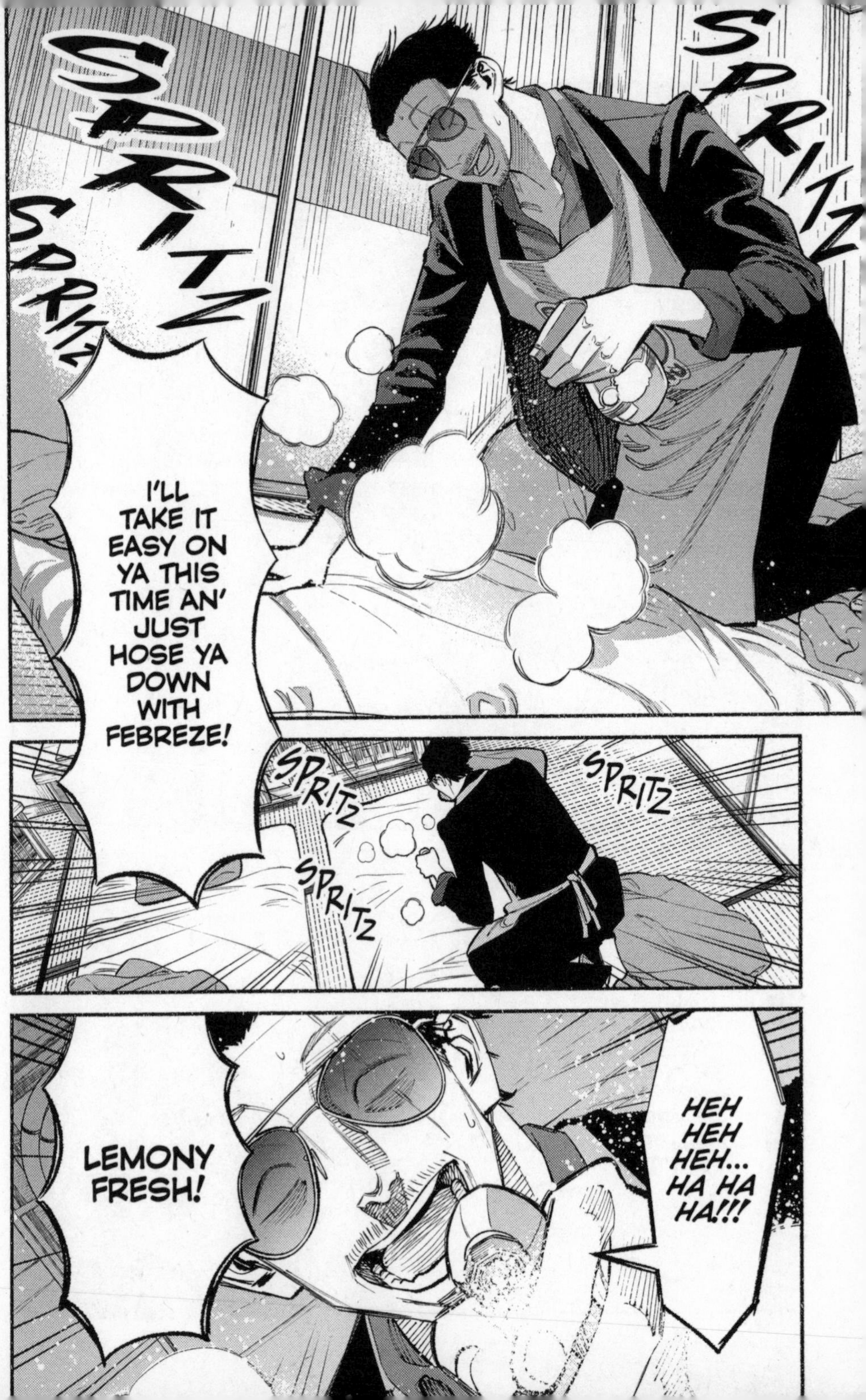
SPRITZ
SPRITZ
SPRITZ
I'LL TAKE IT EASY ON YA THIS TIME AN' JUST HOSE YA DOWN WITH FEBREZE!
SPRITZ
SPRITZ
SPRITZ
HEH HEH HEH... HA HA HA!!!
LEMONY FRESH!

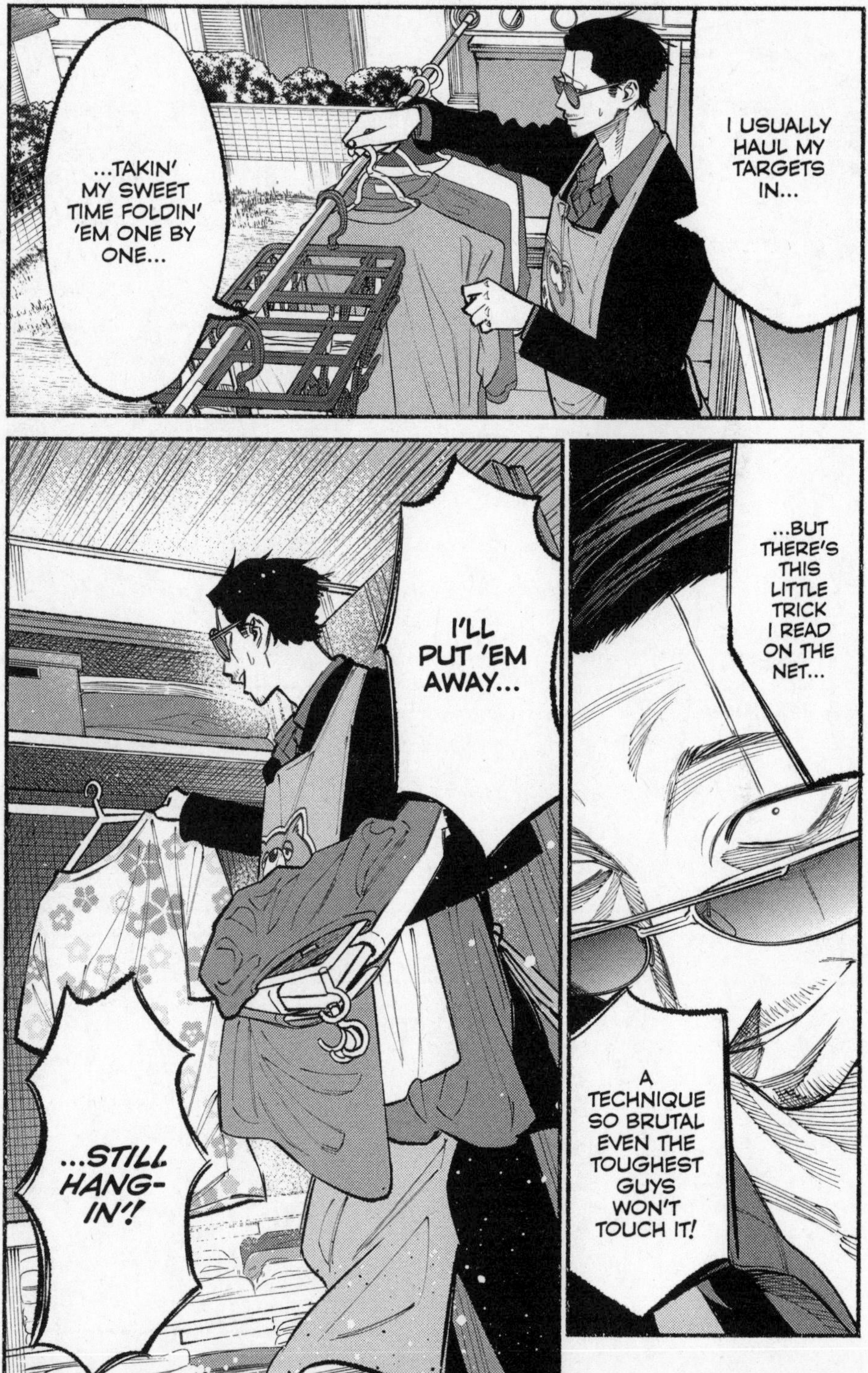
I USUALLY HAUL MY TARGETS IN...
...TAKIN' MY SWEET TIME FOLDIN' 'EM ONE BY ONE...
...BUT THERE'S THIS LITTLE TRICK I READ ON THE NET...
A TECHNIQUE SO BRUTAL EVEN THE TOUGHEST GUYS WON'T TOUCH IT!
I'LL PUT 'EM AWAY...
...STILL HANGIN'!

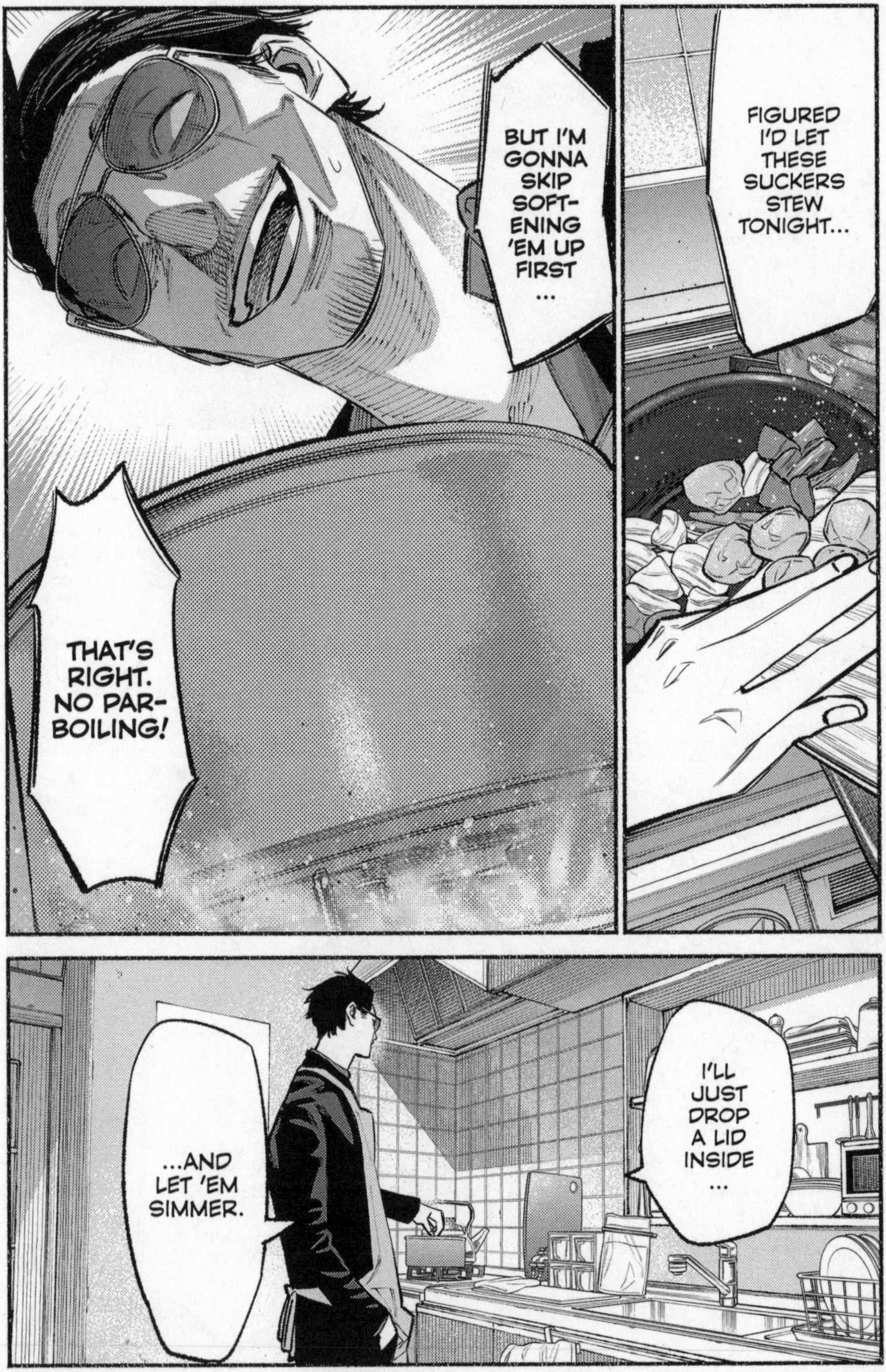
FIGURED I'D LET THESE SUCKERS STEW TONIGHT...
BUT I'M GONNA SKIP SOFT-ENING 'EM UP FIRST ...
THAT'S RIGHT. NO PAR-BOILING!
I'LL JUST DROP A LID INSIDE ...
...AND LET 'EM SIMMER.

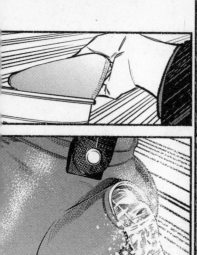

I'VE STAYED CLEAN, BUT I THINK I'LL DIP INTO MY SECRET STASH...

I'M A JUNKIE, ALL RIGHT...

A JUNKIE FOR LUNCHTIME INSTANT NOODLES ...

FWOO!

FWOO, FWOO!

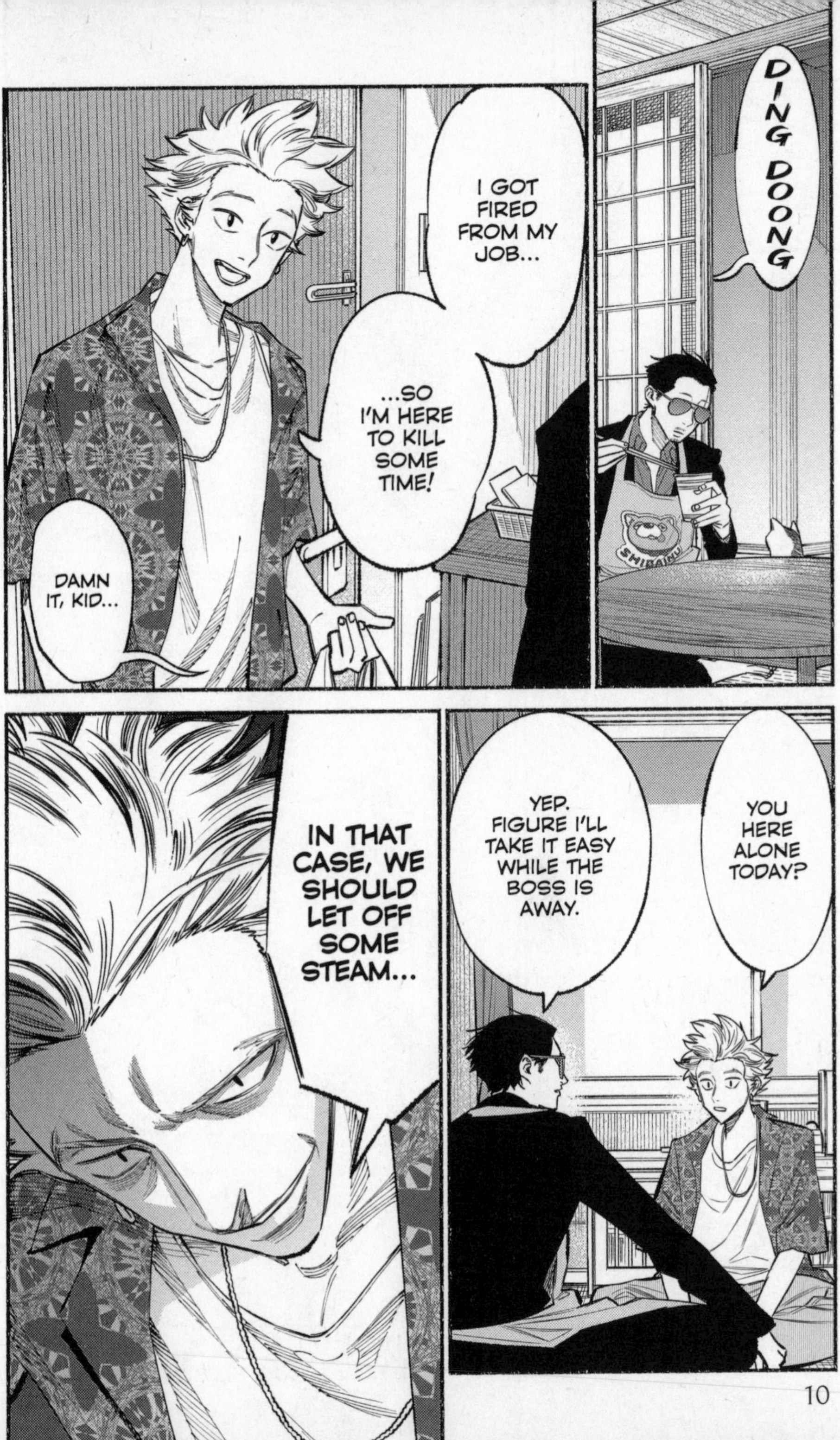
DING DOONG
I GOT FIRED FROM MY JOB...
...SO I'M HERE TO KILL SOME TIME!
DAMN IT, KID...
YOU HERE ALONE TODAY?
YEP. FIGURE I'LL TAKE IT EASY WHILE THE BOSS IS AWAY.
IN THAT CASE, WE SHOULD LET OFF SOME STEAM...

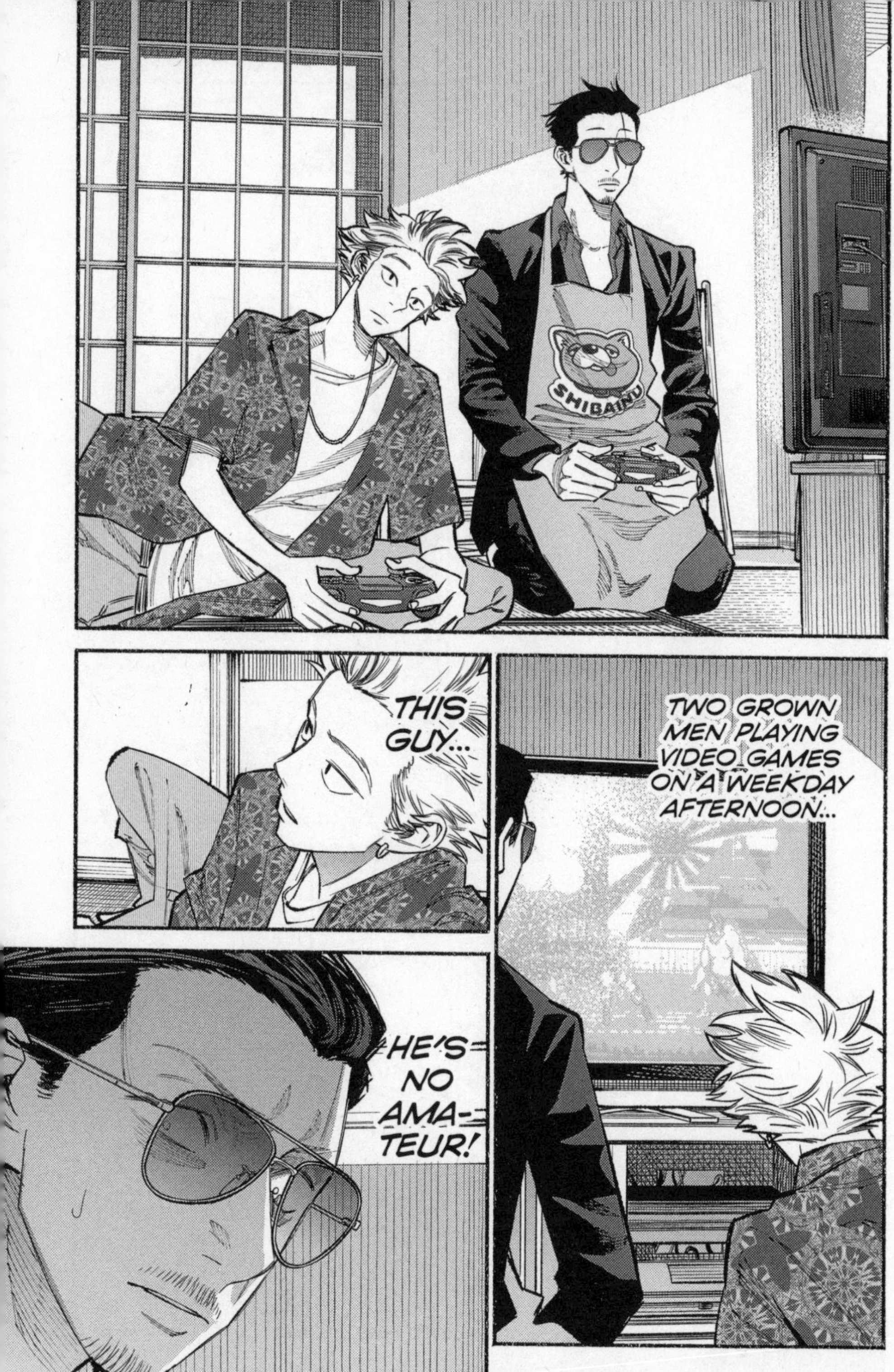
SHIBAINU
TWO GROWN MEN PLAYING VIDEO GAMES ON A WEEKDAY AFTERNOON...
THIS GUY...
HE'S NO AMA-TEUR!

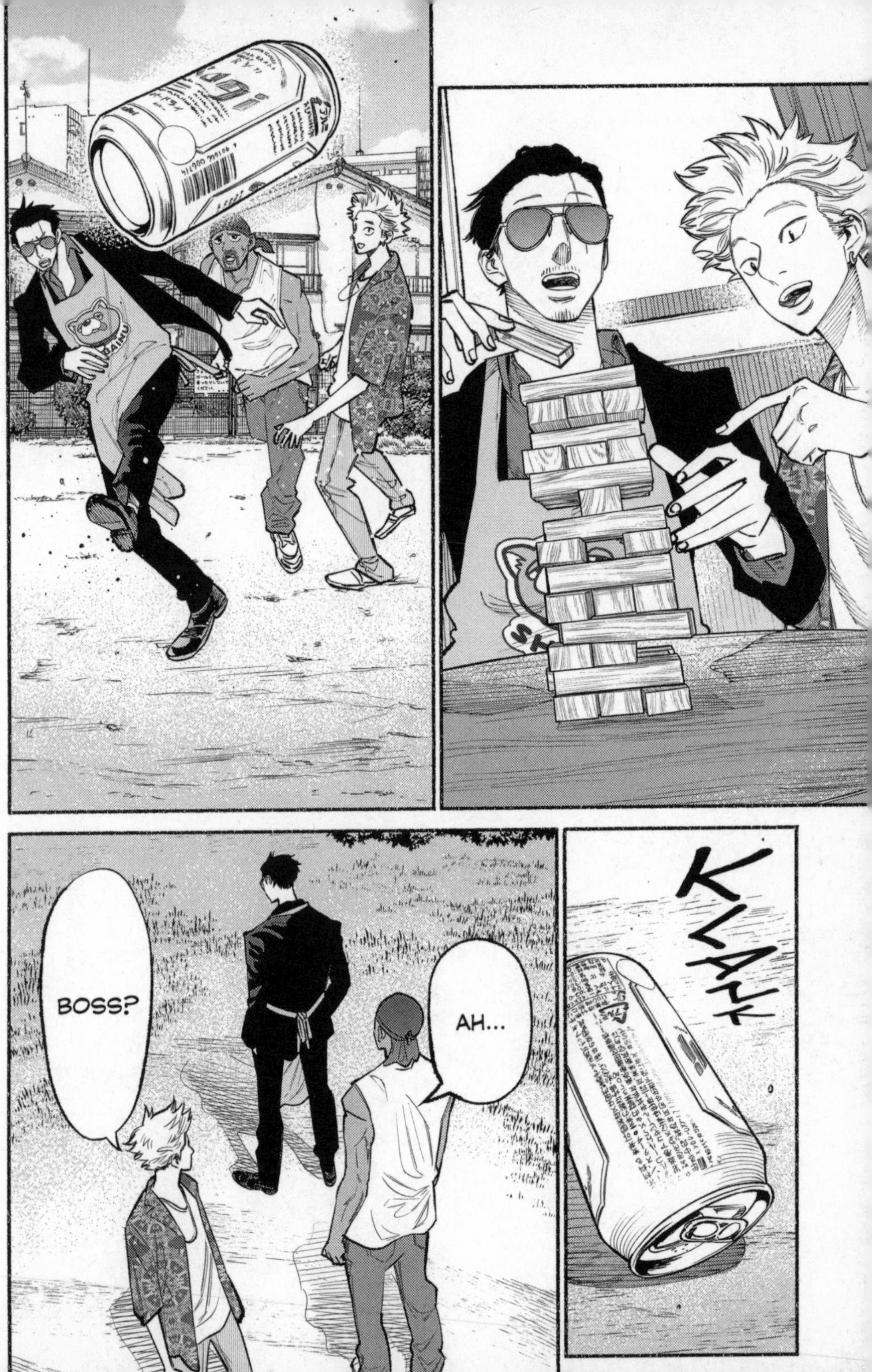
KLANK
AH...
BOSS?

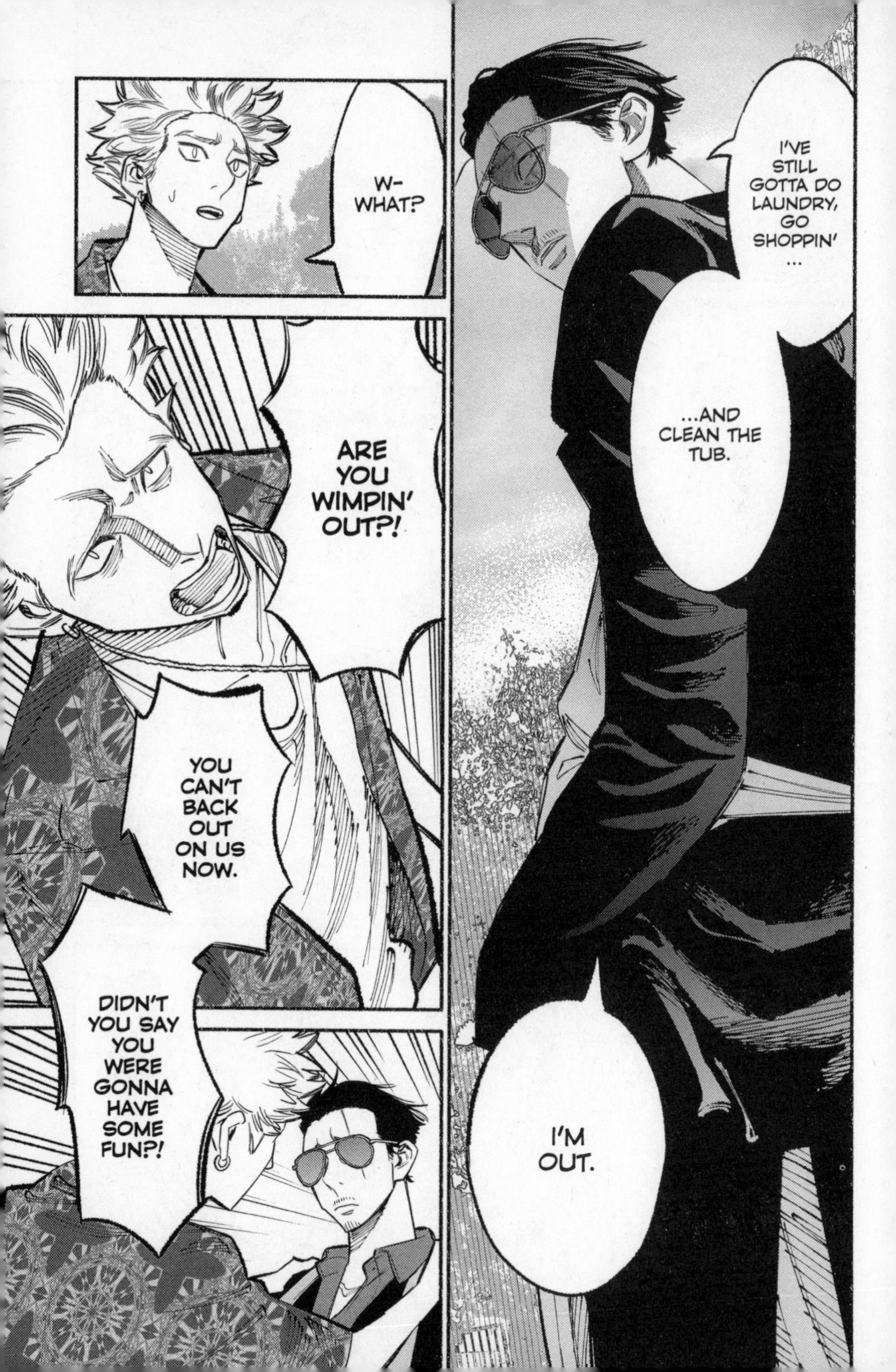
I'VE STILL GOTTA DO LAUNDRY, GO SHOPPIN' ...
...AND CLEAN THE TUB.
I'M OUT.
W-WHAT?
ARE YOU WIMPIN' OUT?!
YOU CAN'T BACK OUT ON US NOW.
DIDN'T YOU SAY YOU WERE GONNA HAVE SOME FUN?!

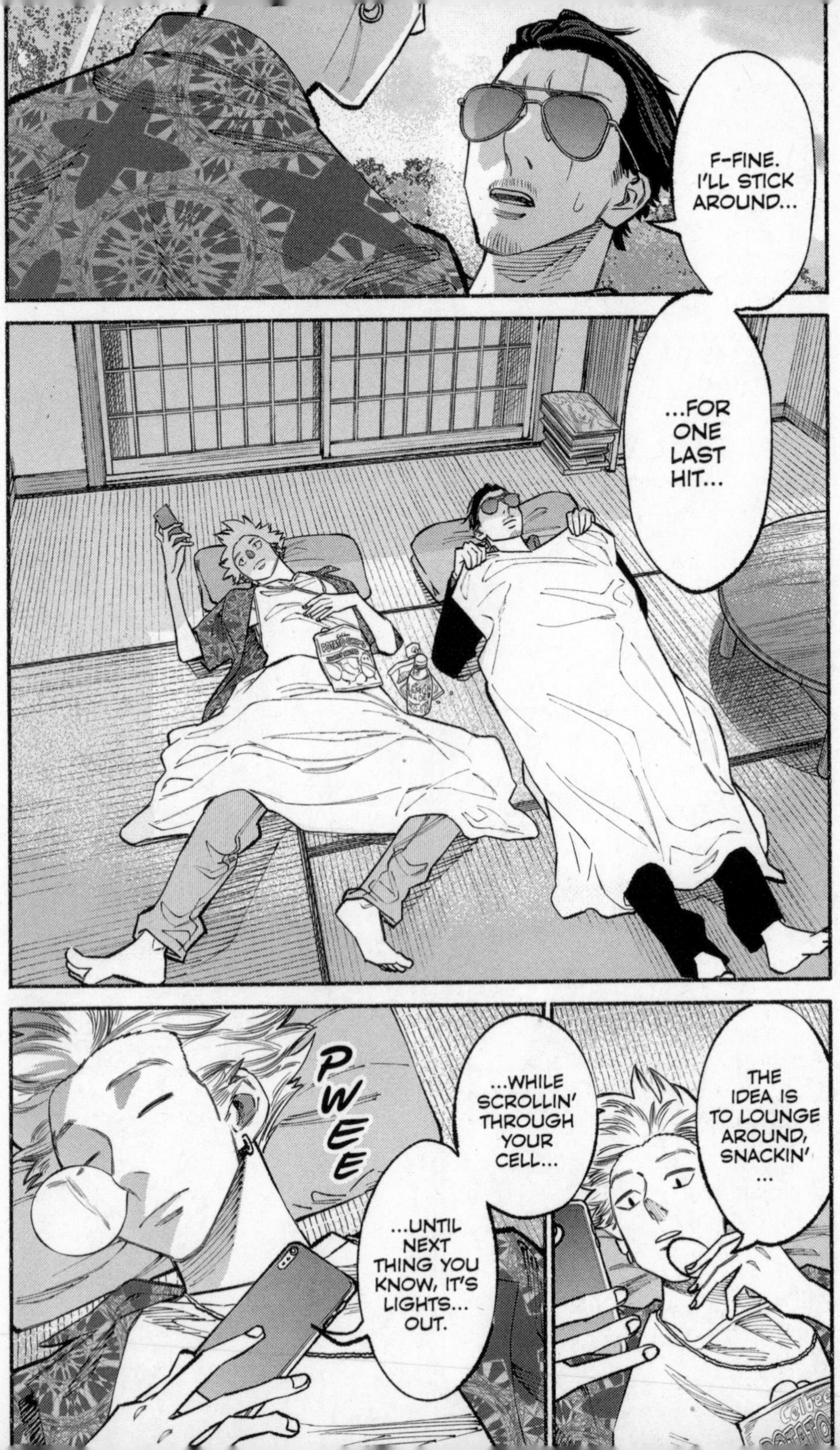
F-FINE. I'LL STICK AROUND...
...FOR ONE LAST HIT...
THE IDEA IS TO LOUNGE AROUND, SNACKIN' ...
...WHILE SCROLLIN' THROUGH YOUR CELL...
PWEE
...UNTIL NEXT THING YOU KNOW, IT'S LIGHTS... OUT.

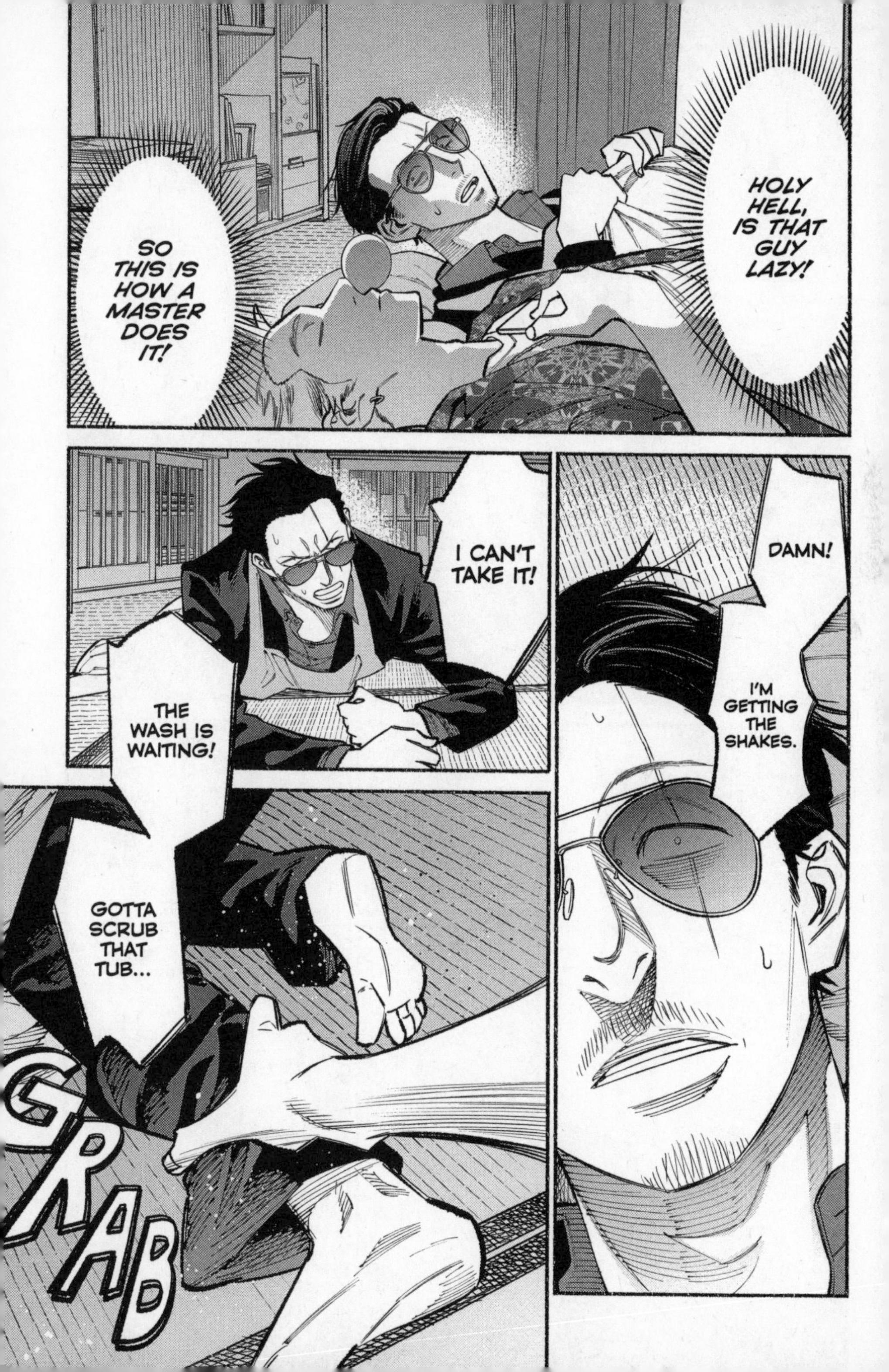
HOLY HELL, IS THAT GUY LAZY!
SO THIS IS HOW A MASTER DOES IT!
DAMN!
I'M GETTING THE SHAKES.
I CAN'T TAKE IT!
THE WASH IS WAITING!
GOTTA SCRUB THAT TUB...
GRAB

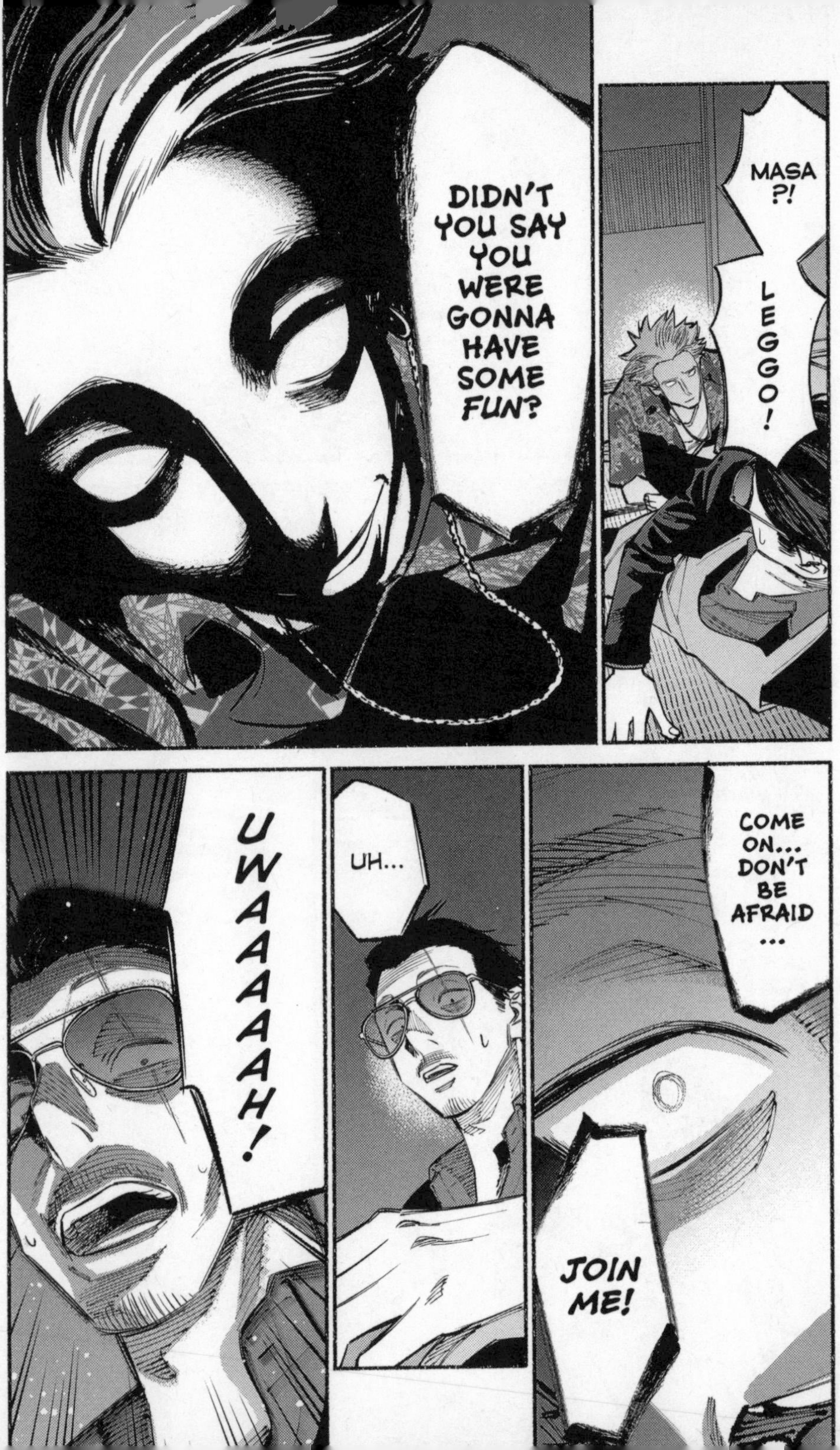
MASA ?!
LEGGO!
DIDN'T YOU SAY YOU WERE GONNA HAVE SOME FUN?
COME ON... DON'T BE AFRAID...
JOIN ME!
UH...
UWAAAAAAAH!

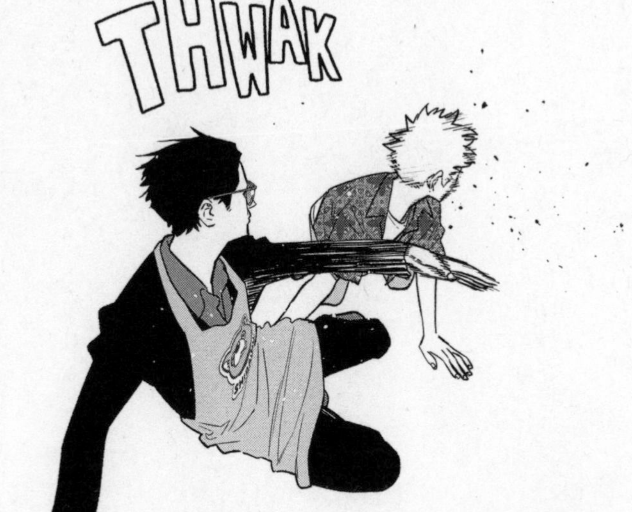
THWAK

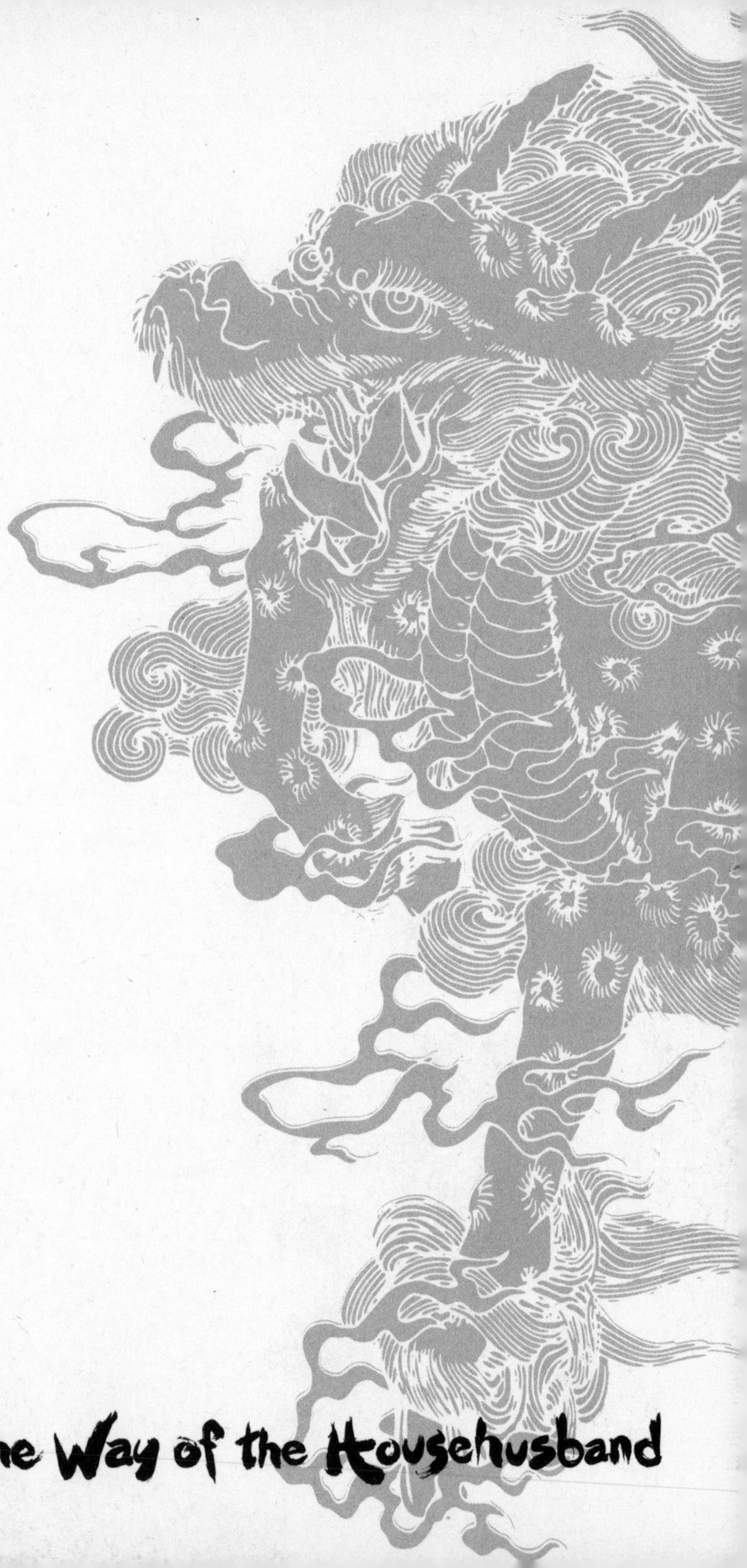

The Way of the Househusband

CHAPTER 38

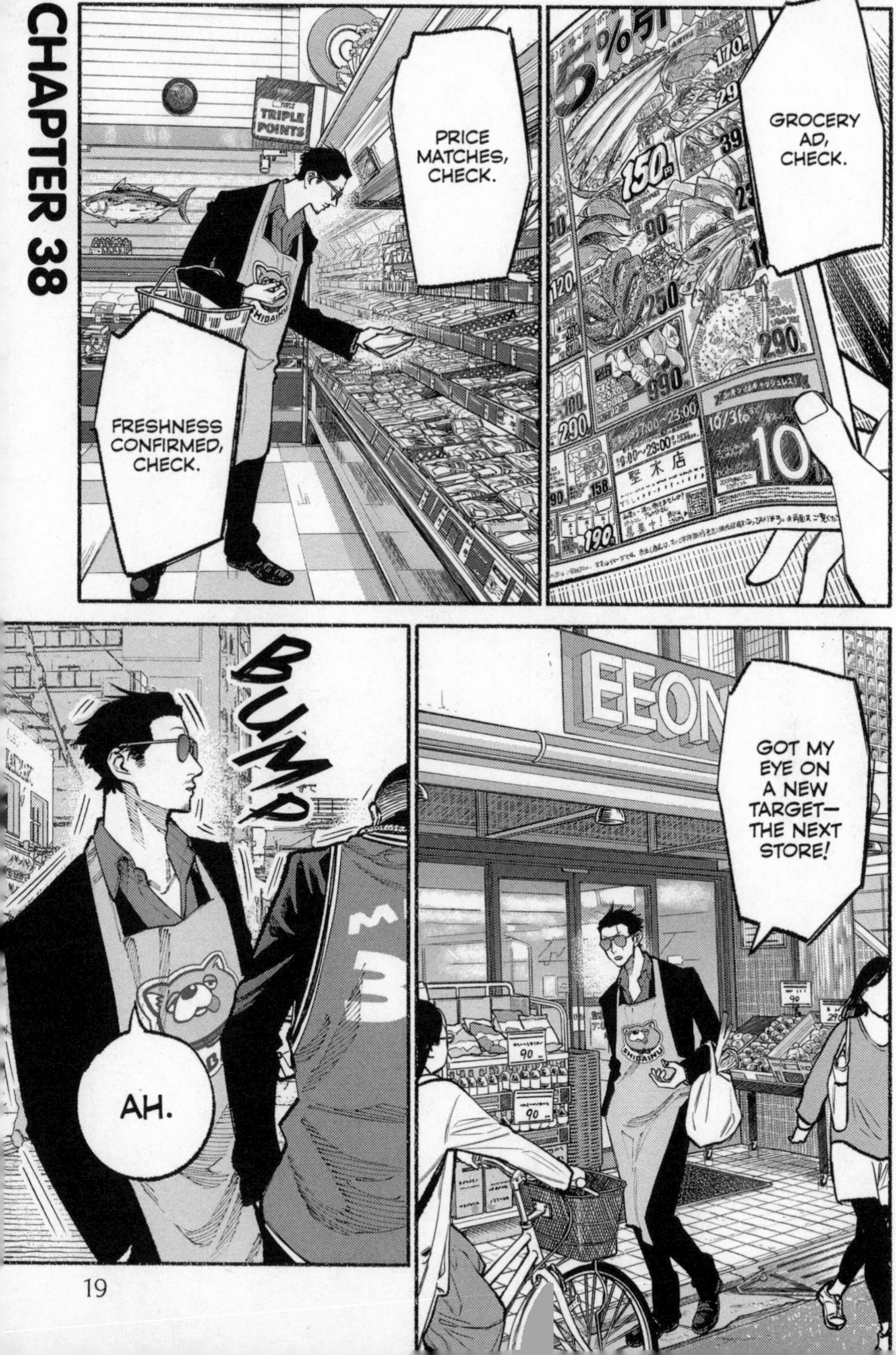

GROCERY AD, CHECK.
TRIPLE POINTS
PRICE MATCHES, CHECK.
FRESHNESS CONFIRMED, CHECK.
EEON
GOT MY EYE ON A NEW TARGET— THE NEXT STORE!
BUMP
AH.

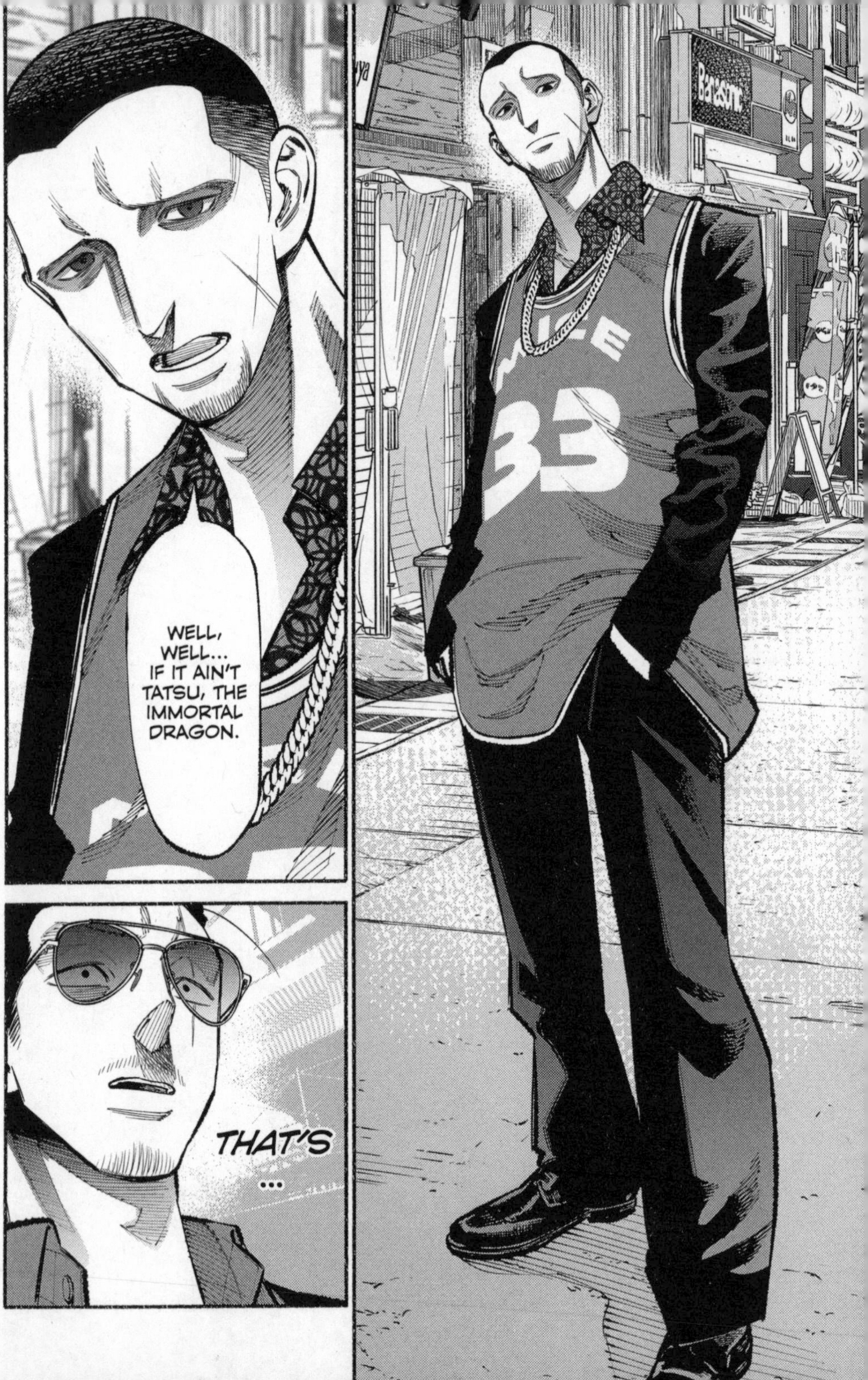
WELL, WELL... IF IT AIN'T TATSU, THE IMMORTAL DRAGON.
THAT'S ...

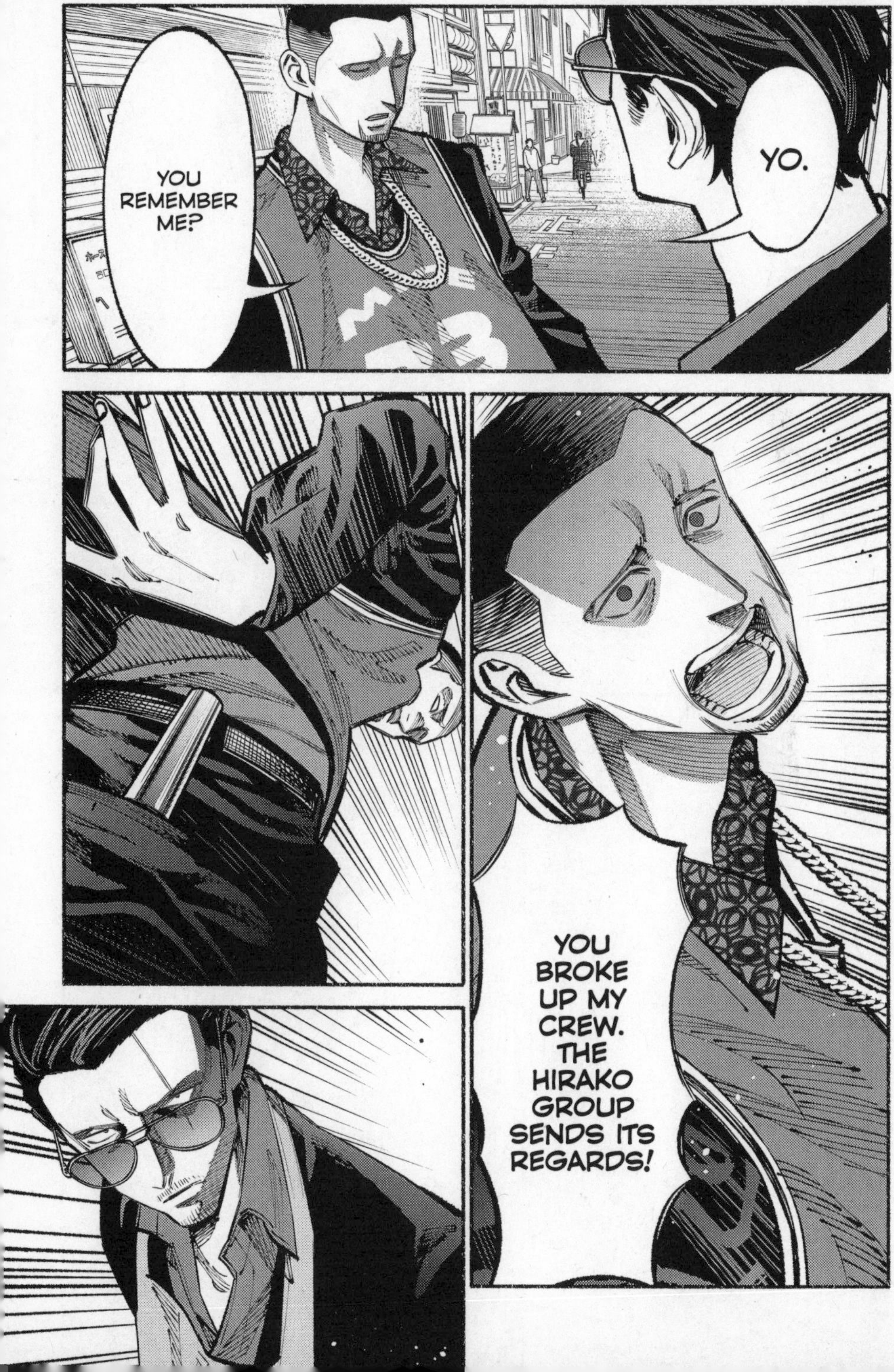
YO.
YOU REMEMBER ME?
YOU BROKE UP MY CREW. THE HIRAKO GROUP SENDS ITS REGARDS!

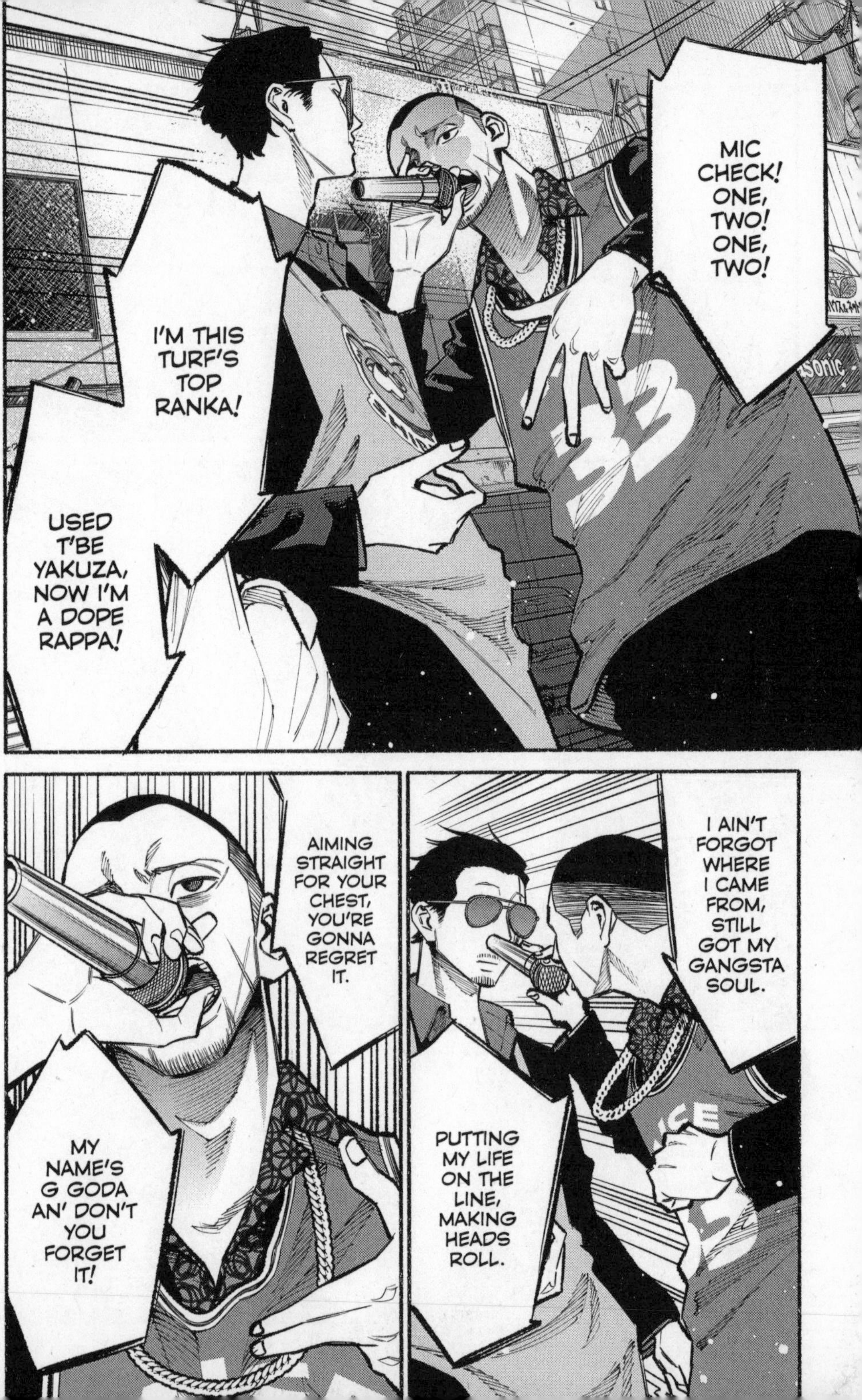
MIC CHECK! ONE, TWO! ONE, TWO!
I'M THIS TURF'S TOP RANKA!
USED T'BE YAKUZA, NOW I'M A DOPE RAPPA!
I AIN'T FORGOT WHERE I CAME FROM, STILL GOT MY GANGSTA SOUL.
PUTTING MY LIFE ON THE LINE, MAKING HEADS ROLL.
AIMING STRAIGHT FOR YOUR CHEST, YOU'RE GONNA REGRET IT.
MY NAME'S G GODA AN' DON'T YOU FORGET IT!

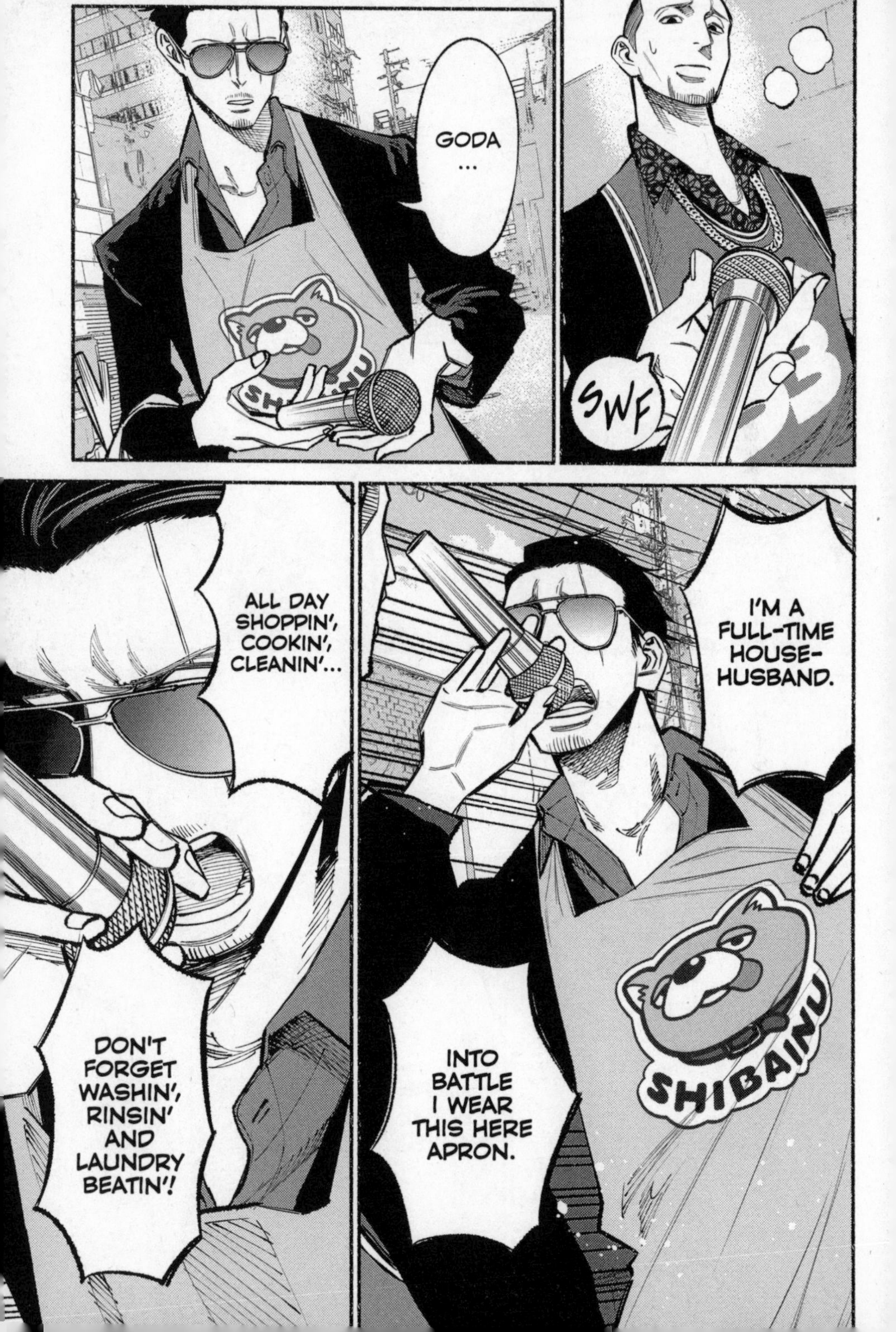
SWF
GODA ...
I'M A FULL-TIME HOUSE-HUSBAND.
INTO BATTLE I WEAR THIS HERE APRON.
SHIBAINU
ALL DAY SHOPPIN', COOKIN', CLEANIN'...
DON'T FORGET WASHIN', RINSIN' AND LAUNDRY BEATIN'!

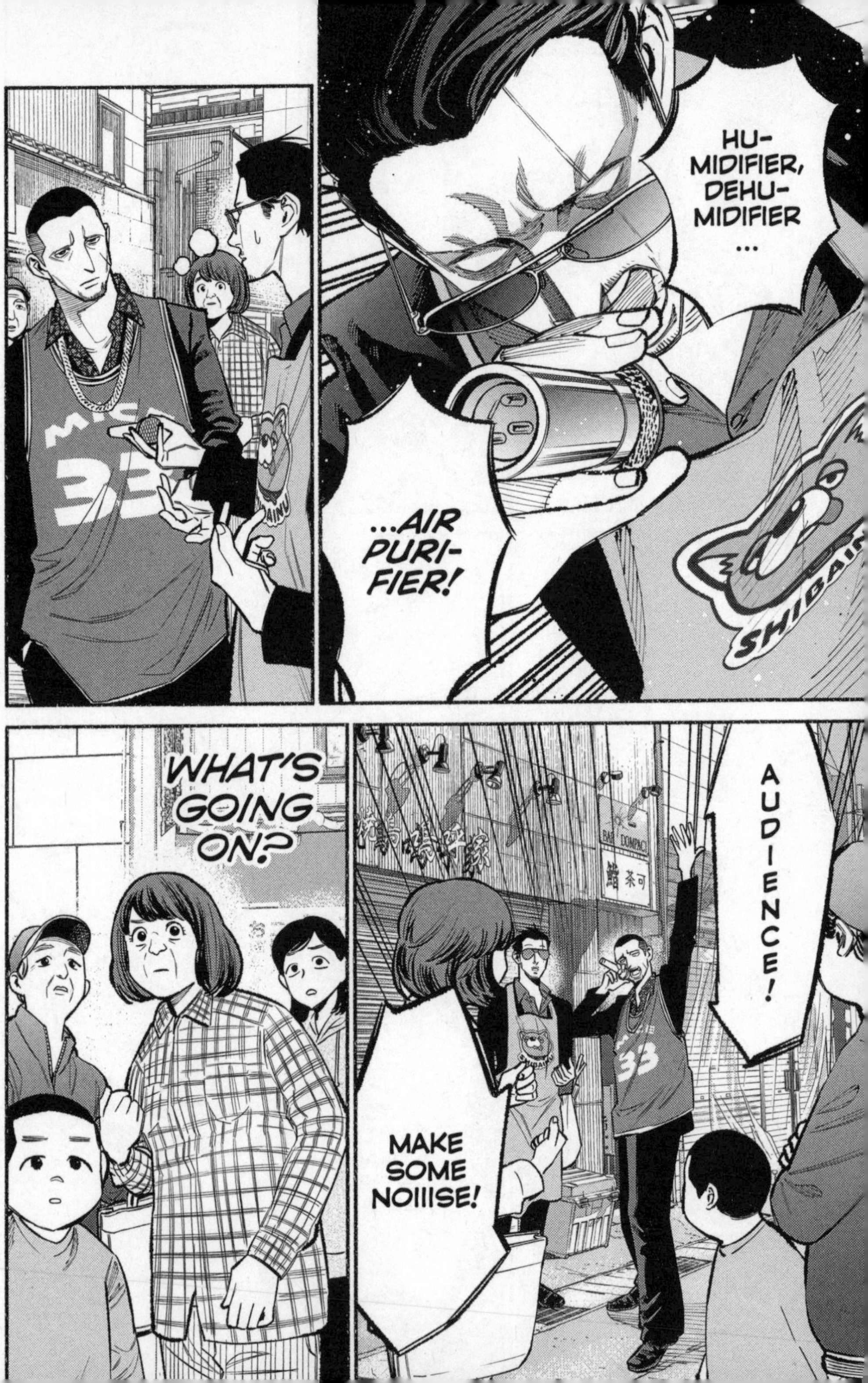
HU-MIDIFIER, DEHU-MIDIFIER ...
...AIR PURIFIER!
AUDIENCE!
MAKE SOME NOIIISE!
WHAT'S GOING ON?

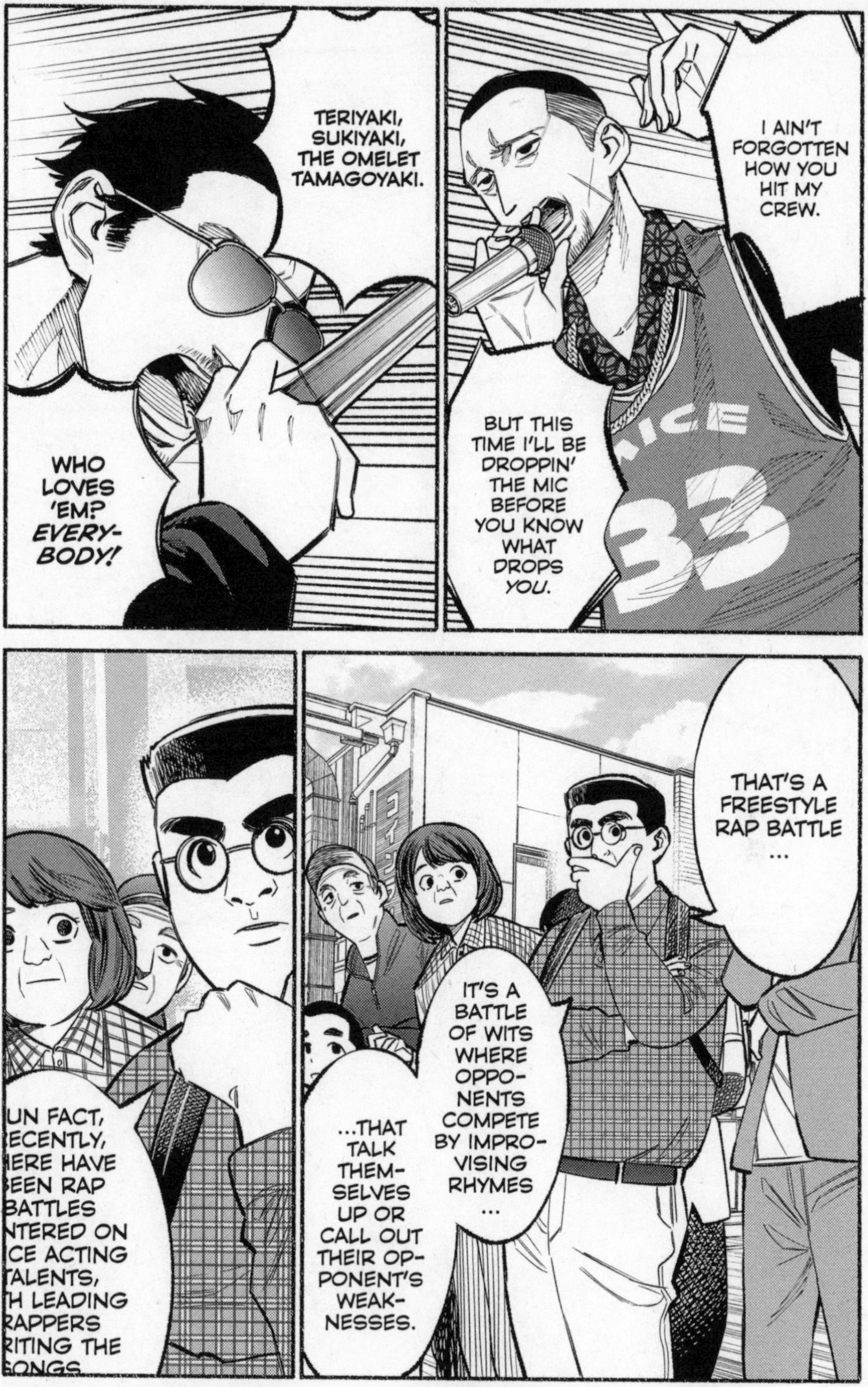
I AIN'T FORGOTTEN HOW YOU HIT MY CREW.
BUT THIS TIME I'LL BE DROPPIN' THE MIC BEFORE YOU KNOW WHAT DROPS *YOU*.
TERIYAKI, SUKIYAKI, THE OMELET TAMAGOYAKI.
WHO LOVES 'EM? *EVERY-BODY!*
THAT'S A FREESTYLE RAP BATTLE ...
IT'S A BATTLE OF WITS WHERE OPPO-NENTS COMPETE BY IMPRO-VISING RHYMES ...
...THAT TALK THEM-SELVES UP OR CALL OUT THEIR OP-PONENT'S WEAK-NESSES.
UN FACT, ECENTLY, HERE HAVE EEN RAP BATTLES NTERED ON CE ACTING TALENTS, TH LEADING RAPPERS RITING THE

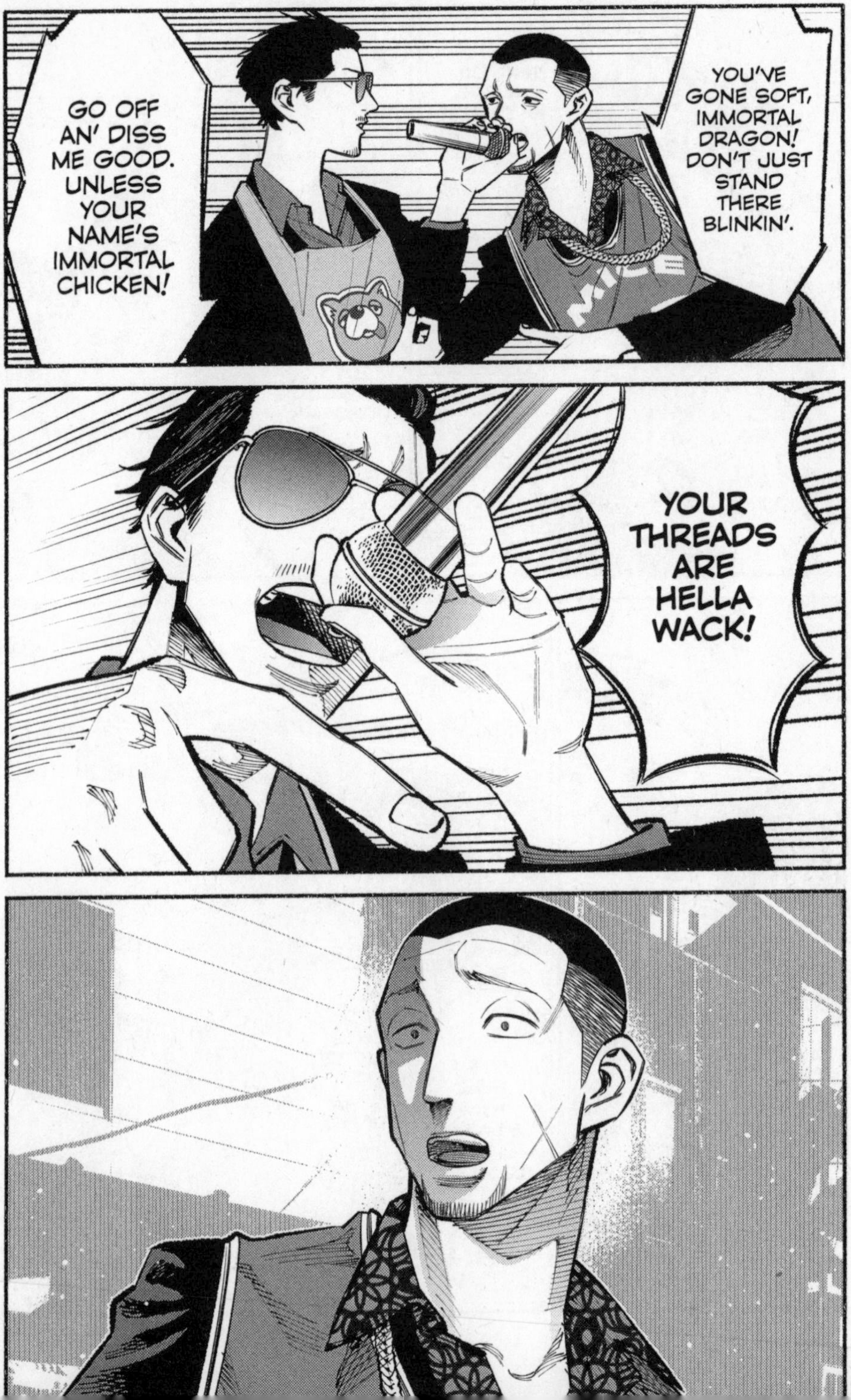
YOU'VE GONE SOFT, IMMORTAL DRAGON! DON'T JUST STAND THERE BLINKIN'.
GO OFF AN' DISS ME GOOD. UNLESS YOUR NAME'S IMMORTAL CHICKEN!
YOUR THREADS ARE HELLA WACK!

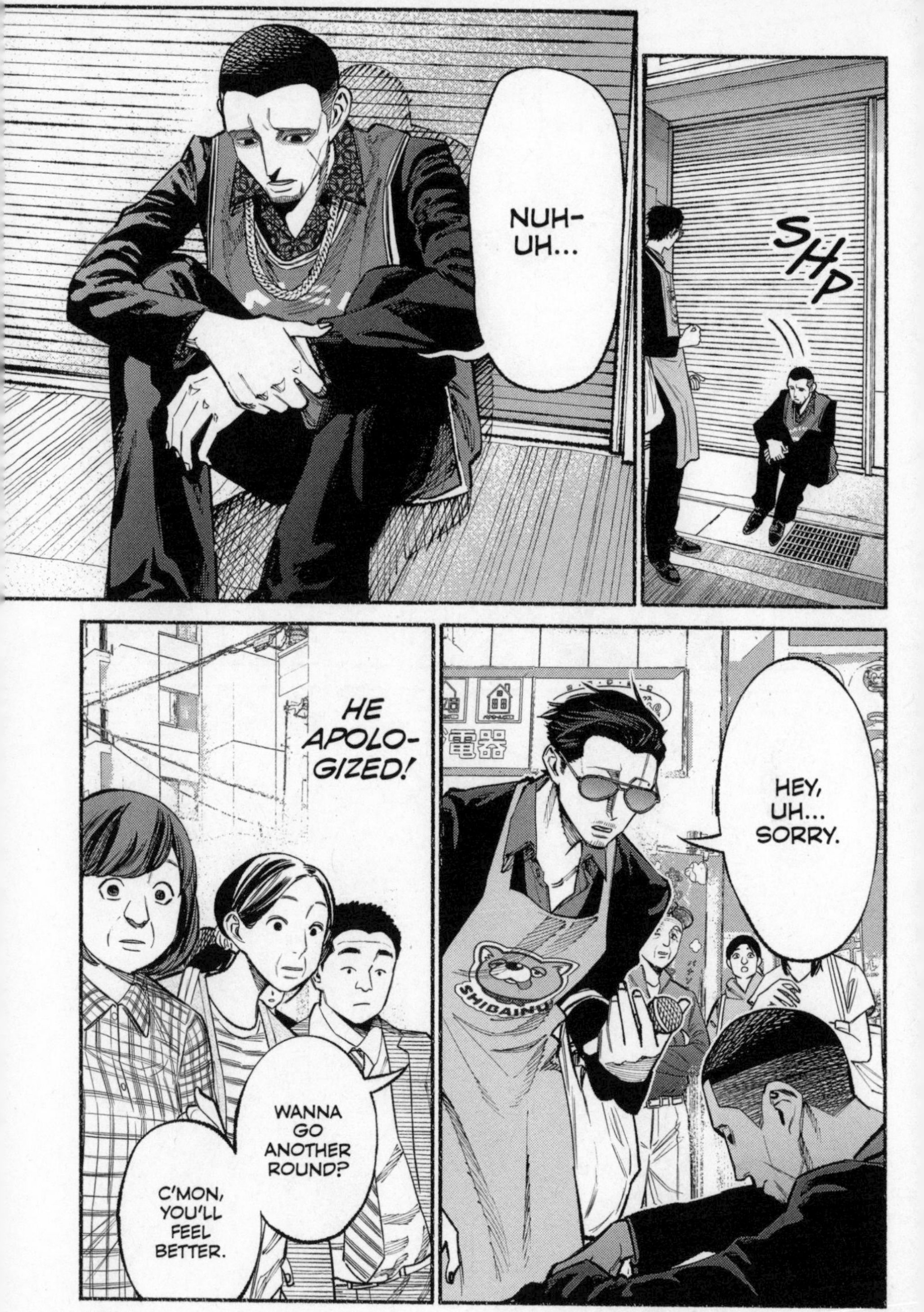
SHP
NUH-UH...
電器
SHIBAINU
HEY, UH... SORRY.
HE APOLOGIZED!
WANNA GO ANOTHER ROUND?
C'MON, YOU'LL FEEL BETTER.

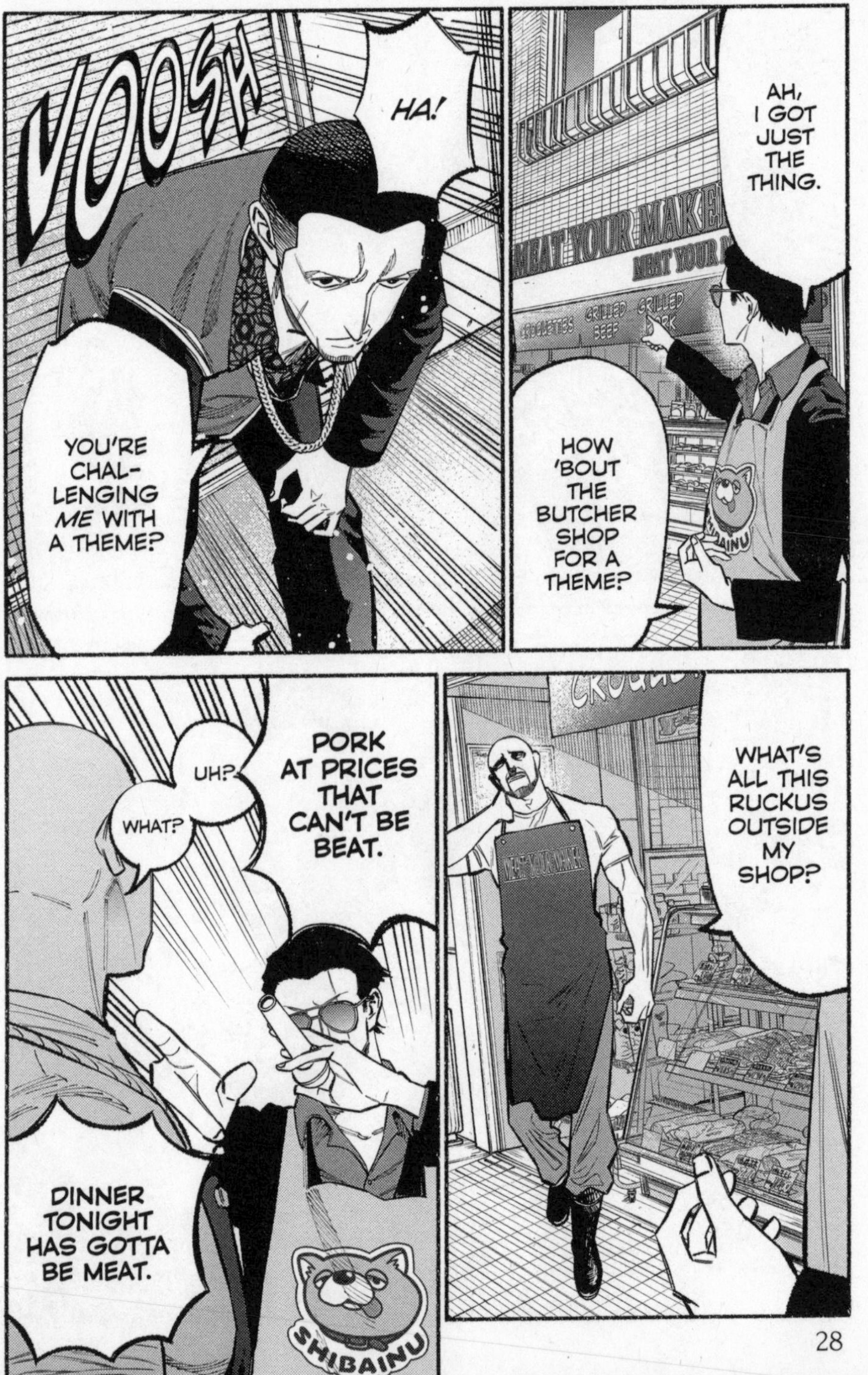
AH, I GOT JUST THE THING.
CROQUETTES
GRILLED BEEF
HOW 'BOUT THE BUTCHER SHOP FOR A THEME?
HA!
VOOSH
YOU'RE CHAL-LENGING *ME* WITH A THEME?
WHAT'S ALL THIS RUCKUS OUTSIDE MY SHOP?
PORK AT PRICES THAT CAN'T BE BEAT.
UH?
WHAT?
DINNER TONIGHT HAS GOTTA BE MEAT.
SHIBAINU

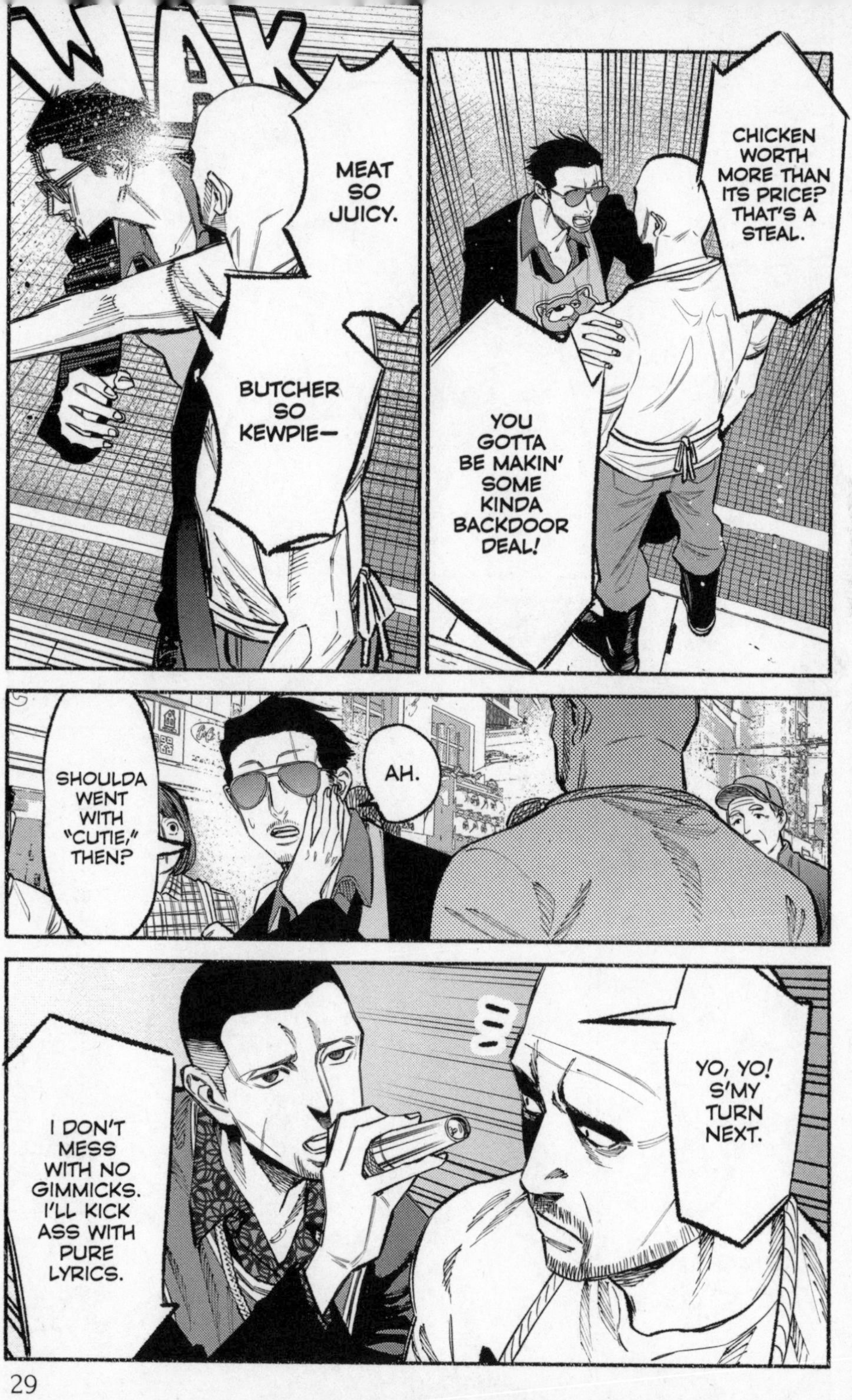

CHICKEN WORTH MORE THAN ITS PRICE? THAT'S A STEAL.
YOU GOTTA BE MAKIN' SOME KINDA BACKDOOR DEAL!
WAK
MEAT SO JUICY.
BUTCHER SO KEWPIE—
AH.
SHOULDA WENT WITH "CUTIE," THEN?
YO, YO! S'MY TURN NEXT.
I DON'T MESS WITH NO GIMMICKS. I'LL KICK ASS WITH PURE LYRICS.

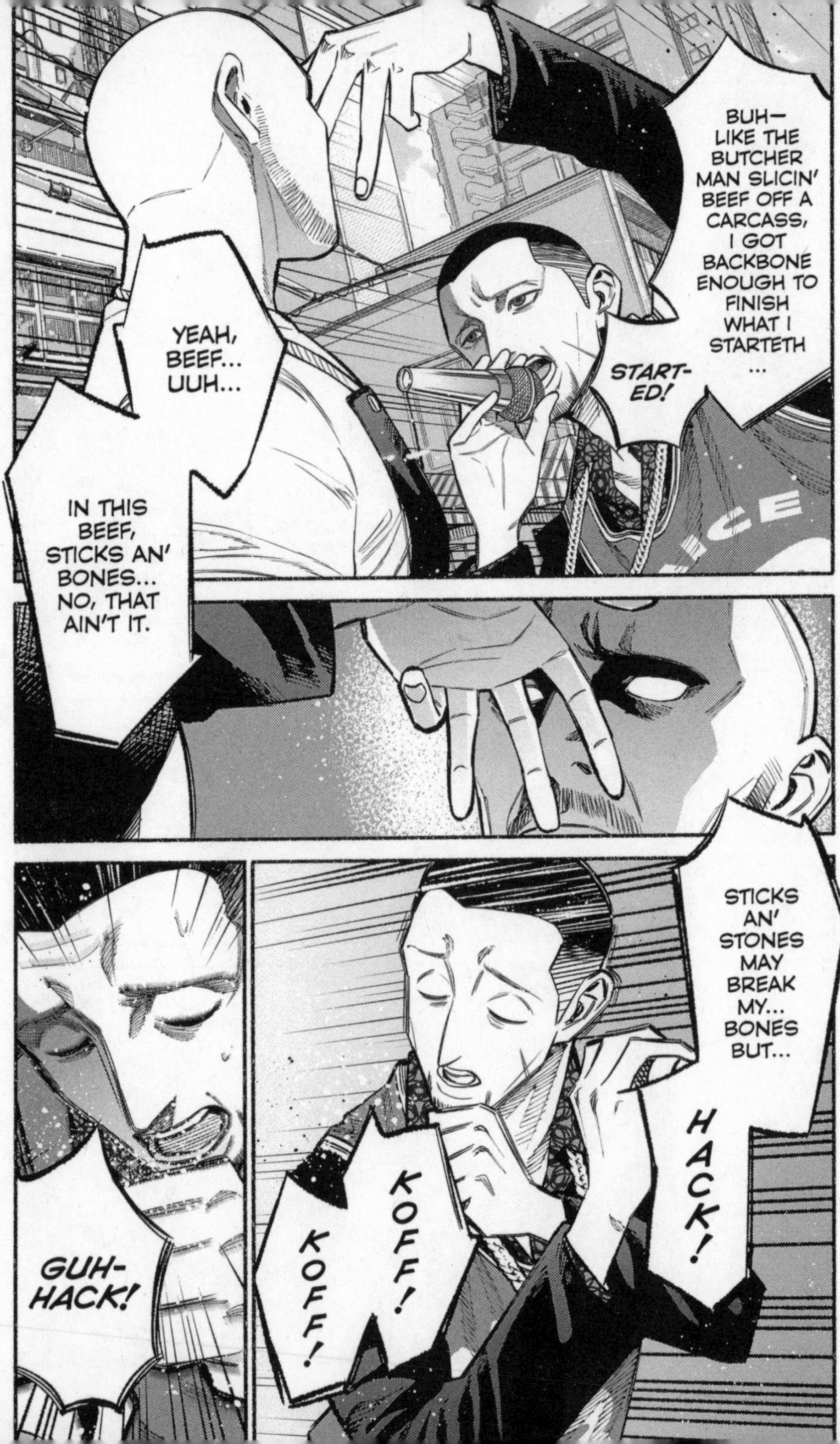
BUH— LIKE THE BUTCHER MAN SLICIN' BEEF OFF A CARCASS, I GOT BACKBONE ENOUGH TO FINISH WHAT I STARTETH ...
START-ED!
YEAH, BEEF... UUH...
IN THIS BEEF, STICKS AN' BONES... NO, THAT AIN'T IT.
STICKS AN' STONES MAY BREAK MY... BONES BUT...
HACK!
KOFF!
KOFF!
GUH-HACK!

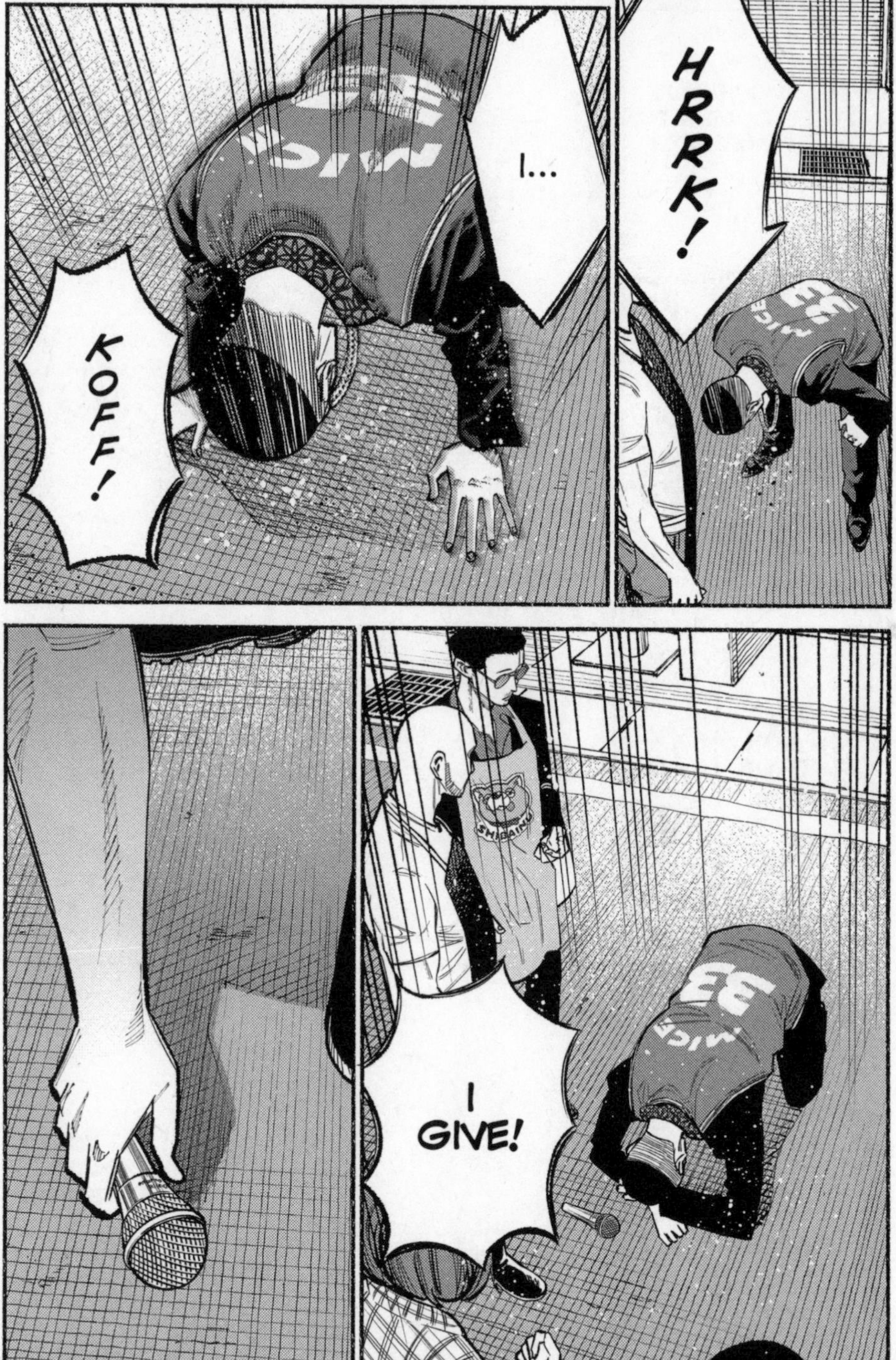
HRRK!
I...
KOFF!
I GIVE!

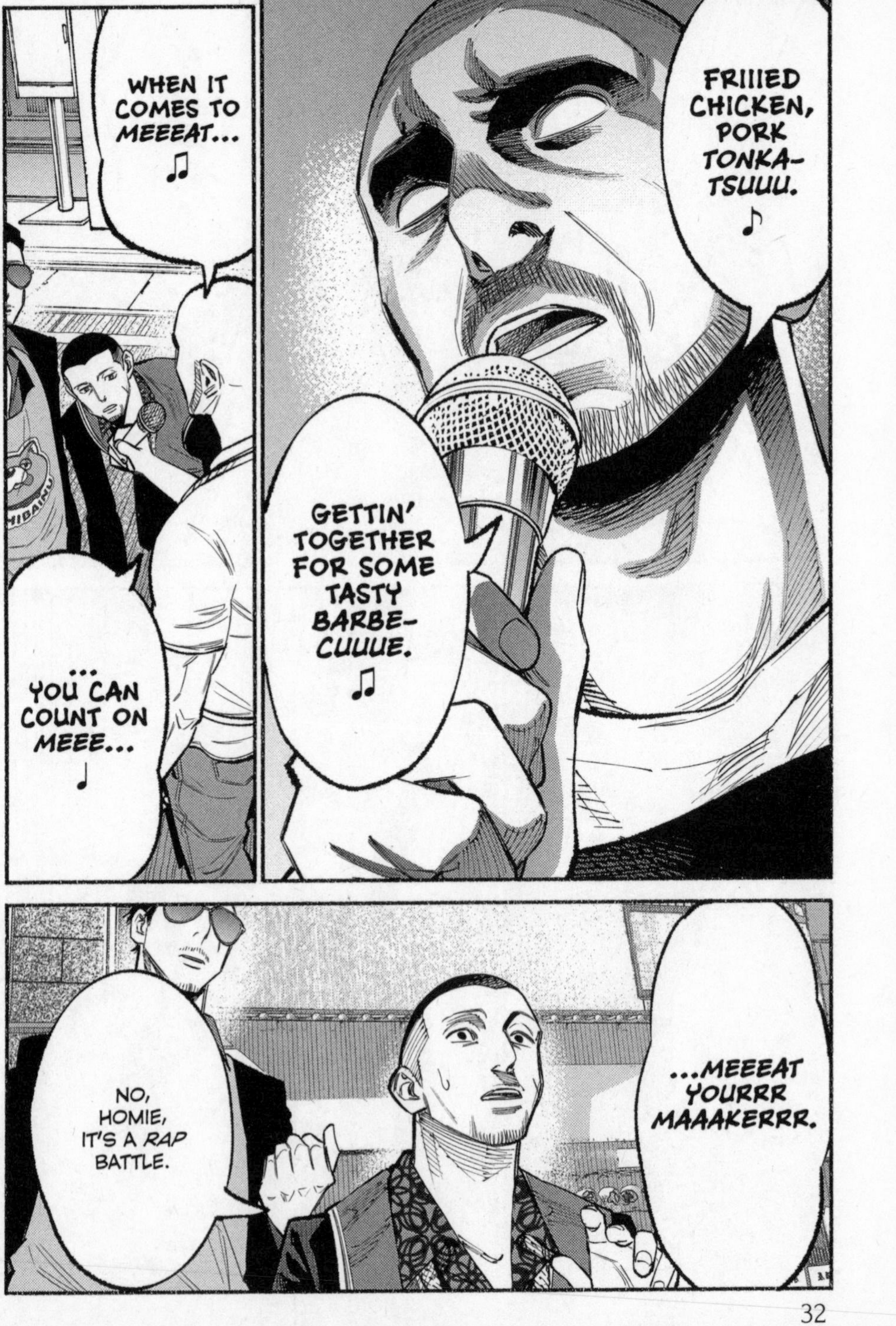
FRIIIED CHICKEN, PORK TONKA-TSUUU. ♪
GETTIN' TOGETHER FOR SOME TASTY BARBE-CUUUE. ♫
WHEN IT COMES TO MEEEAT... ♫
... YOU CAN COUNT ON MEEE... ♩
...MEEEAT YOURRR MAAAKERRR.
NO, HOMIE, IT'S A *RAP* BATTLE.

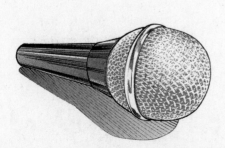

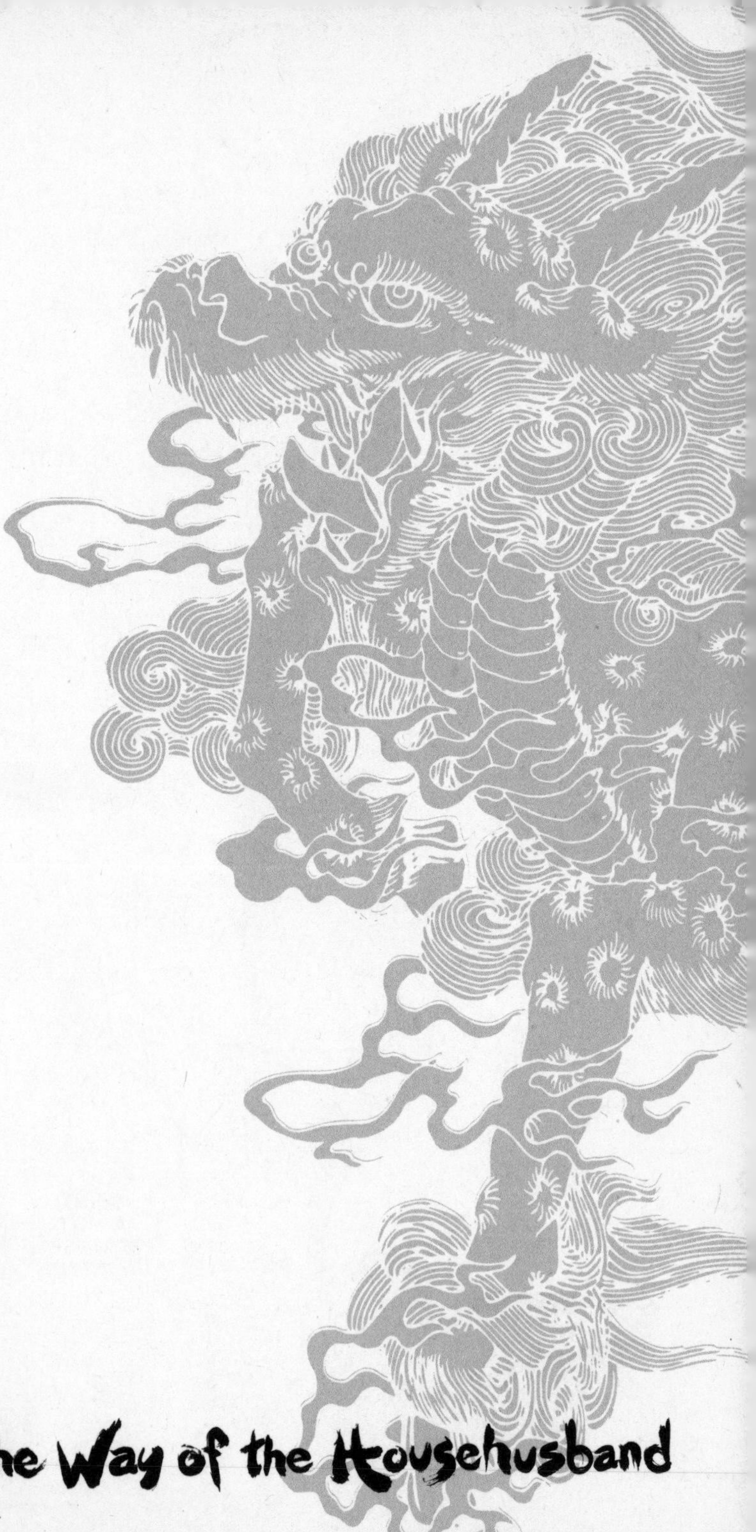

The Way of the Househusband

CHAPTER 39

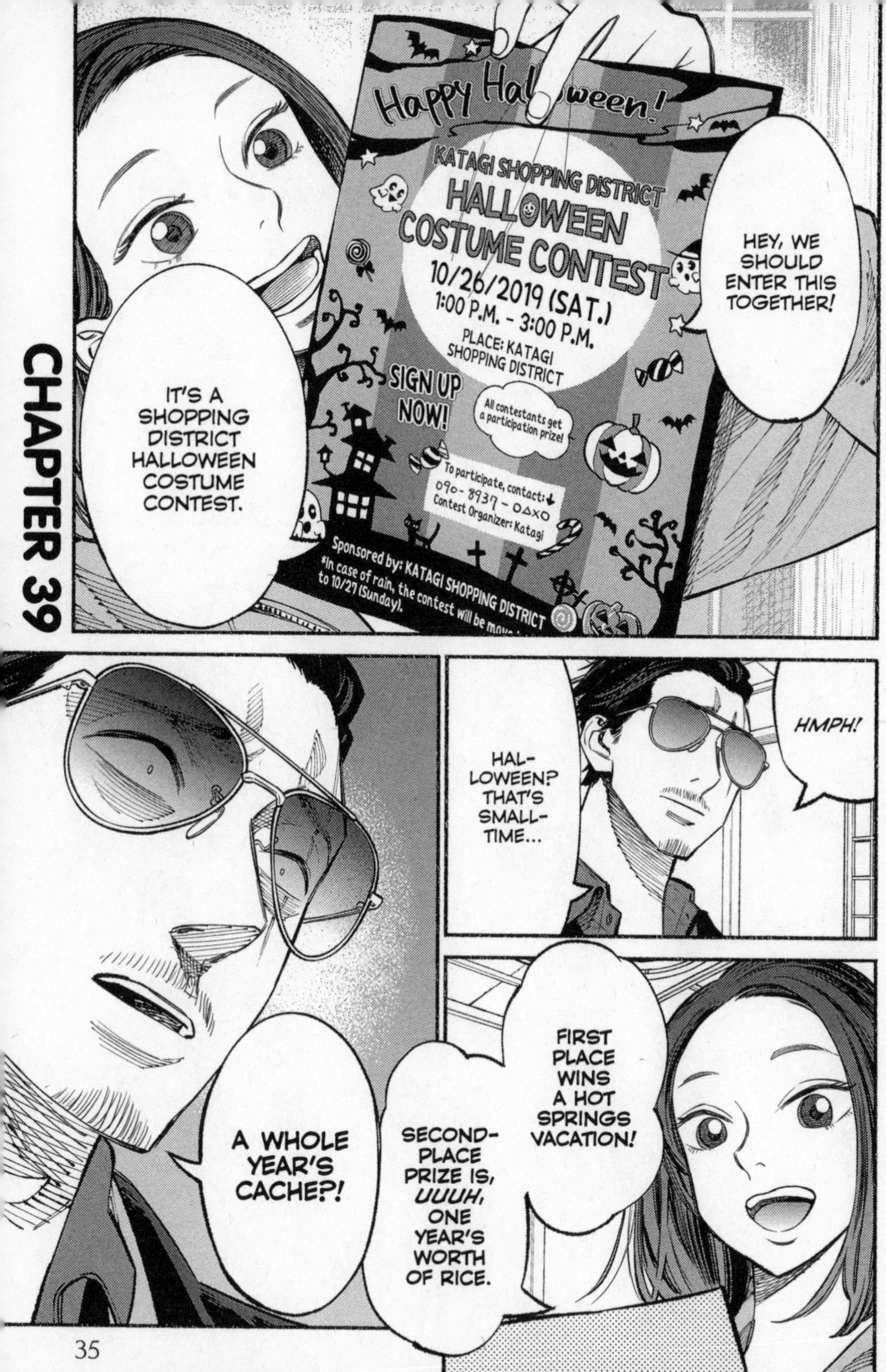
HEY, WE SHOULD ENTER THIS TOGETHER!
Happy Halloween!
KATAGI SHOPPING DISTRICT
HALLOWEEN COSTUME CONTEST
10/26/2019 (SAT.)
1:00 P.M. - 3:00 P.M.
PLACE: KATAGI SHOPPING DISTRICT
SIGN UP NOW!
All contestants get a participation prize!
To participate, contact:
090-8937-○△×○
Contest Organizer: Katagi
Sponsored by: KATAGI SHOPPING DISTRICT
*In case of rain, the contest will be
to 10/27 (Sunday).
IT'S A SHOPPING DISTRICT HALLOWEEN COSTUME CONTEST.
HMPH!
HAL-LOWEEN? THAT'S SMALL-TIME...
FIRST PLACE WINS A HOT SPRINGS VACATION!
SECOND-PLACE PRIZE IS, *UUUH*, ONE YEAR'S WORTH OF RICE.
A WHOLE YEAR'S CACHE?!

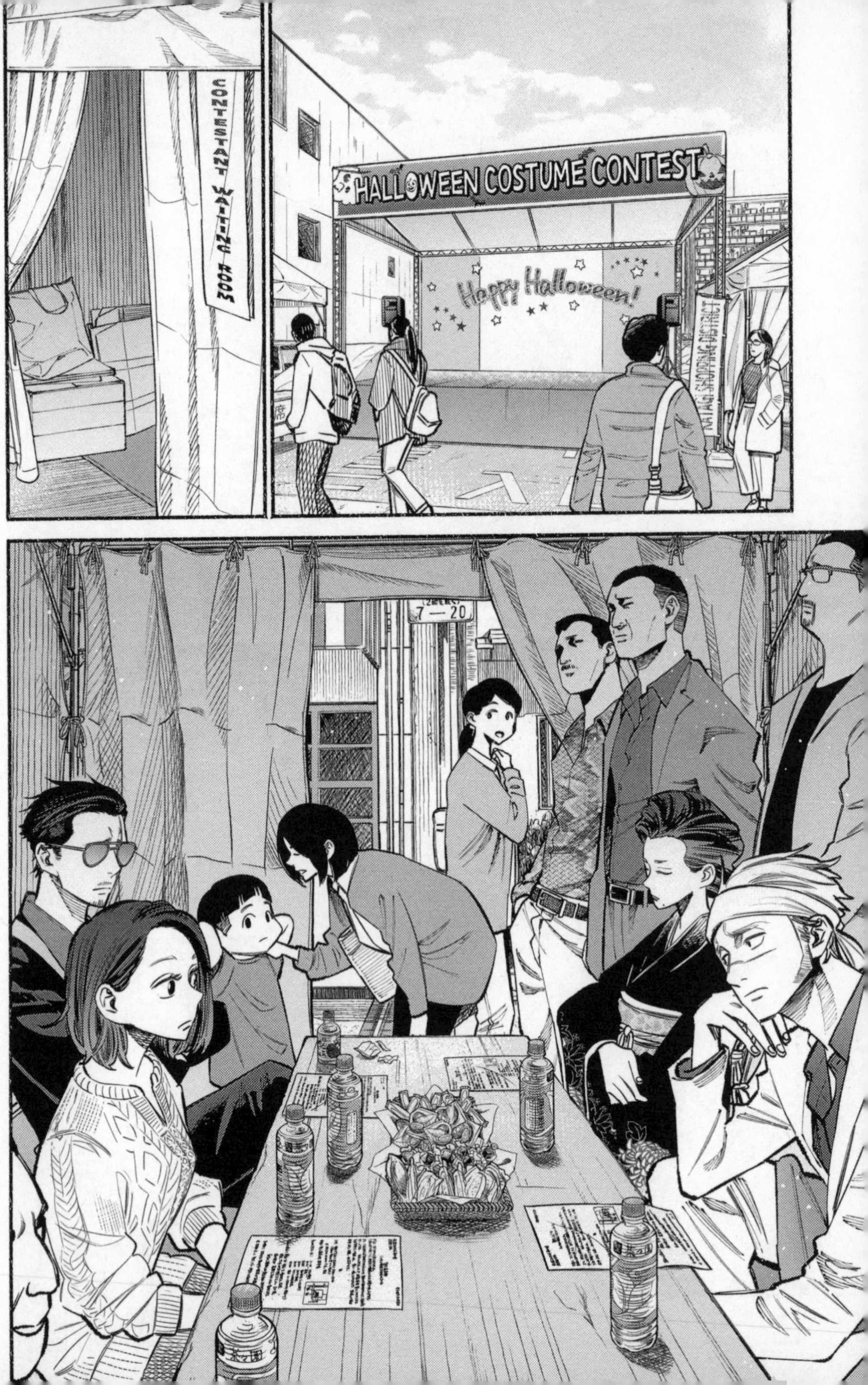
HALLOWEEN COSTUME CONTEST
Happy Halloween!
CONTESTANT WAITING ROOM
7—20

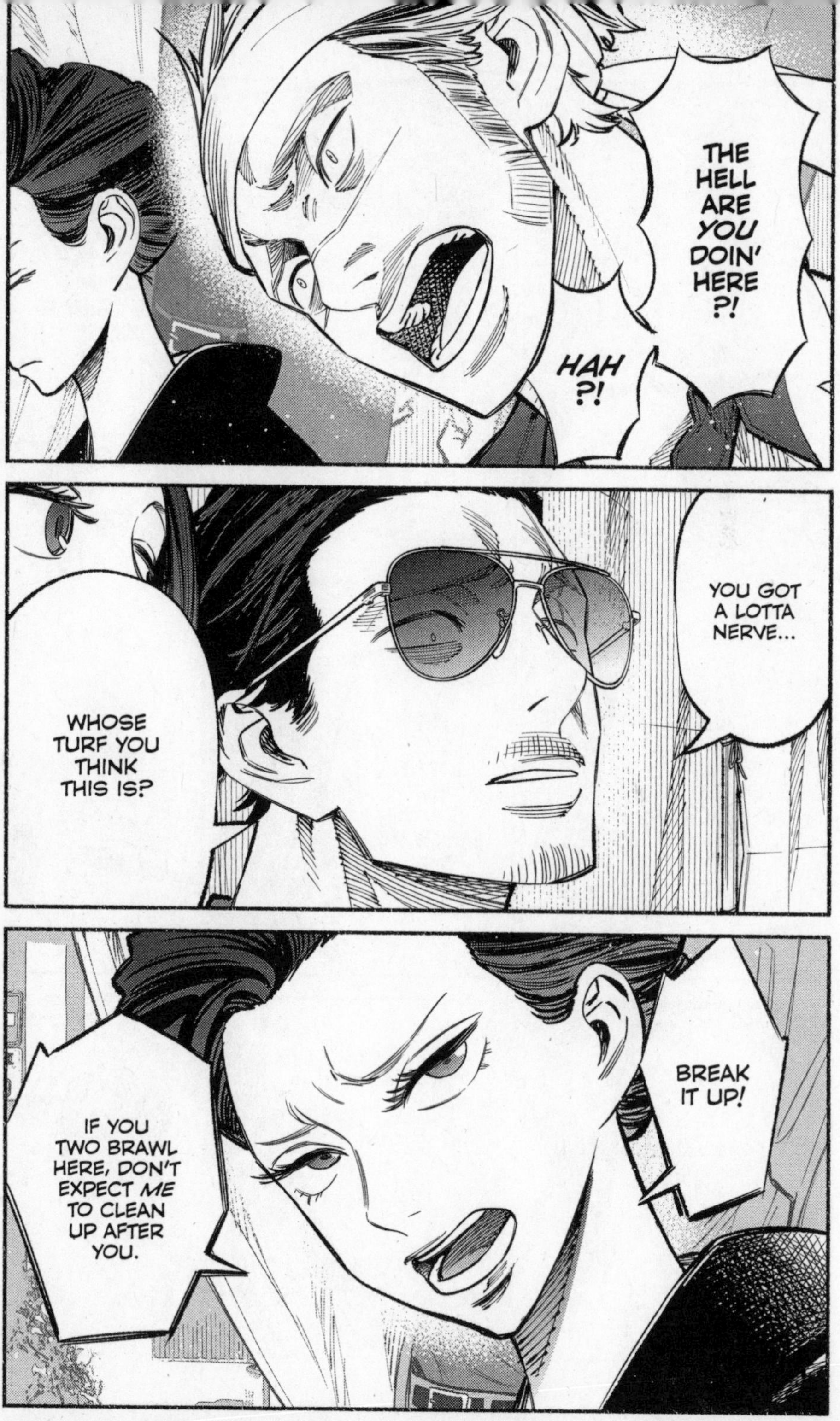
THE HELL ARE *YOU* DOIN' HERE ?!
HAH ?!
YOU GOT A LOTTA NERVE...
WHOSE TURF YOU THINK THIS IS?
BREAK IT UP!
IF YOU TWO BRAWL HERE, DON'T EXPECT *ME* TO CLEAN UP AFTER YOU.

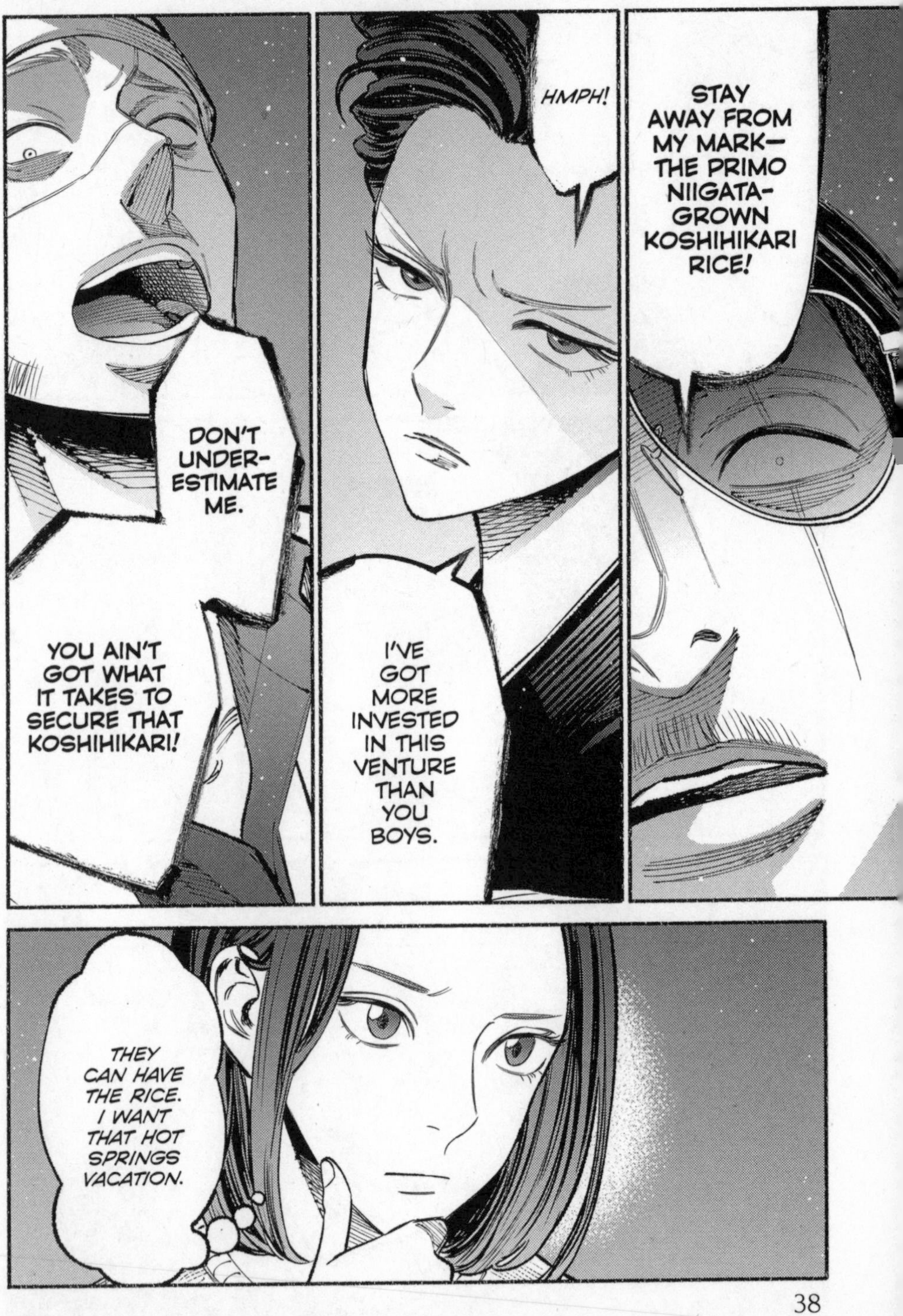
STAY AWAY FROM MY MARK— THE PRIMO NIIGATA-GROWN KOSHIHIKARI RICE!
HMPH!
I'VE GOT MORE INVESTED IN THIS VENTURE THAN YOU BOYS.
DON'T UNDER-ESTIMATE ME.
YOU AIN'T GOT WHAT IT TAKES TO SECURE THAT KOSHIHIKARI!
THEY CAN HAVE THE RICE. I WANT THAT HOT SPRINGS VACATION.

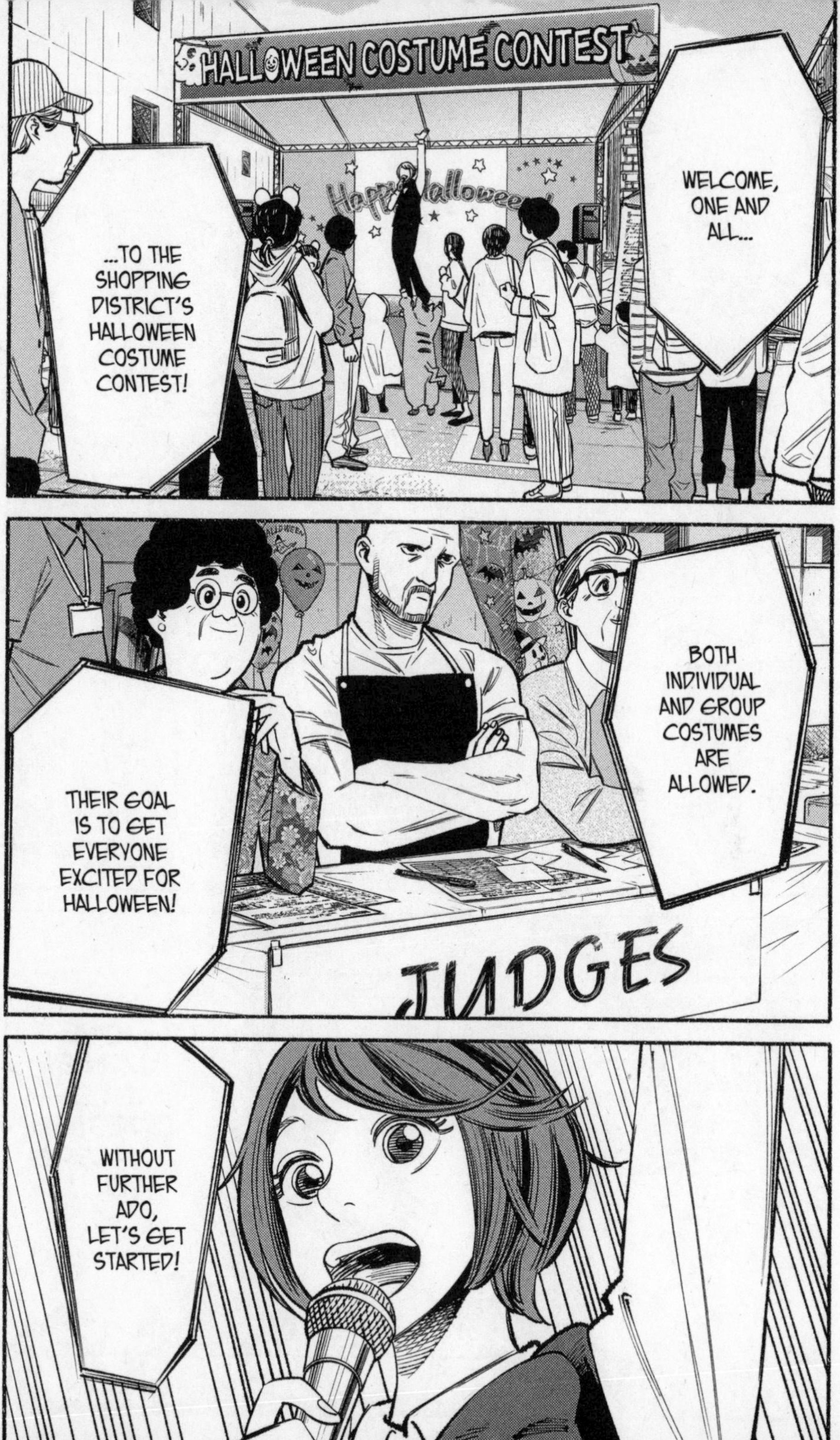
HALLOWEEN COSTUME CONTEST
WELCOME, ONE AND ALL...
...TO THE SHOPPING DISTRICT'S HALLOWEEN COSTUME CONTEST!
BOTH INDIVIDUAL AND GROUP COSTUMES ARE ALLOWED.
THEIR GOAL IS TO GET EVERYONE EXCITED FOR HALLOWEEN!
JUDGES
WITHOUT FURTHER ADO, LET'S GET STARTED!

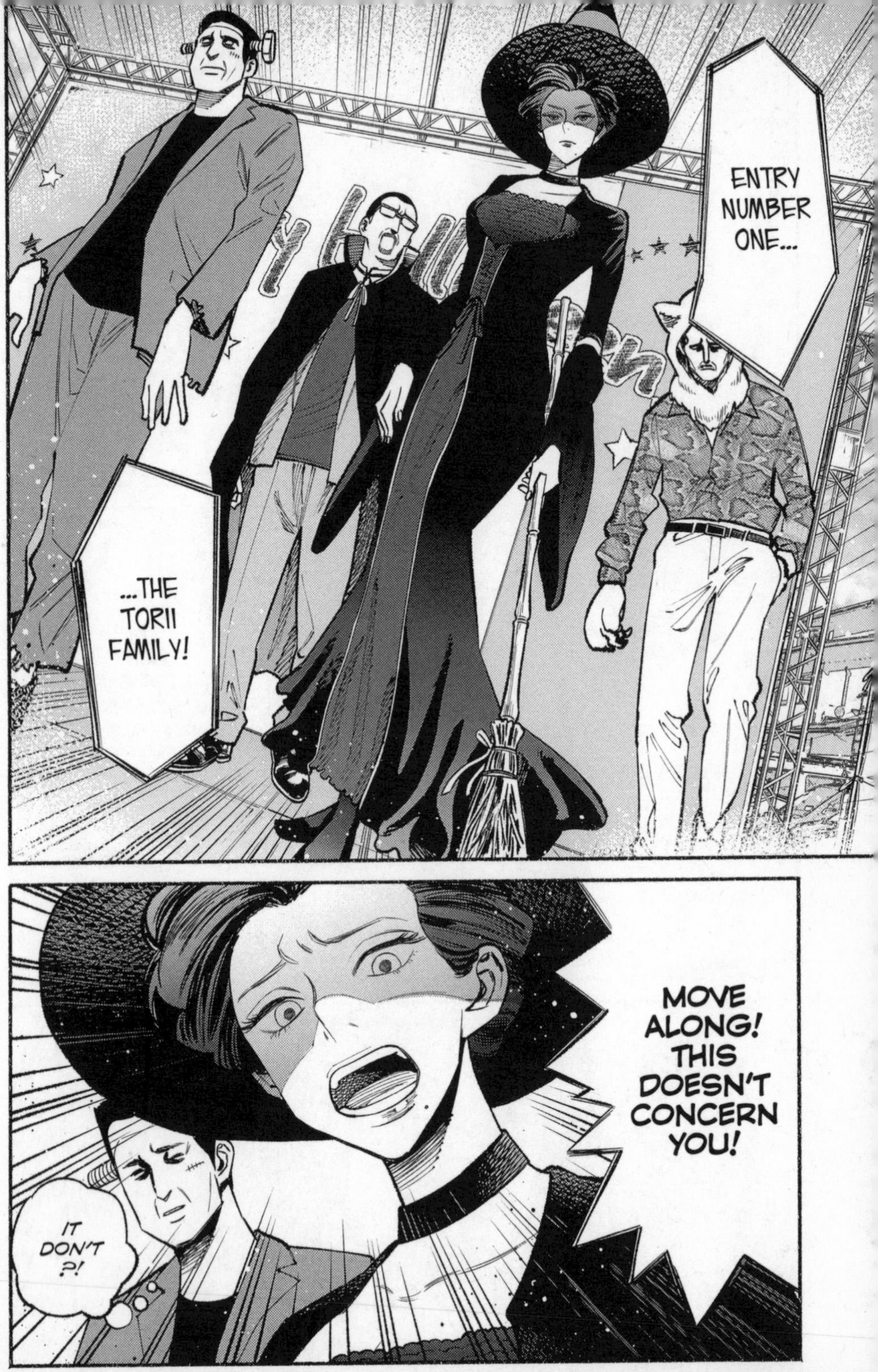
ENTRY NUMBER ONE...
...THE TORII FAMILY!
MOVE ALONG! THIS DOESN'T CONCERN YOU!
IT DON'T ?!

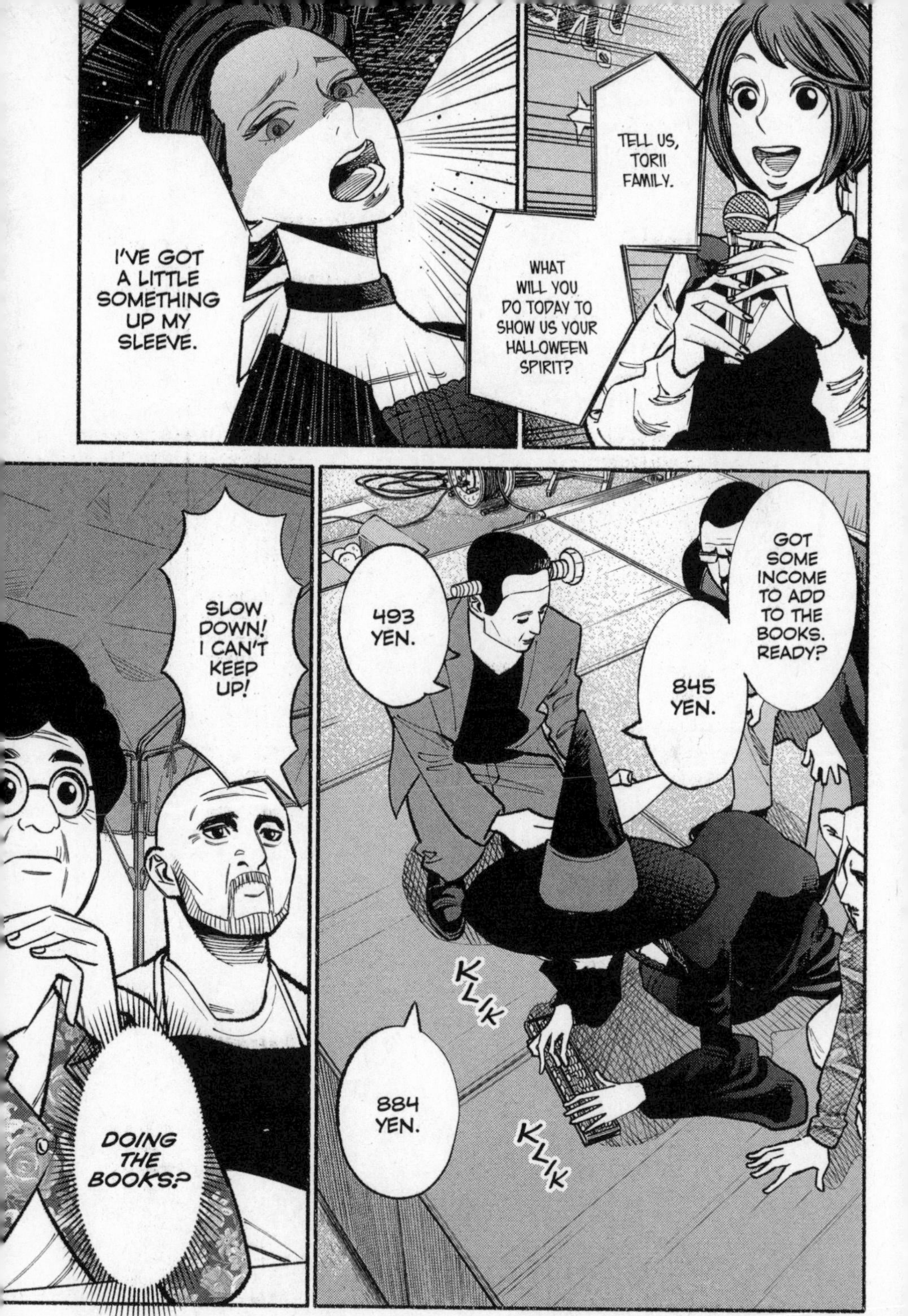
TELL US, TORII FAMILY.
WHAT WILL YOU DO TODAY TO SHOW US YOUR HALLOWEEN SPIRIT?
I'VE GOT A LITTLE SOMETHING UP MY SLEEVE.
GOT SOME INCOME TO ADD TO THE BOOKS. READY?
845 YEN.
493 YEN.
KLIK
884 YEN.
KLIK
SLOW DOWN! I CAN'T KEEP UP!
DOING THE BOOKS?

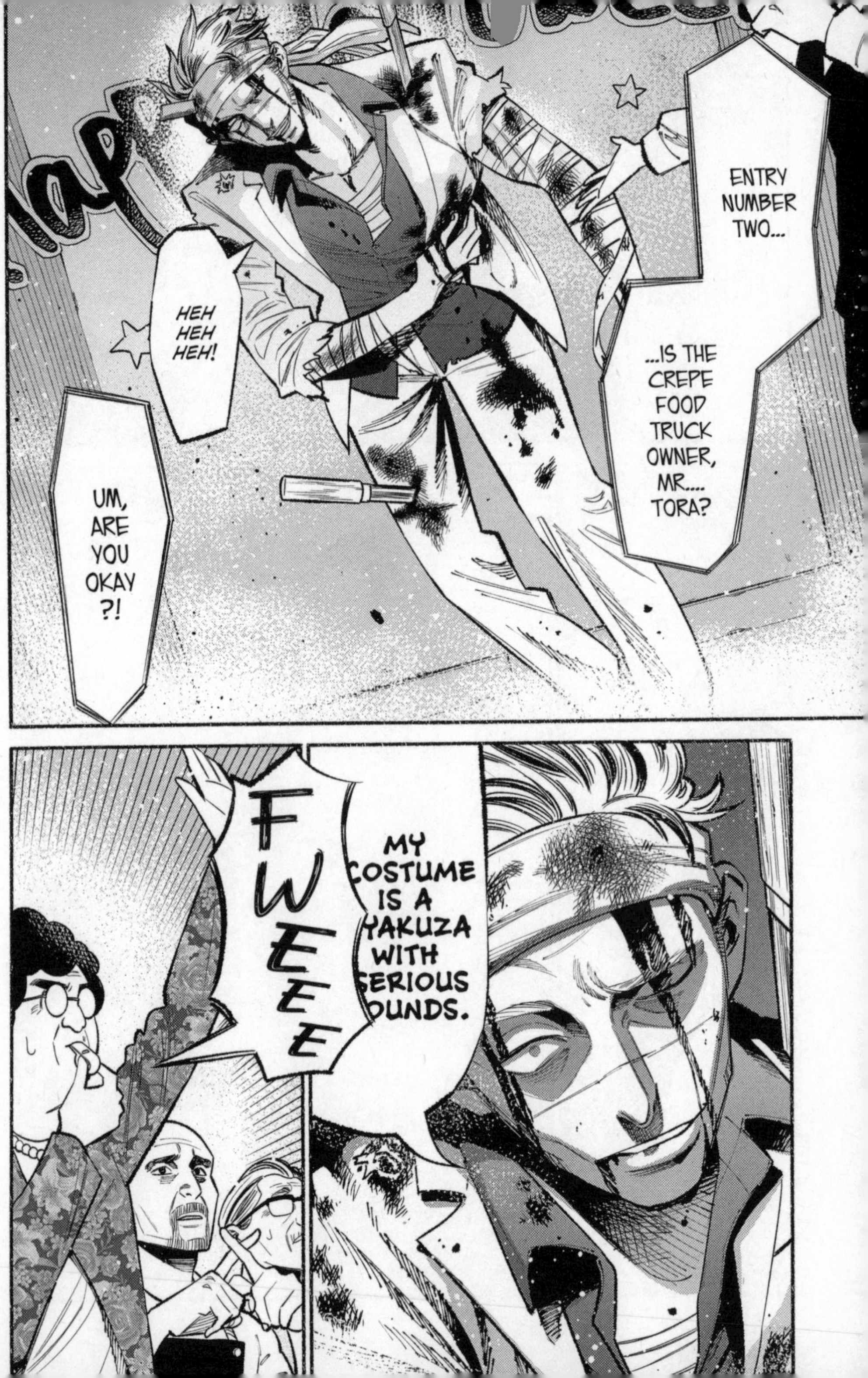
ENTRY NUMBER TWO...
...IS THE CREPE FOOD TRUCK OWNER, MR.... TORA?
HEH HEH HEH!
UM, ARE YOU OKAY ?!
MY COSTUME IS A YAKUZA WITH SERIOUS WOUNDS.
FWEEEE

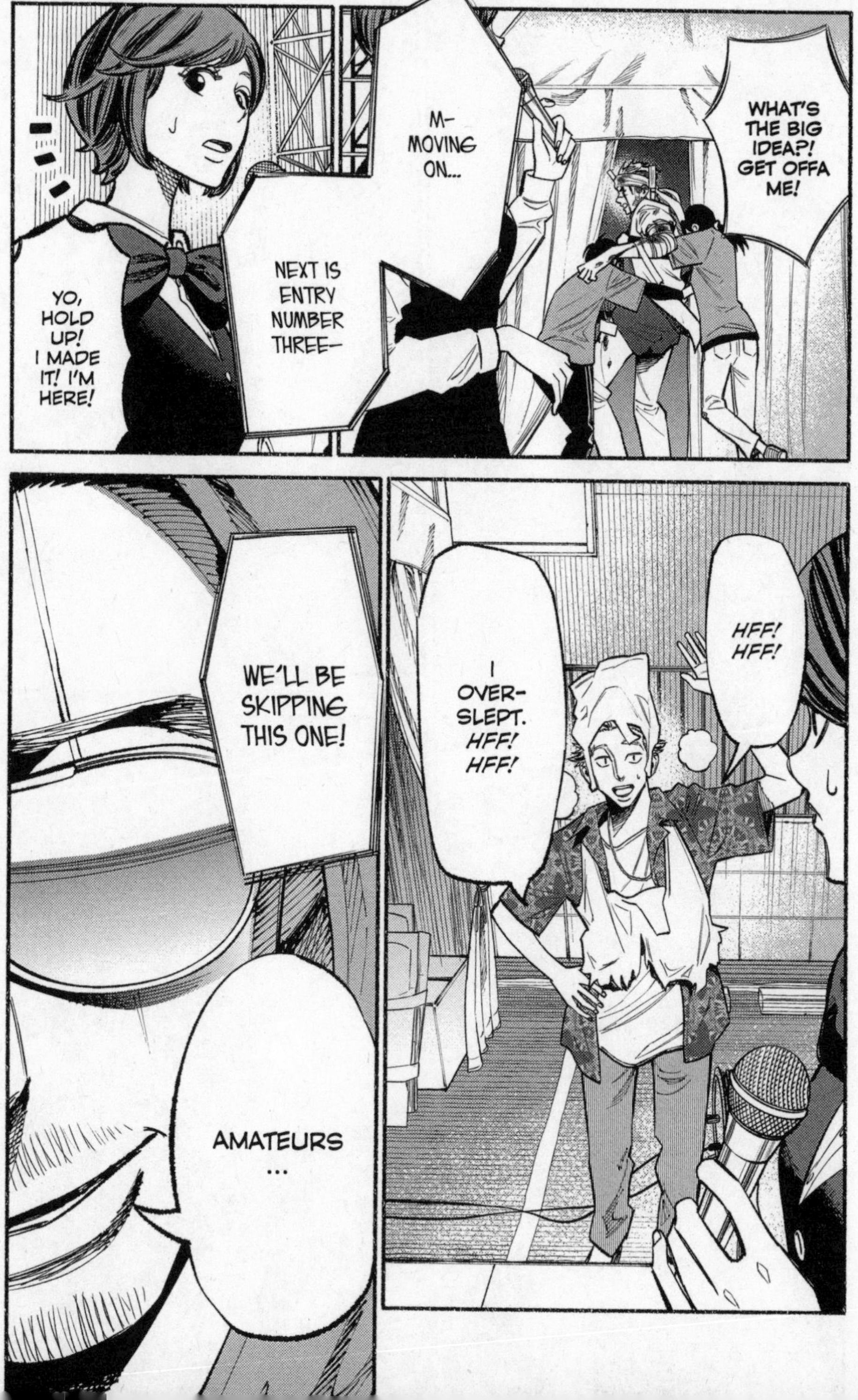
WHAT'S THE BIG IDEA?! GET OFFA ME!
M-MOVING ON...
NEXT IS ENTRY NUMBER THREE-
YO, HOLD UP! I MADE IT! I'M HERE!
HFF! HFF!
I OVER-SLEPT. HFF! HFF!
WE'LL BE SKIPPING THIS ONE!
AMATEURS...

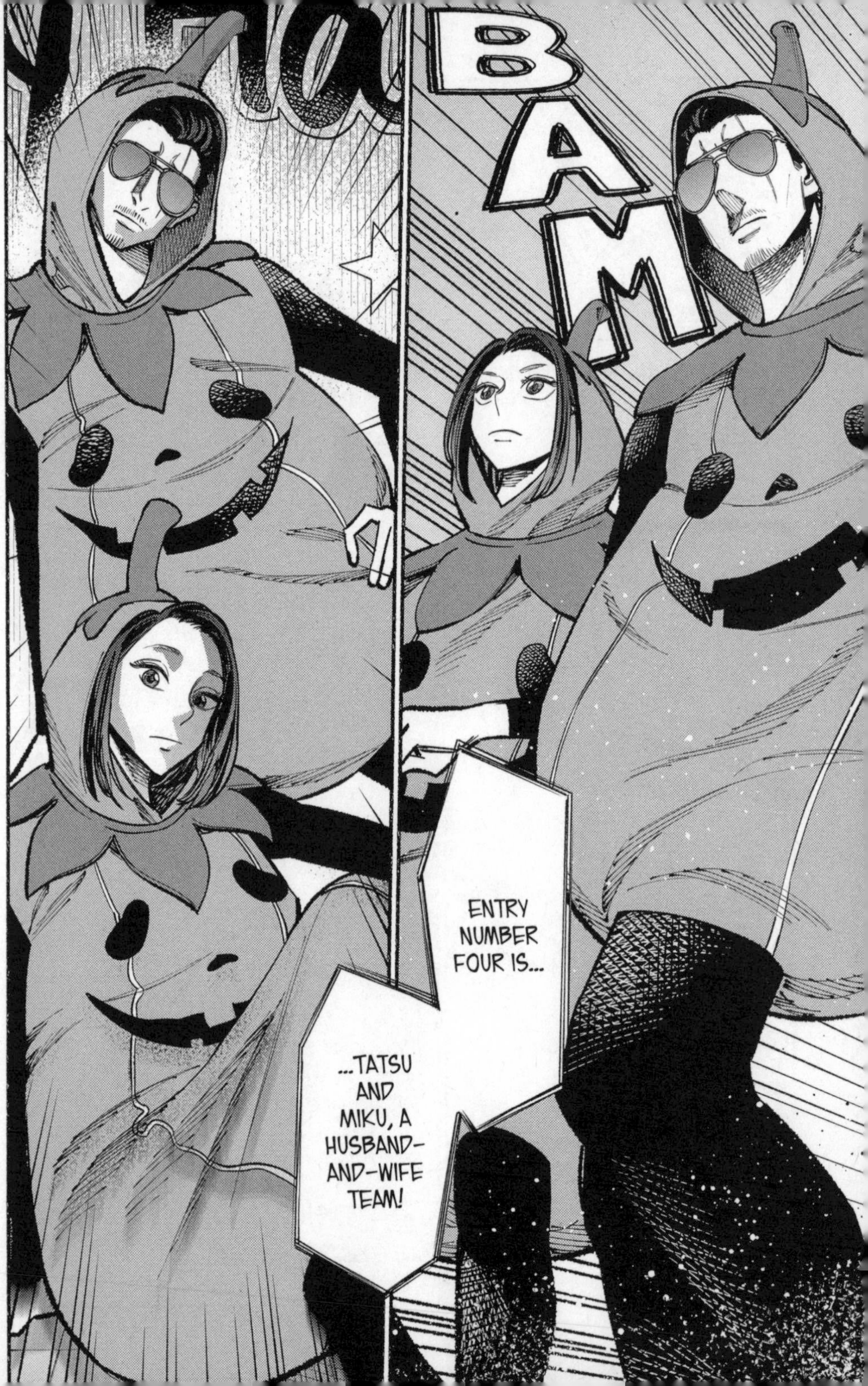
BAM
ENTRY NUMBER FOUR IS...
...TATSU AND MIKU, A HUSBAND-AND-WIFE TEAM!

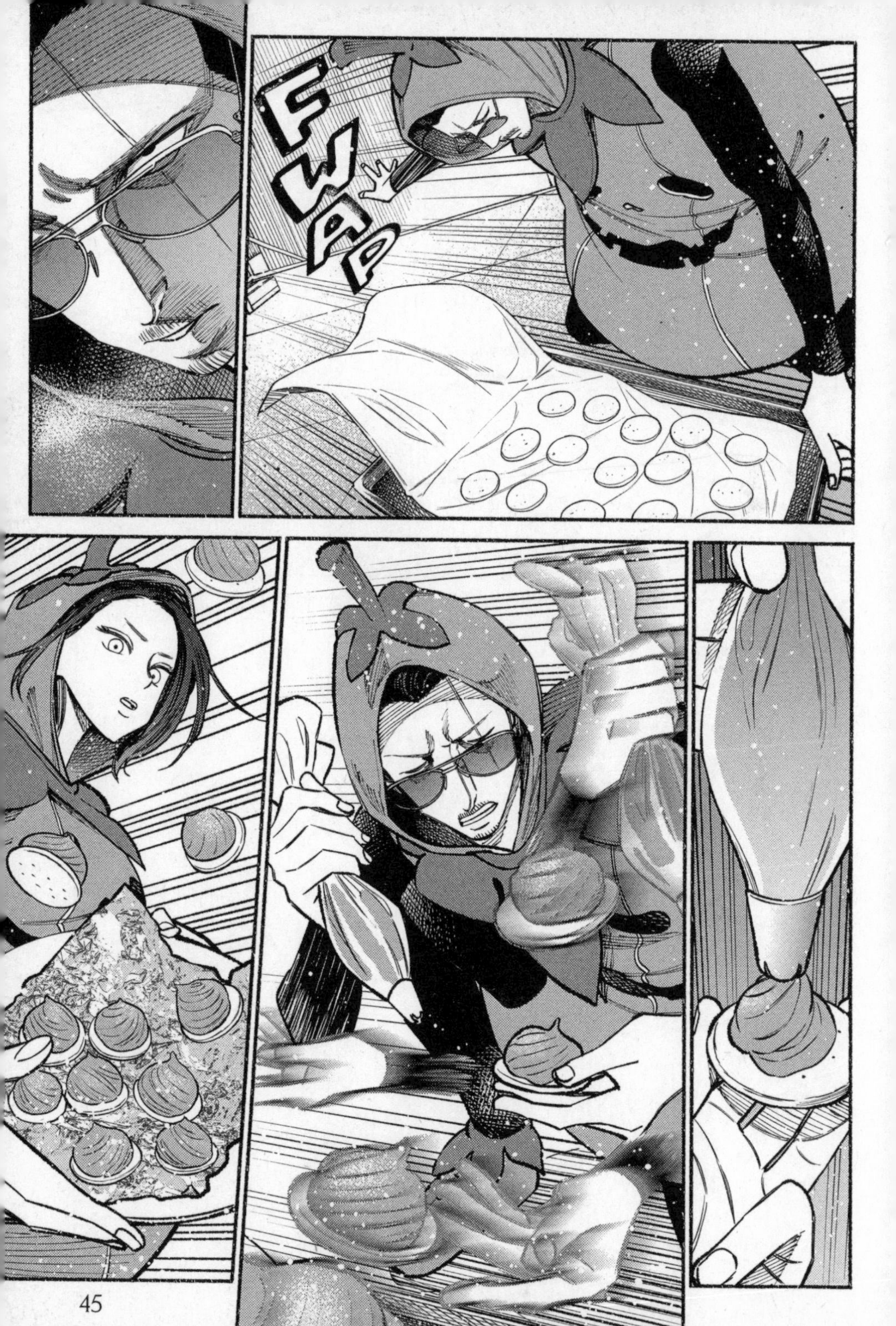
FWAP

SLAM

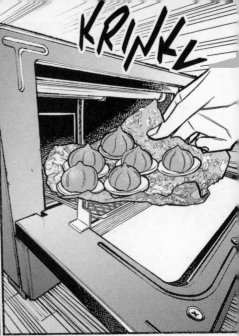

KRINKL

CHIK
CHIK
CHIK

WHMMM

WHMMM

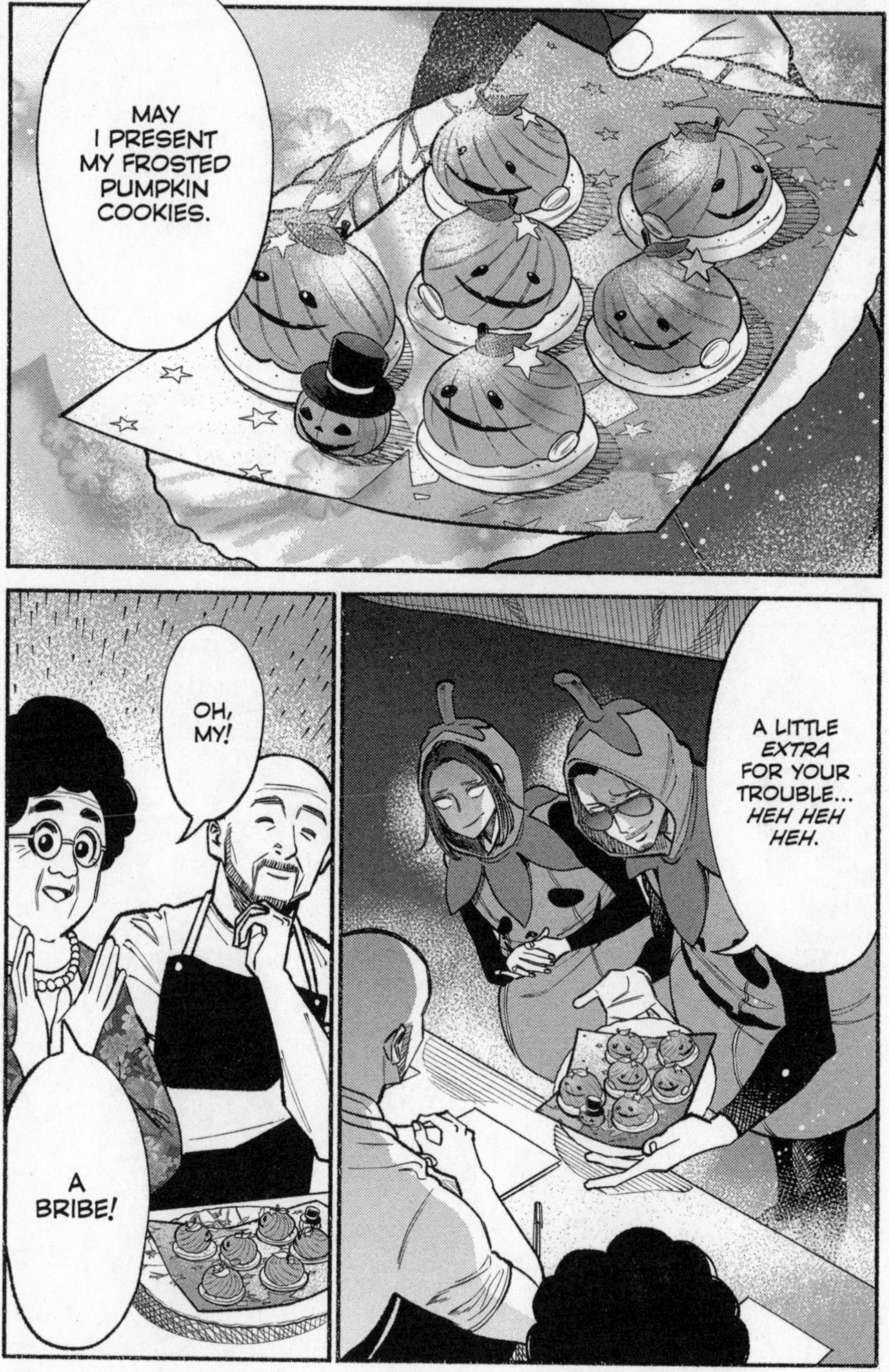
MAY I PRESENT MY FROSTED PUMPKIN COOKIES.
A LITTLE *EXTRA* FOR YOUR TROUBLE... *HEH HEH HEH.*
OH, MY!
A BRIBE!

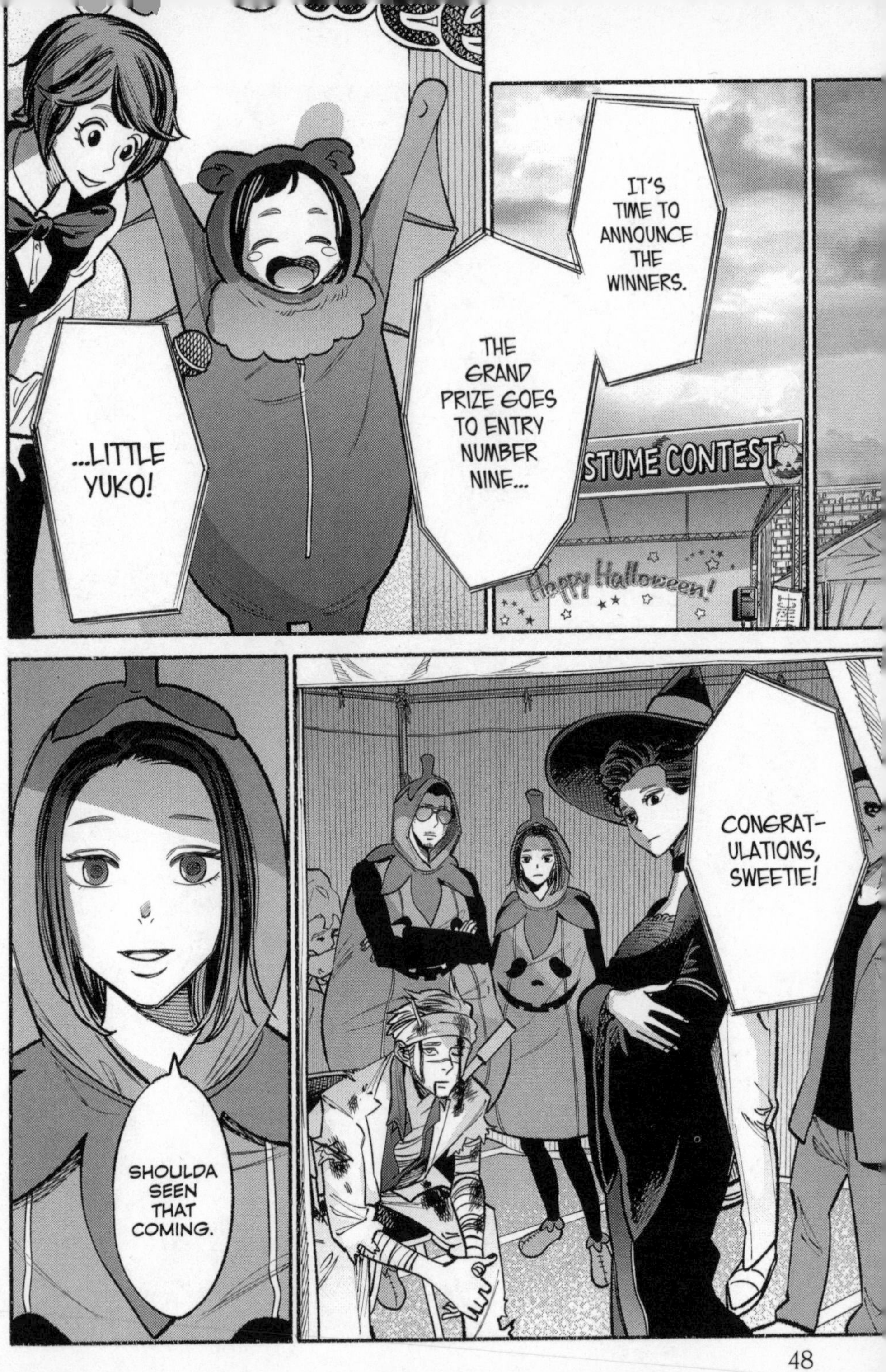
IT'S TIME TO ANNOUNCE THE WINNERS.
THE GRAND PRIZE GOES TO ENTRY NUMBER NINE...
STUME CONTEST
Happy Halloween!
...LITTLE YUKO!
CONGRAT-ULATIONS, SWEETIE!
SHOULDA SEEN THAT COMING.

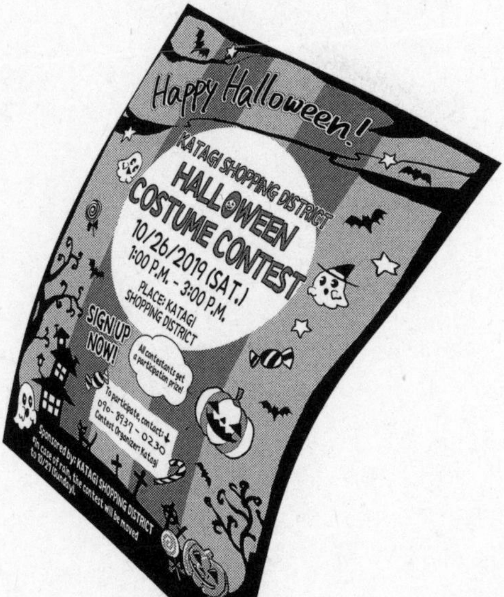
Happy Halloween!
KATAGI SHOPPING DISTRICT
HALLOWEEN COSTUME CONTEST
10/26/2019 (SAT.)
1:00 P.M. - 3:00 P.M.
PLACE: KATAGI SHOPPING DISTRICT
SIGN UP NOW!
All contestants get a participation prize!
To participate, contact: ↓
090- 8937 - 0230
Contest Organizer: Katagi
Sponsored by: KATAGI SHOPPING DISTRICT
*In case of rain, the contest will be moved to 10/27 (Sunday).

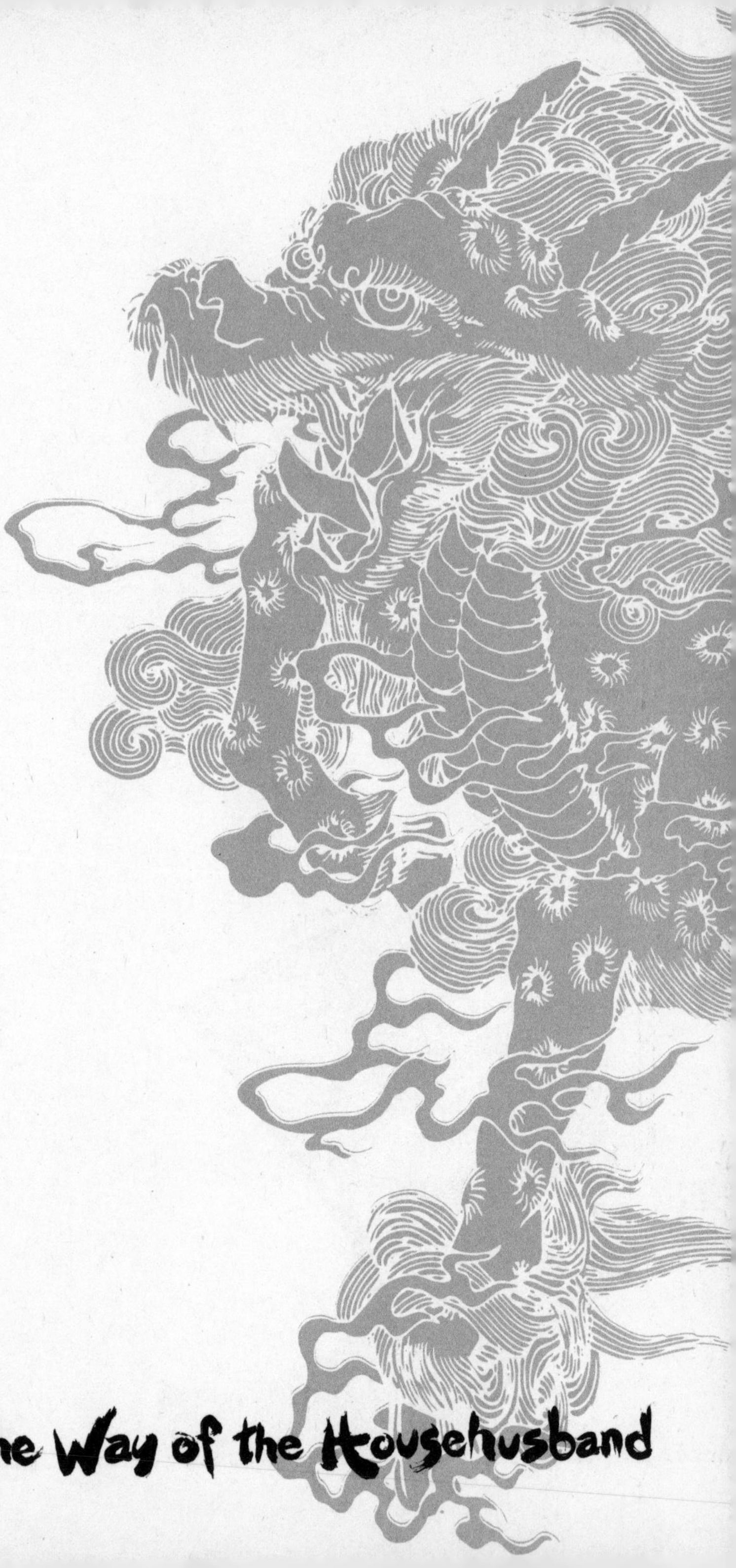

The Way of the Househusband

CHAPTER 40

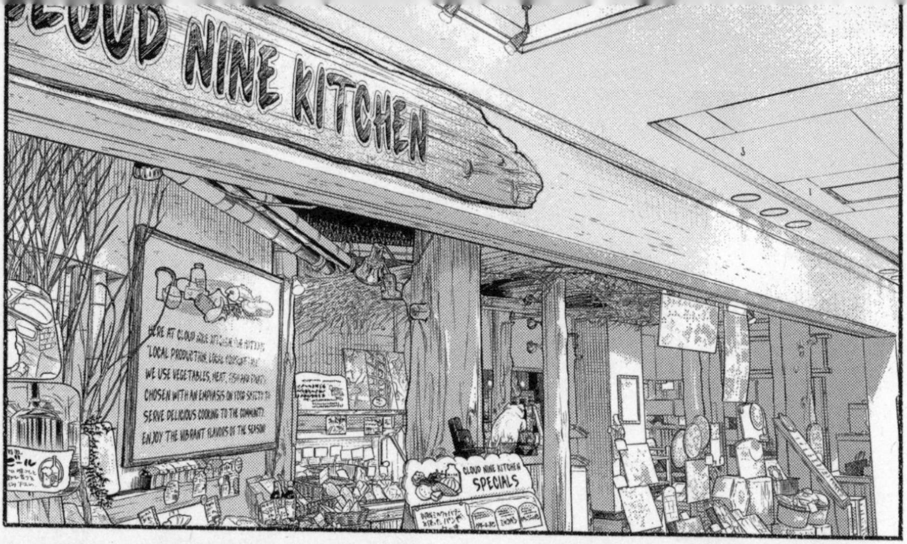

CLOUD NINE KITCHEN
HERE AT CLOUD
"LOCAL PRODUCTION,
WE USE VEGETABLES,
CHOSEN WITH AN EMPHASIS ON
SERVE DELICIOUS COOKING TO THE
ENJOY THE VIBRANT
CLOUD NINE KITCHEN
SPECIALS

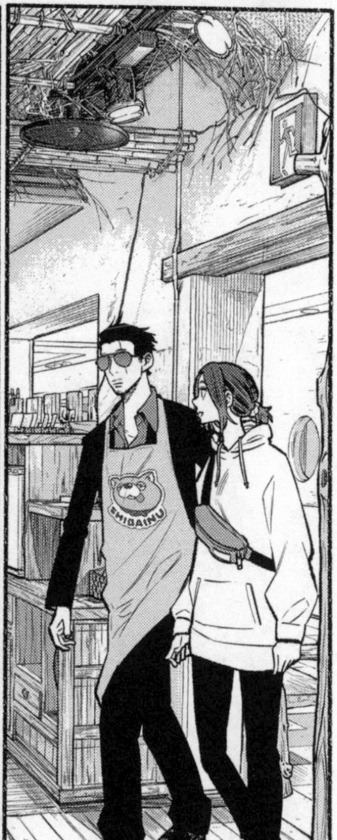

SHIBAINU

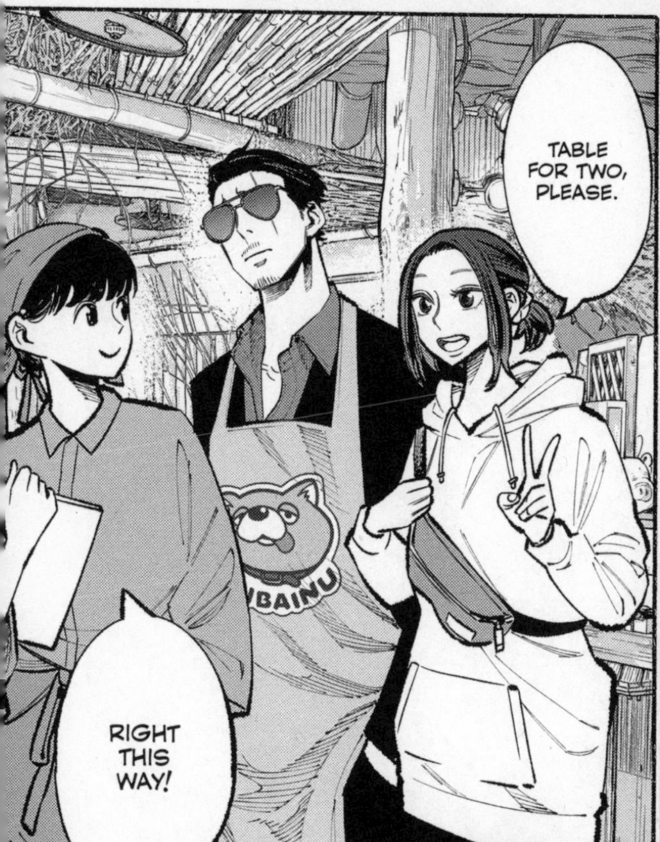

TABLE FOR TWO, PLEASE.
SHIBAINU
RIGHT THIS WAY!

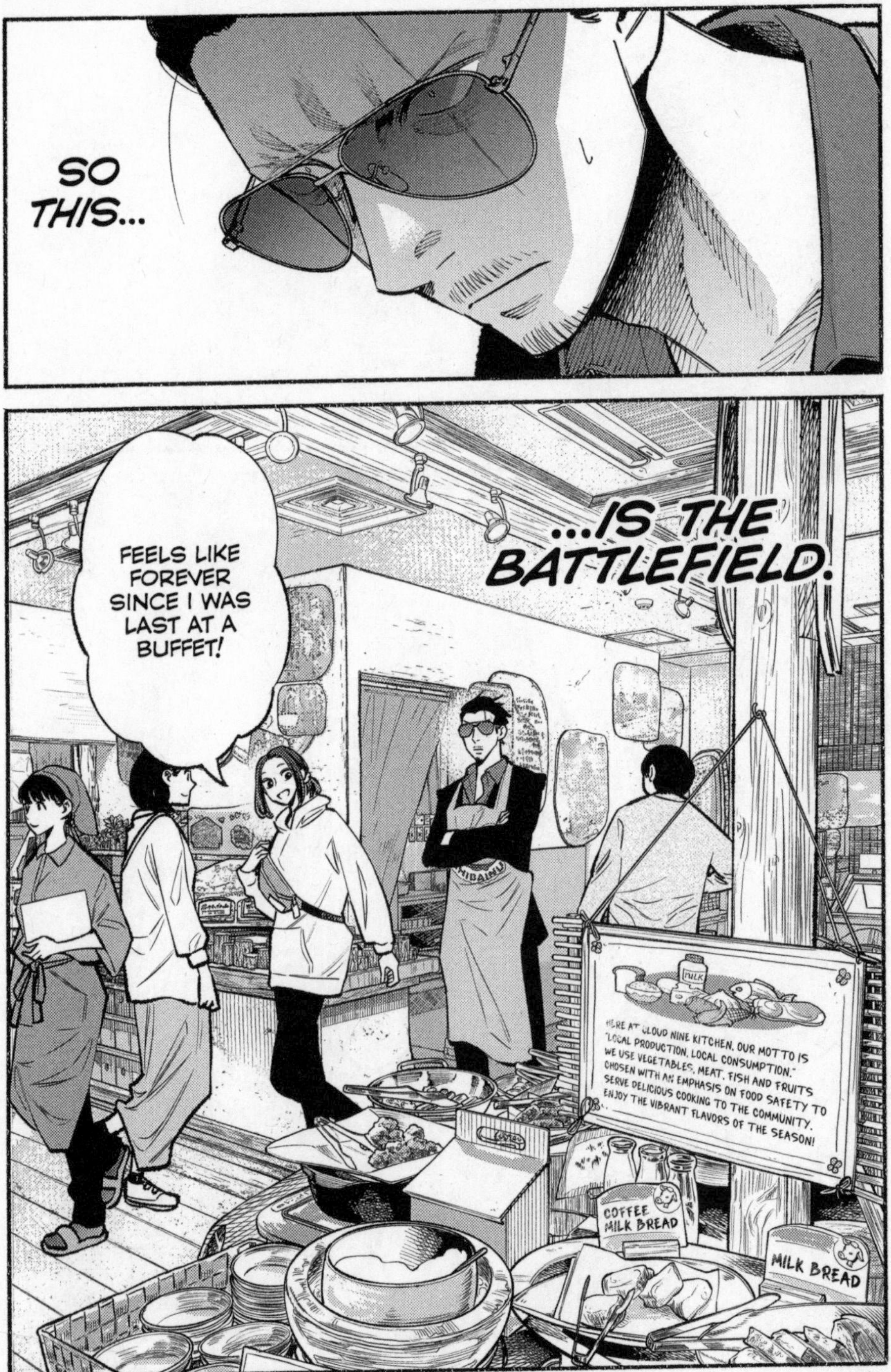
SO THIS...
...IS THE BATTLEFIELD.
FEELS LIKE FOREVER SINCE I WAS LAST AT A BUFFET!
MILK
HERE AT CLOUD NINE KITCHEN, OUR MOTTO IS "LOCAL PRODUCTION, LOCAL CONSUMPTION." WE USE VEGETABLES, MEAT, FISH AND FRUITS CHOSEN WITH AN EMPHASIS ON FOOD SAFETY TO SERVE DELICIOUS COOKING TO THE COMMUNITY. ENJOY THE VIBRANT FLAVORS OF THE SEASON!
COFFEE MILK BREAD
MILK BREAD

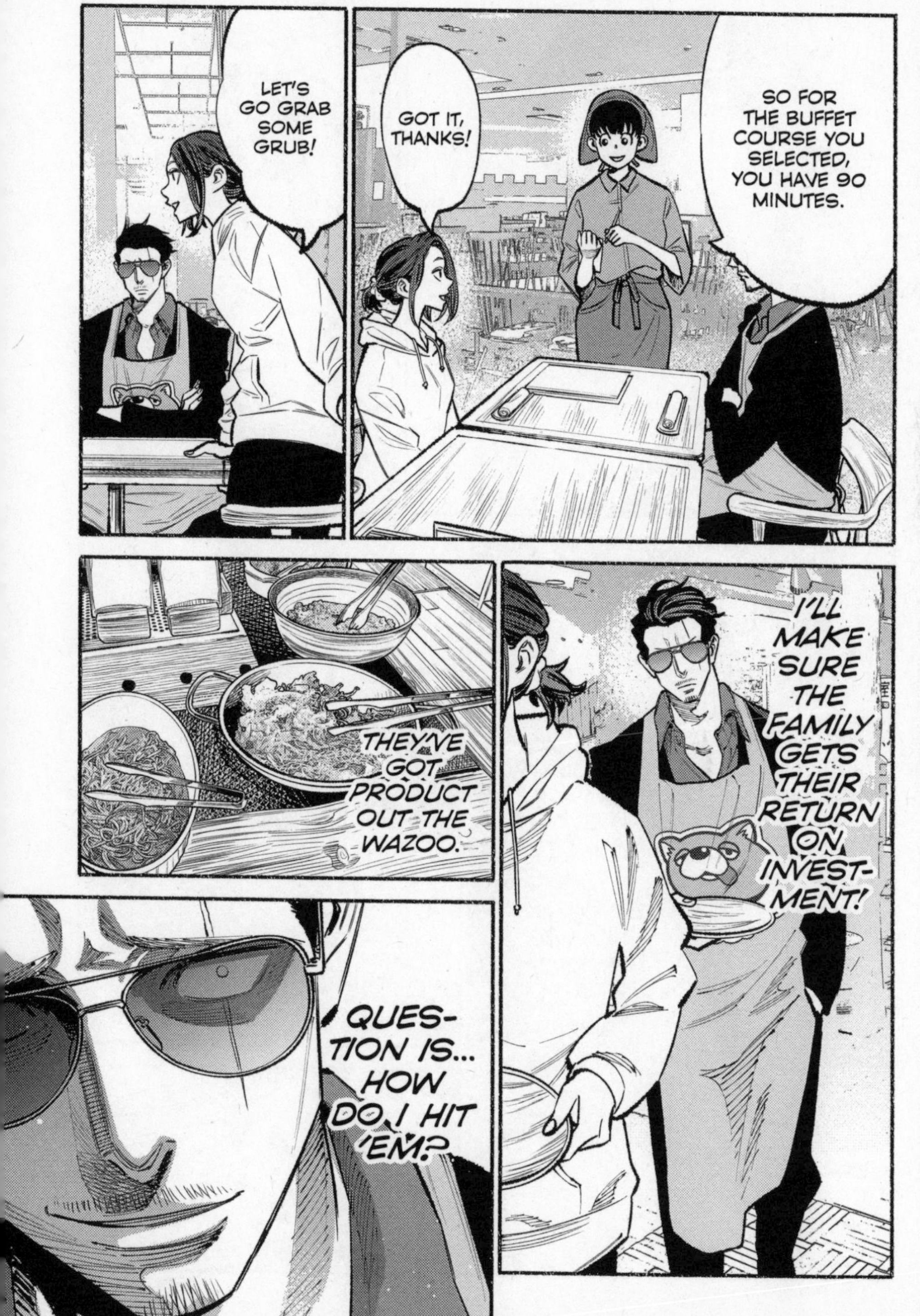
SO FOR THE BUFFET COURSE YOU SELECTED, YOU HAVE 90 MINUTES.
GOT IT, THANKS!
LET'S GO GRAB SOME GRUB!
I'LL MAKE SURE THE FAMILY GETS THEIR RETURN ON INVEST-MENT!
THEY'VE GOT PRODUCT OUT THE WAZOO.
QUES-TION IS... HOW DO I HIT 'EM?

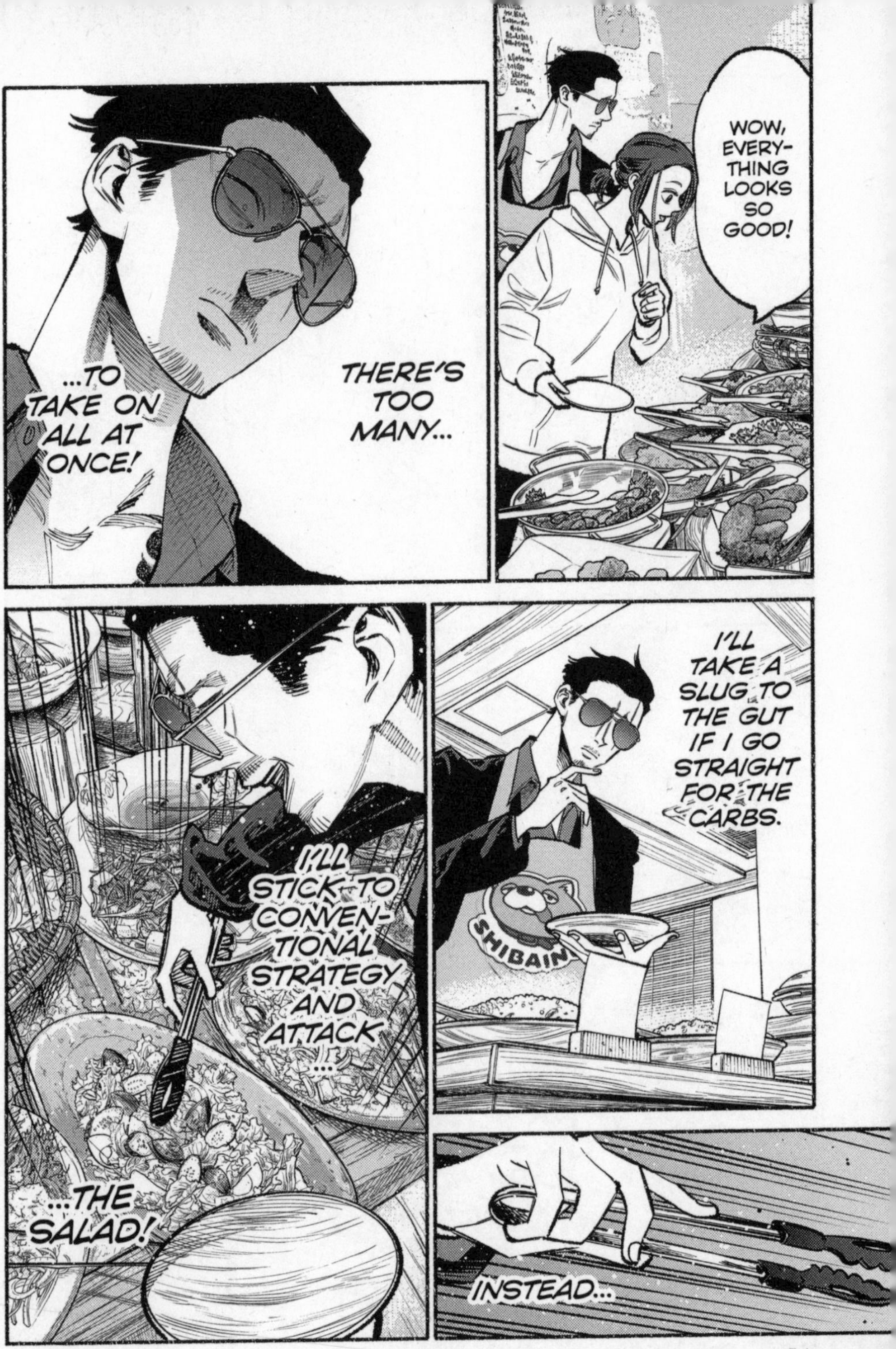
WOW, EVERY-THING LOOKS SO GOOD!
THERE'S TOO MANY...
...TO TAKE ON ALL AT ONCE!
I'LL TAKE A SLUG TO THE GUT IF I GO STRAIGHT FOR THE CARBS.
INSTEAD...
I'LL STICK TO CONVEN-TIONAL STRATEGY AND ATTACK ...
...THE SALAD!
SHIBAIN

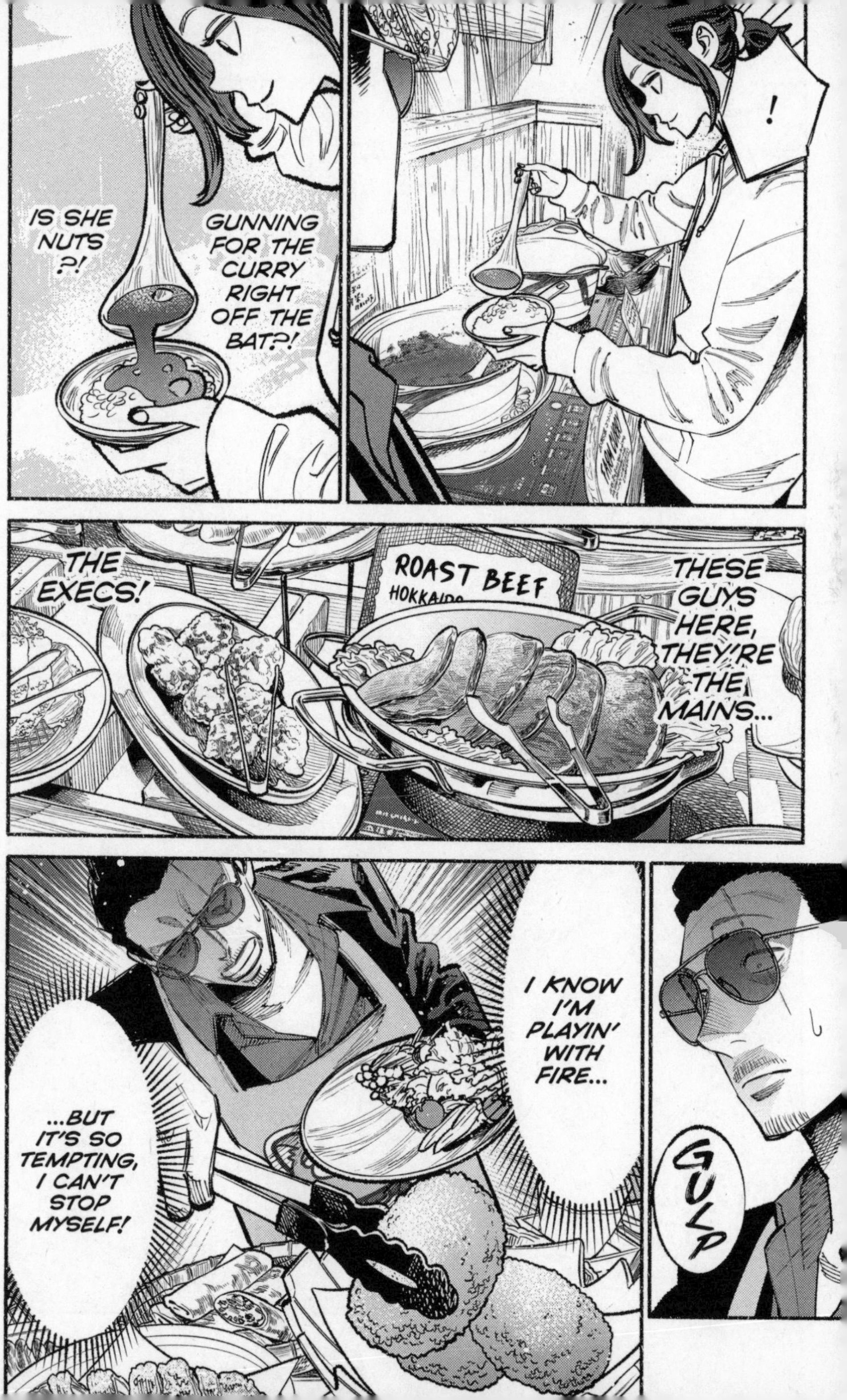
!
GUNNING FOR THE CURRY RIGHT OFF THE BAT?!
IS SHE NUTS?!
THESE GUYS HERE, THEY'RE THE MAINS...
ROAST BEEF
HOKKAIDO
THE EXECS!
GULP
I KNOW I'M PLAYIN' WITH FIRE...
...BUT IT'S SO TEMPTING, I CAN'T STOP MYSELF!

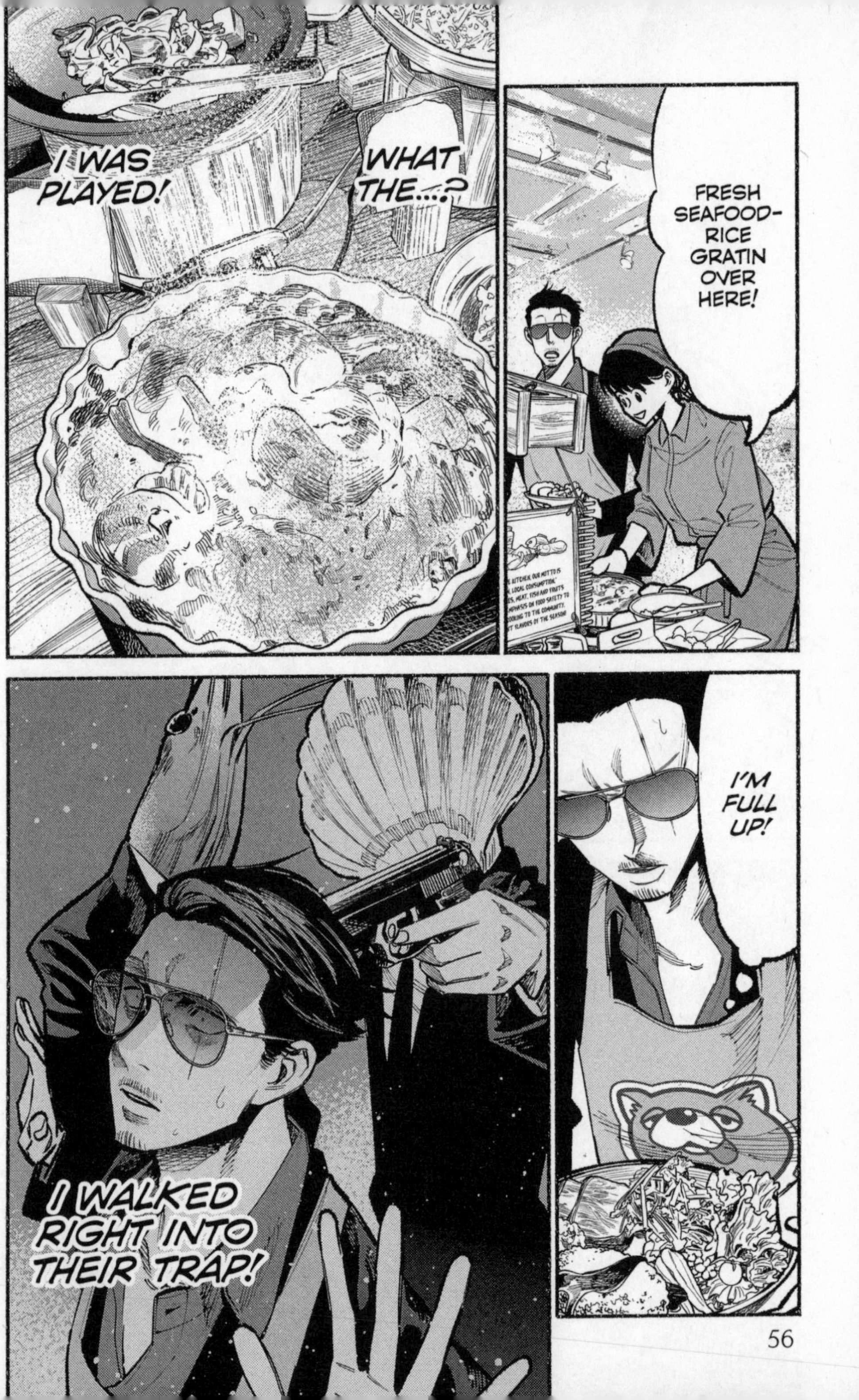

FRESH SEAFOOD-RICE GRATIN OVER HERE!
WHAT THE...?
I WAS PLAYED!
I'M FULL UP!
I WALKED RIGHT INTO THEIR TRAP!

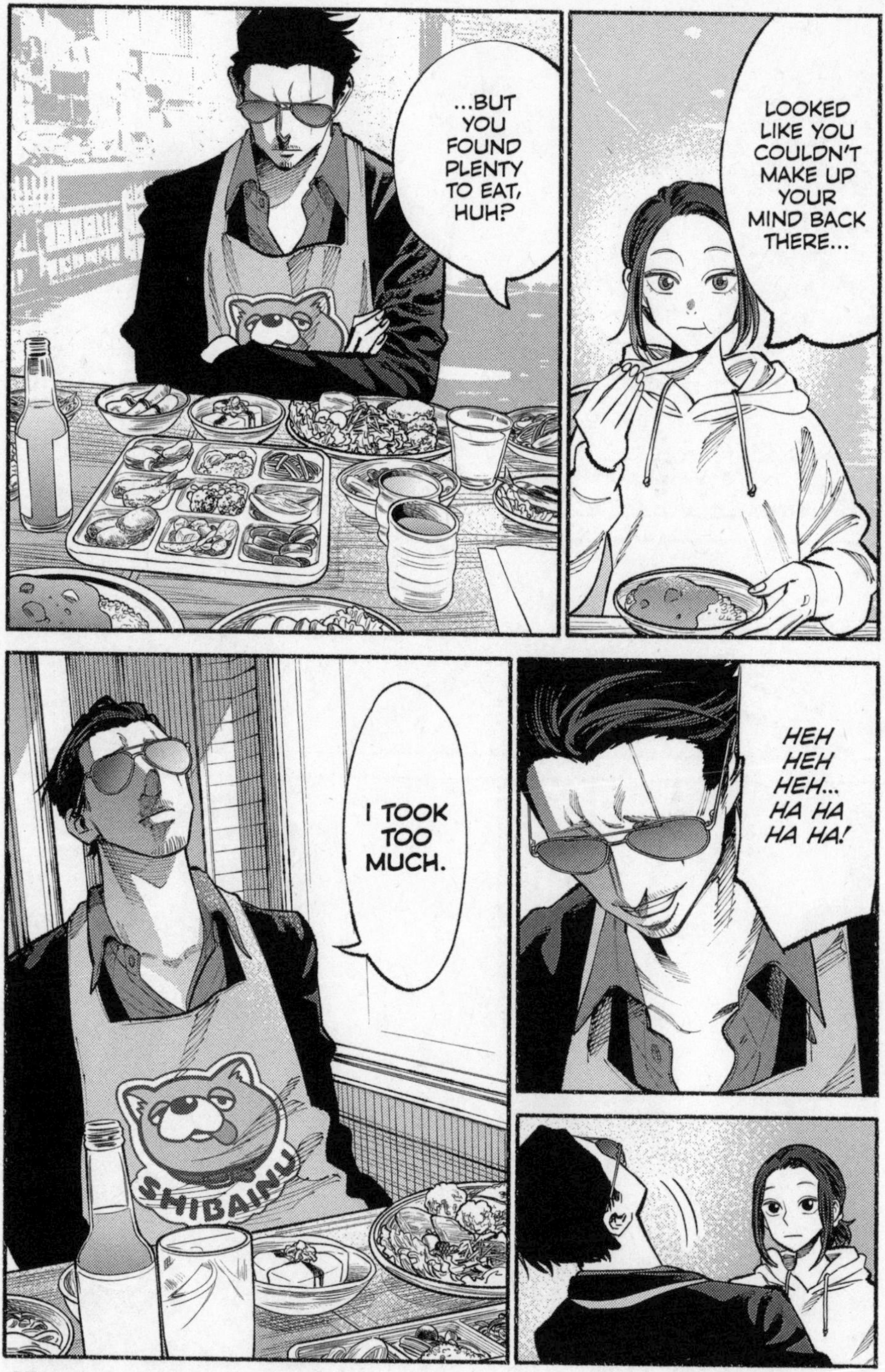
LOOKED LIKE YOU COULDN'T MAKE UP YOUR MIND BACK THERE...
...BUT YOU FOUND PLENTY TO EAT, HUH?
HEH HEH HEH... HA HA HA HA!
I TOOK TOO MUCH.
SHIBAINU

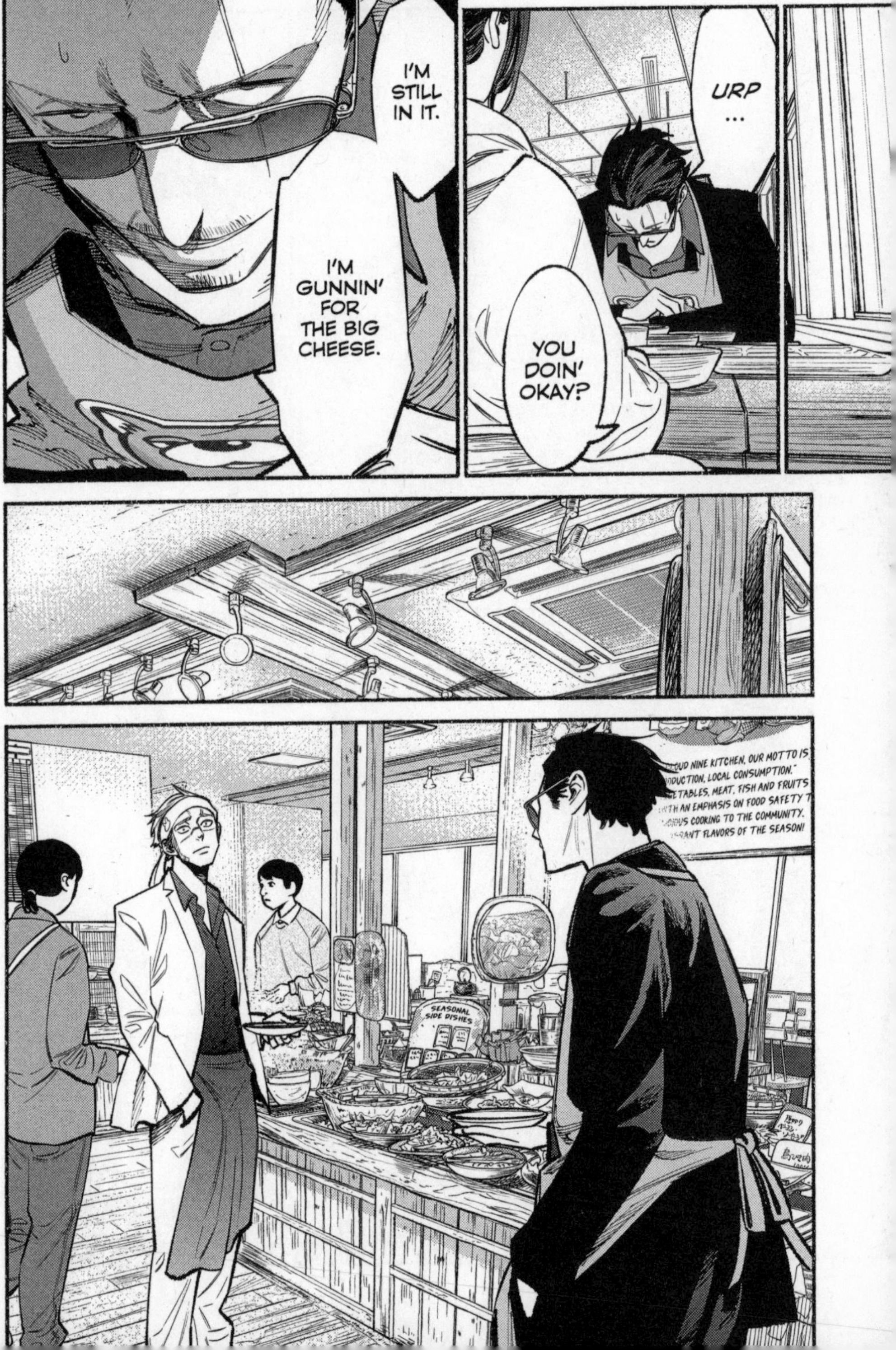
URP ...
YOU DOIN' OKAY?
I'M STILL IN IT.
I'M GUNNIN' FOR THE BIG CHEESE.
OUD NINE KITCHEN, OUR MOTTO IS
DUCTION, LOCAL CONSUMPTION."
TABLES, MEAT, FISH AND FRUITS
TH AN EMPHASIS ON FOOD SAFETY
S COOKING TO THE COMMUNITY.
ANT FLAVORS OF THE SEASON!
SEASONAL SIDE DISHES

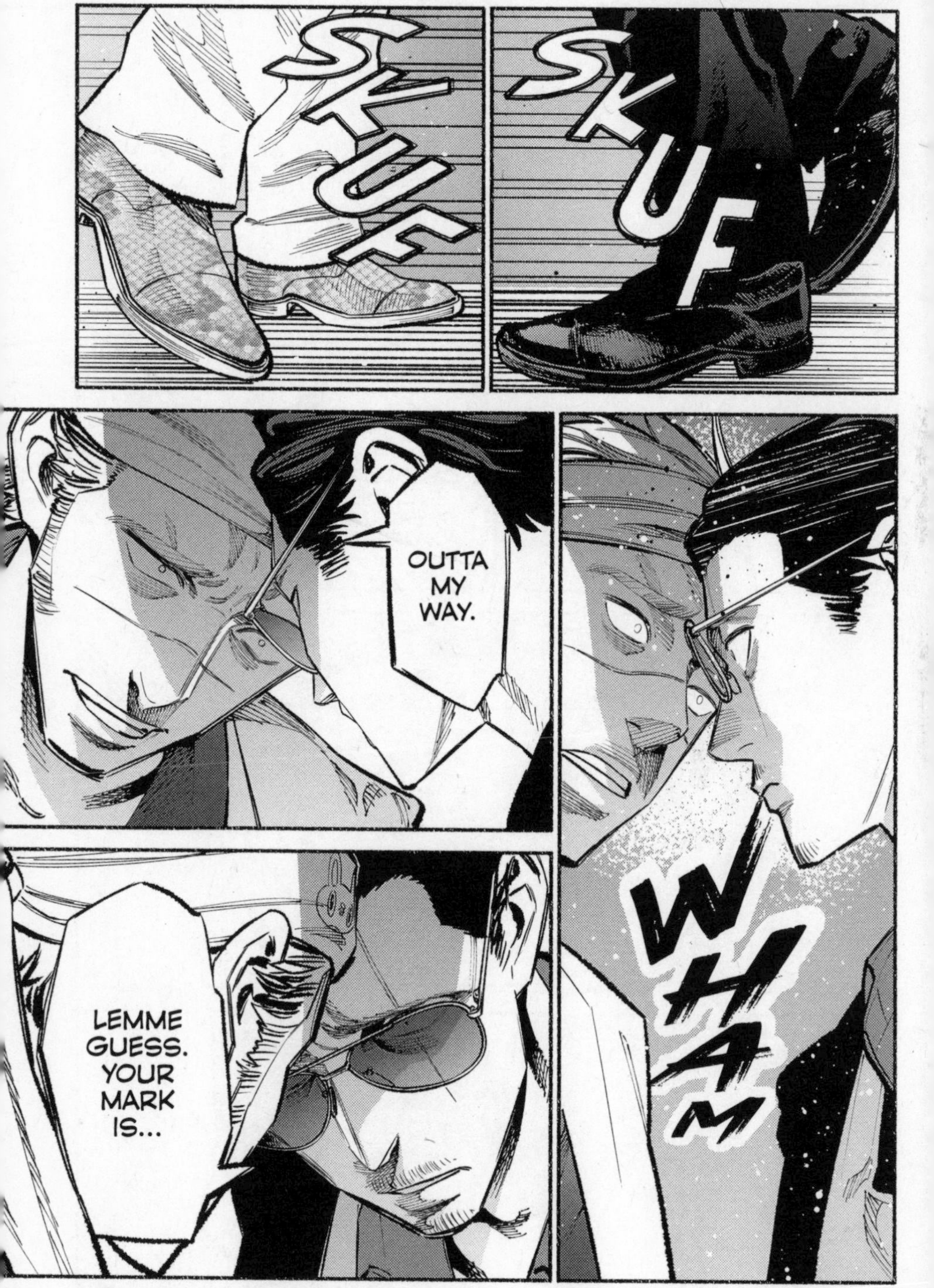
SKUF
SKUF
WHAM
OUTTA MY WAY.
LEMME GUESS. YOUR MARK IS...

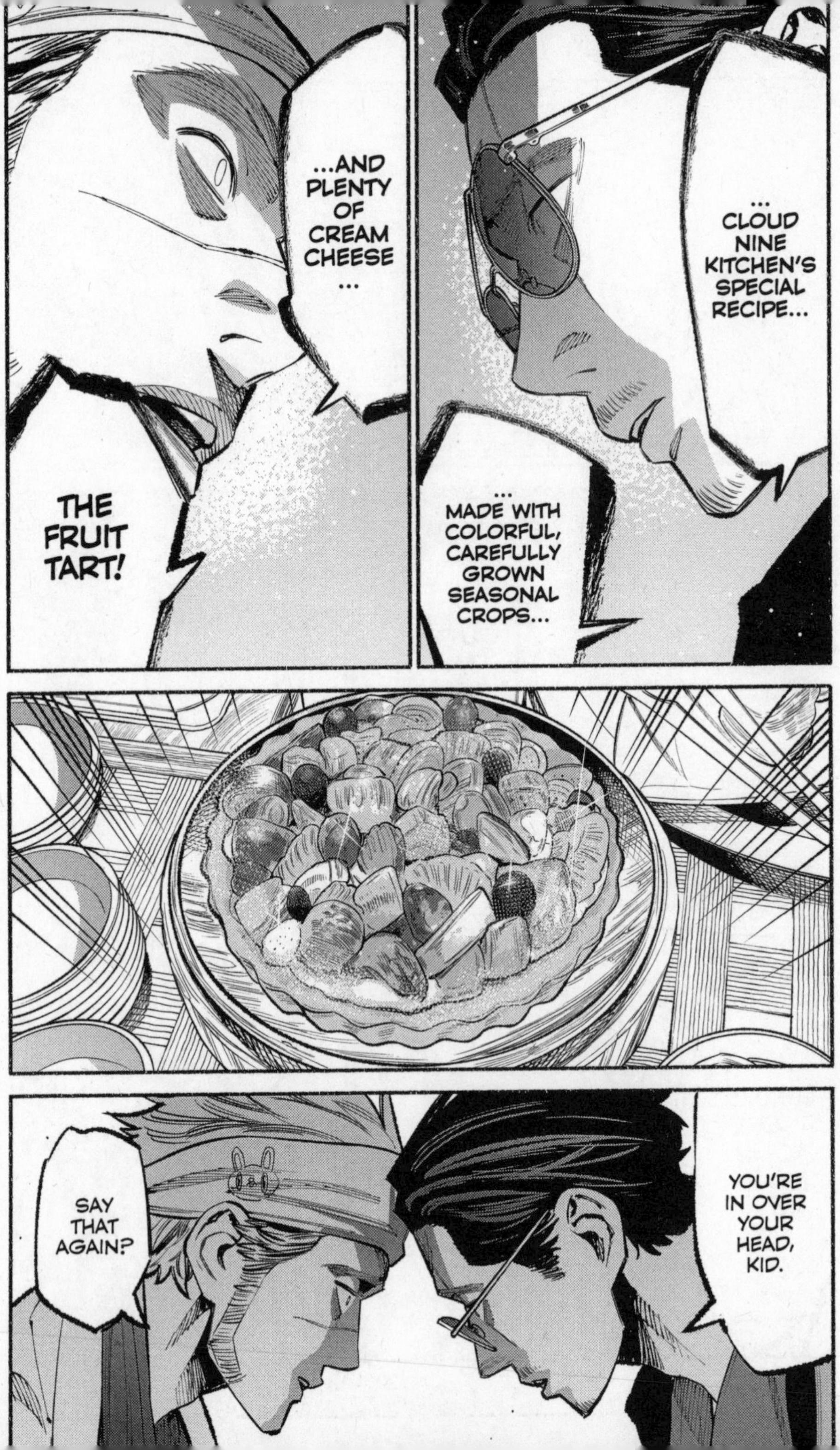
... CLOUD NINE KITCHEN'S SPECIAL RECIPE...
... MADE WITH COLORFUL, CAREFULLY GROWN SEASONAL CROPS...
...AND PLENTY OF CREAM CHEESE ...
THE FRUIT TART!
YOU'RE IN OVER YOUR HEAD, KID.
SAY THAT AGAIN?

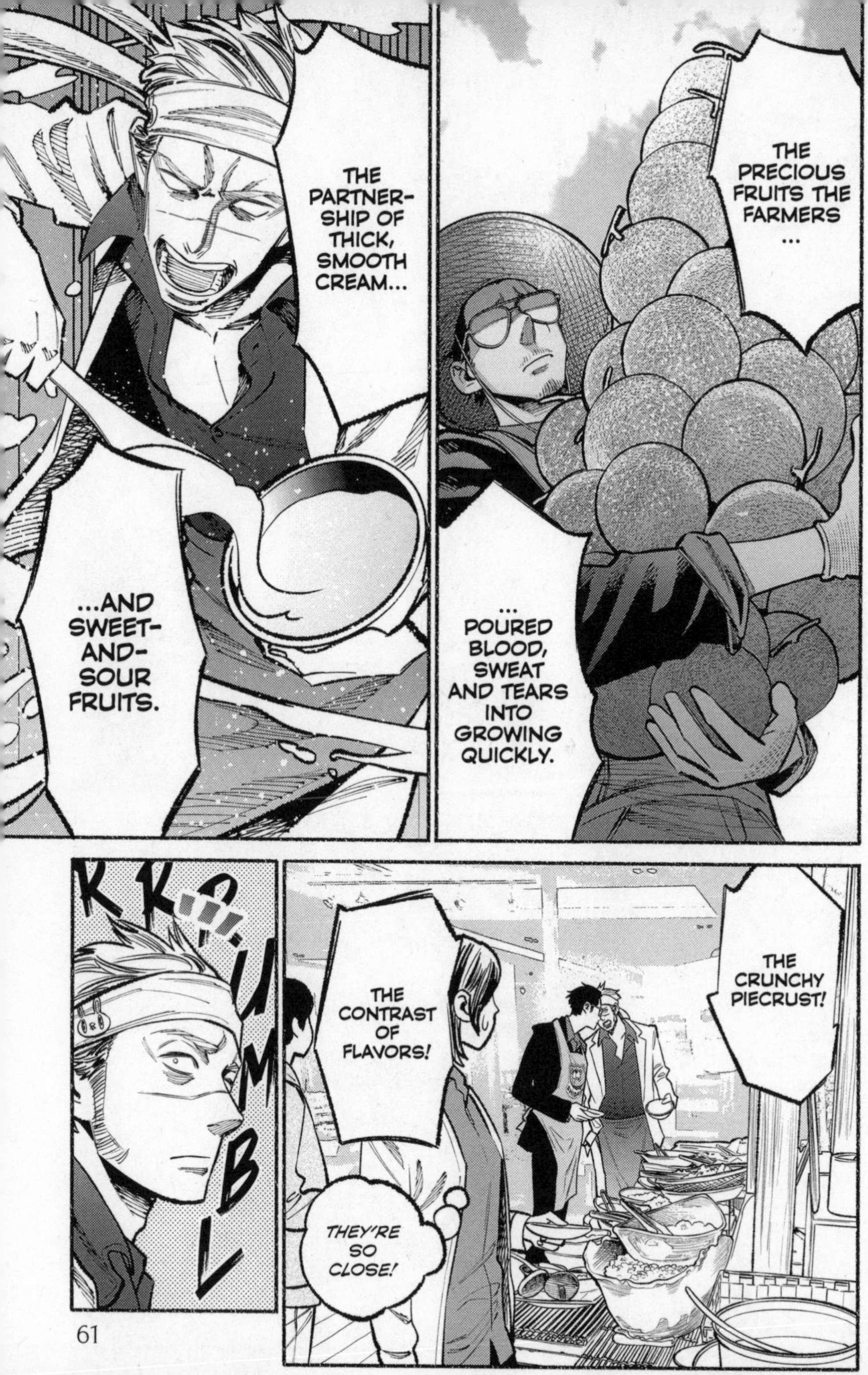
THE PRECIOUS FRUITS THE FARMERS ...
... POURED BLOOD, SWEAT AND TEARS INTO GROWING QUICKLY.
THE PARTNERSHIP OF THICK, SMOOTH CREAM...
...AND SWEET-AND-SOUR FRUITS.
THE CRUNCHY PIECRUST!
THE CONTRAST OF FLAVORS!
THEY'RE SO CLOSE!

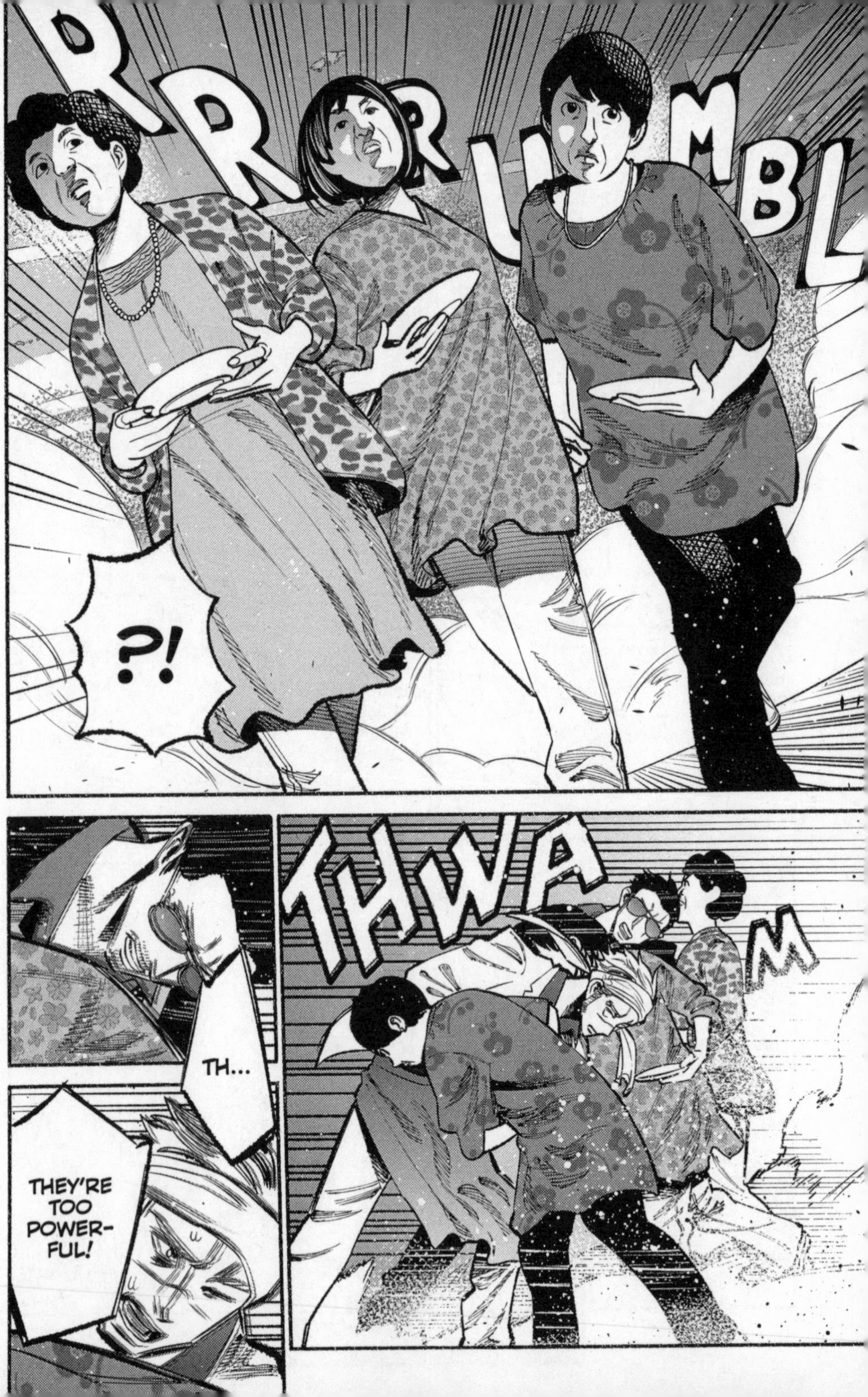
RRRUMBL
?!
THWAM
TH...
THEY'RE TOO POWER-FUL!

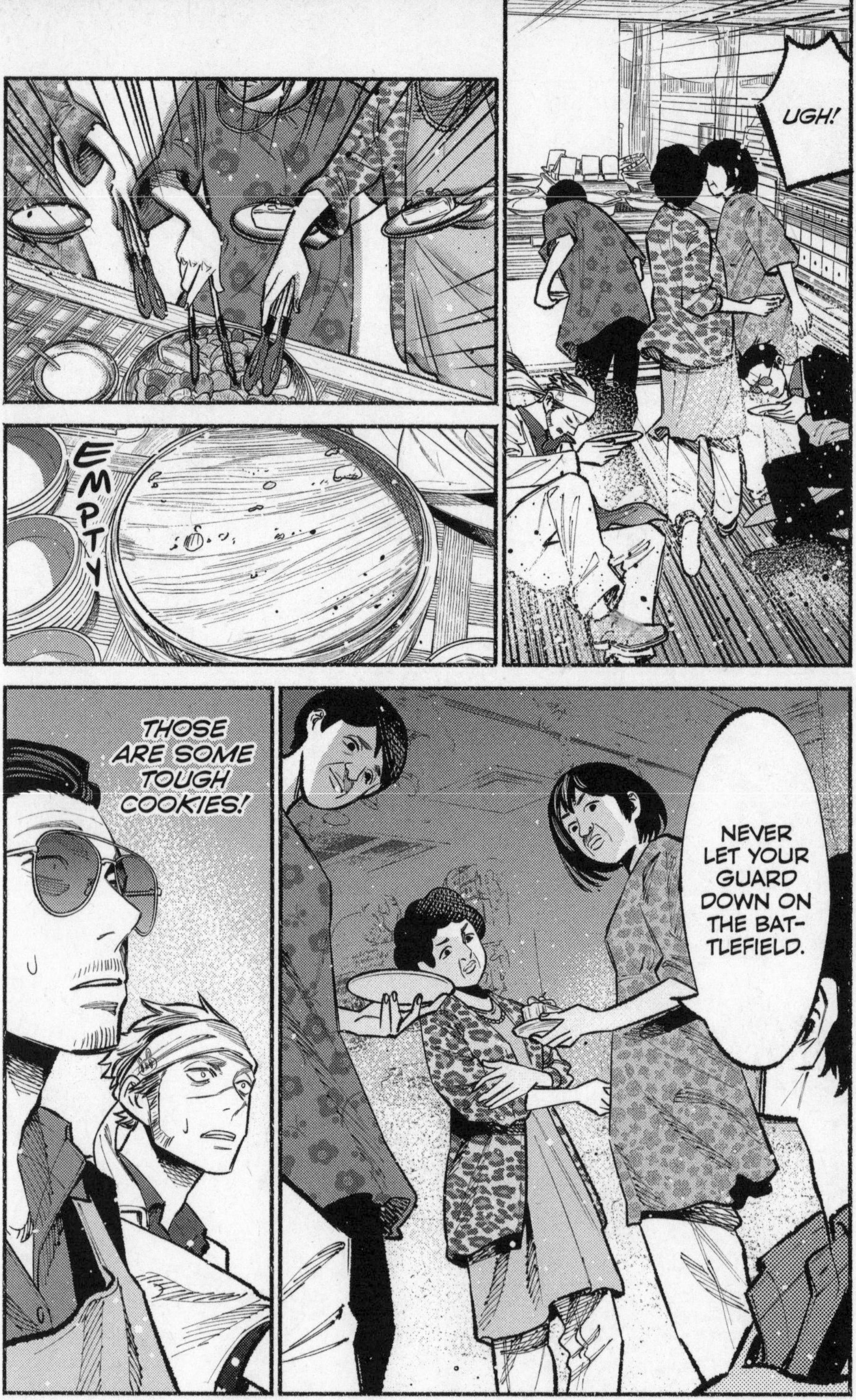
UGH!
EMPTY
NEVER LET YOUR GUARD DOWN ON THE BAT-TLEFIELD.
THOSE ARE SOME TOUGH COOKIES!

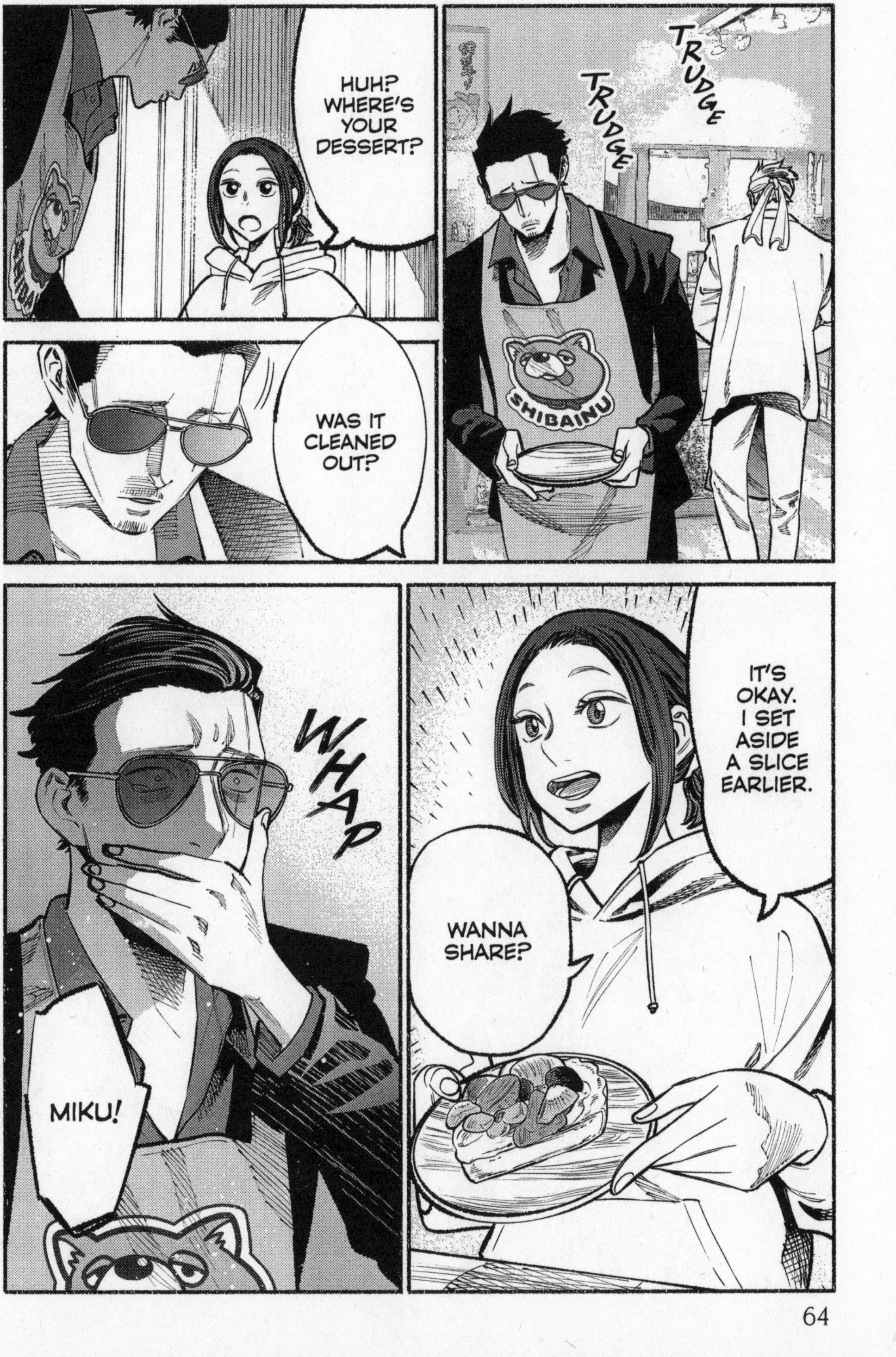
TRUDGE
TRUDGE
HUH? WHERE'S YOUR DESSERT?
WAS IT CLEANED OUT?
IT'S OKAY. I SET ASIDE A SLICE EARLIER.
WANNA SHARE?
WHAP
MIKU!

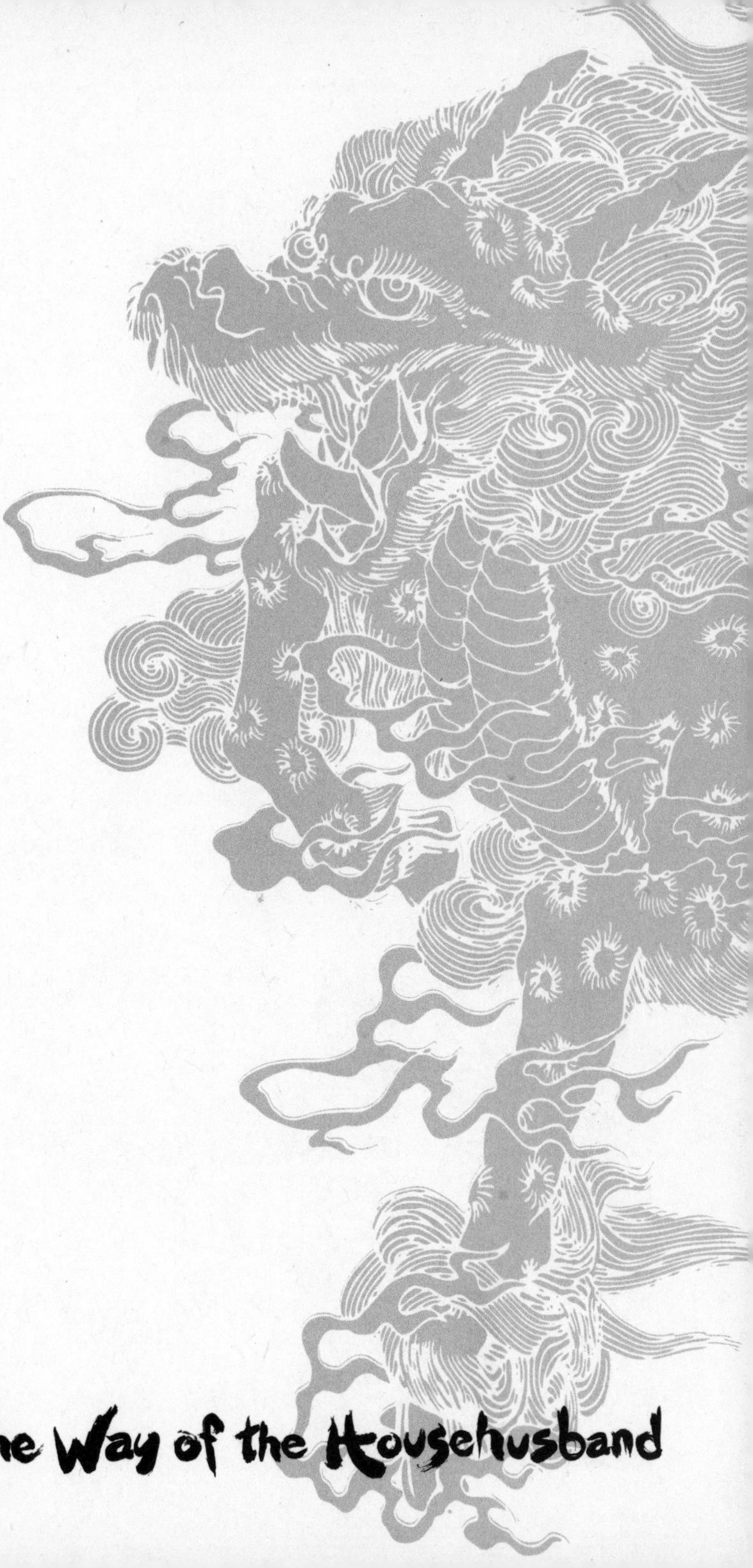

The Way of the Househusband

CHAPTER 41

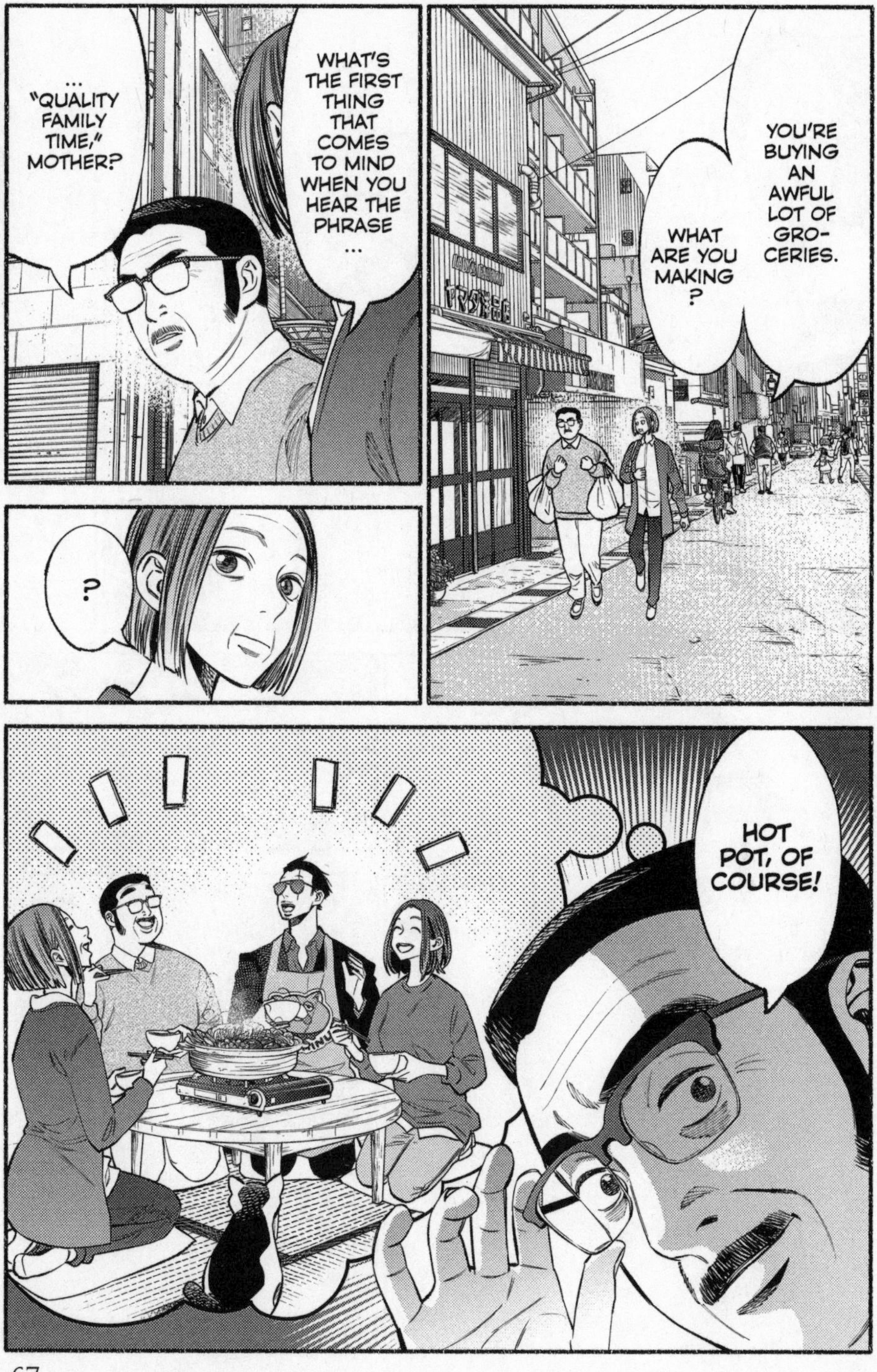
YOU'RE BUYING AN AWFUL LOT OF GRO-CERIES.
WHAT ARE YOU MAKING?
WHAT'S THE FIRST THING THAT COMES TO MIND WHEN YOU HEAR THE PHRASE...
..."QUALITY FAMILY TIME," MOTHER?
?
HOT POT, OF COURSE!

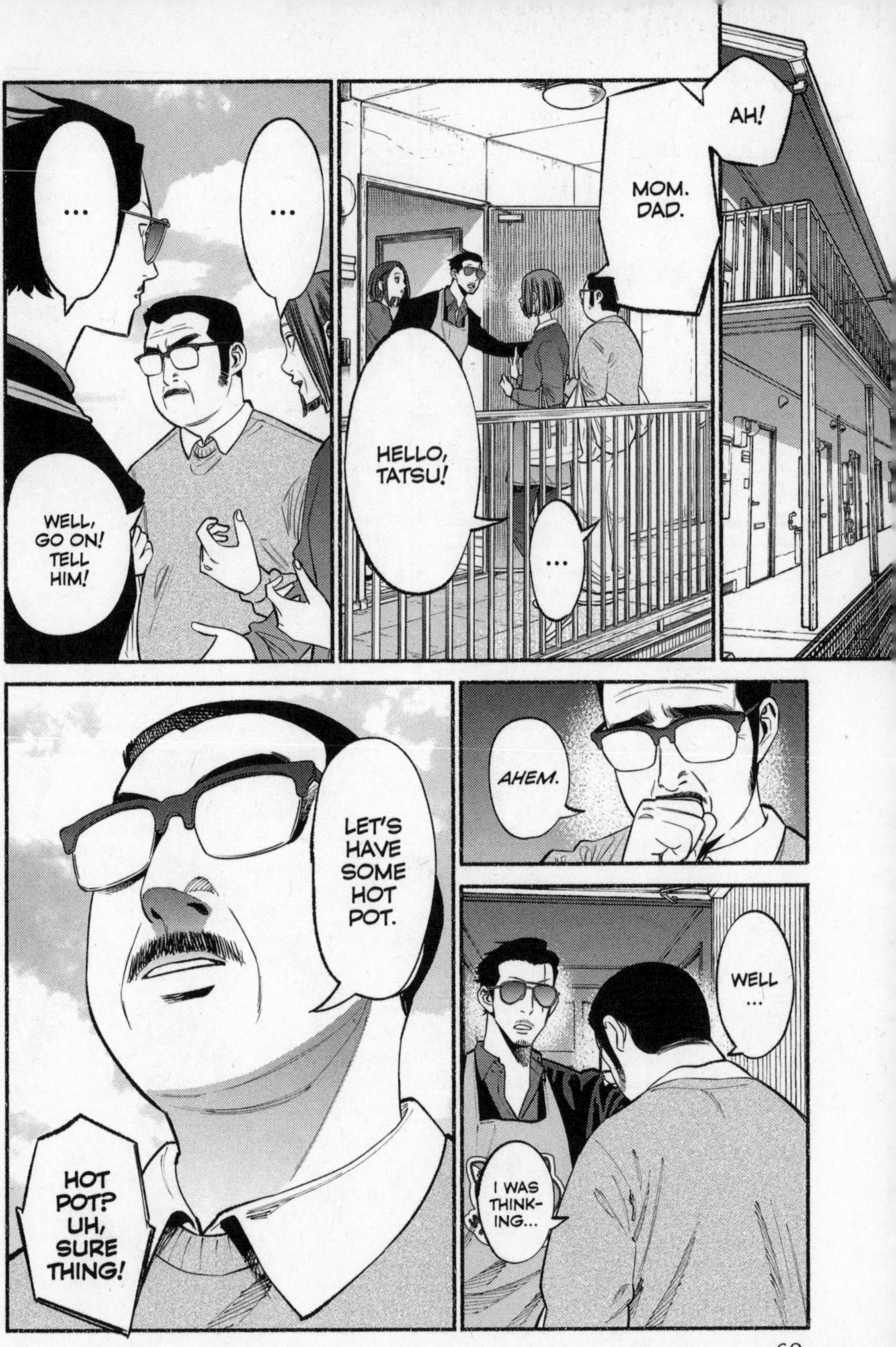
AH!
MOM. DAD.
HELLO, TATSU!
...
...
...
WELL, GO ON! TELL HIM!
AHEM.
WELL ...
I WAS THINK-ING...
LET'S HAVE SOME HOT POT.
HOT POT? UH, SURE THING!

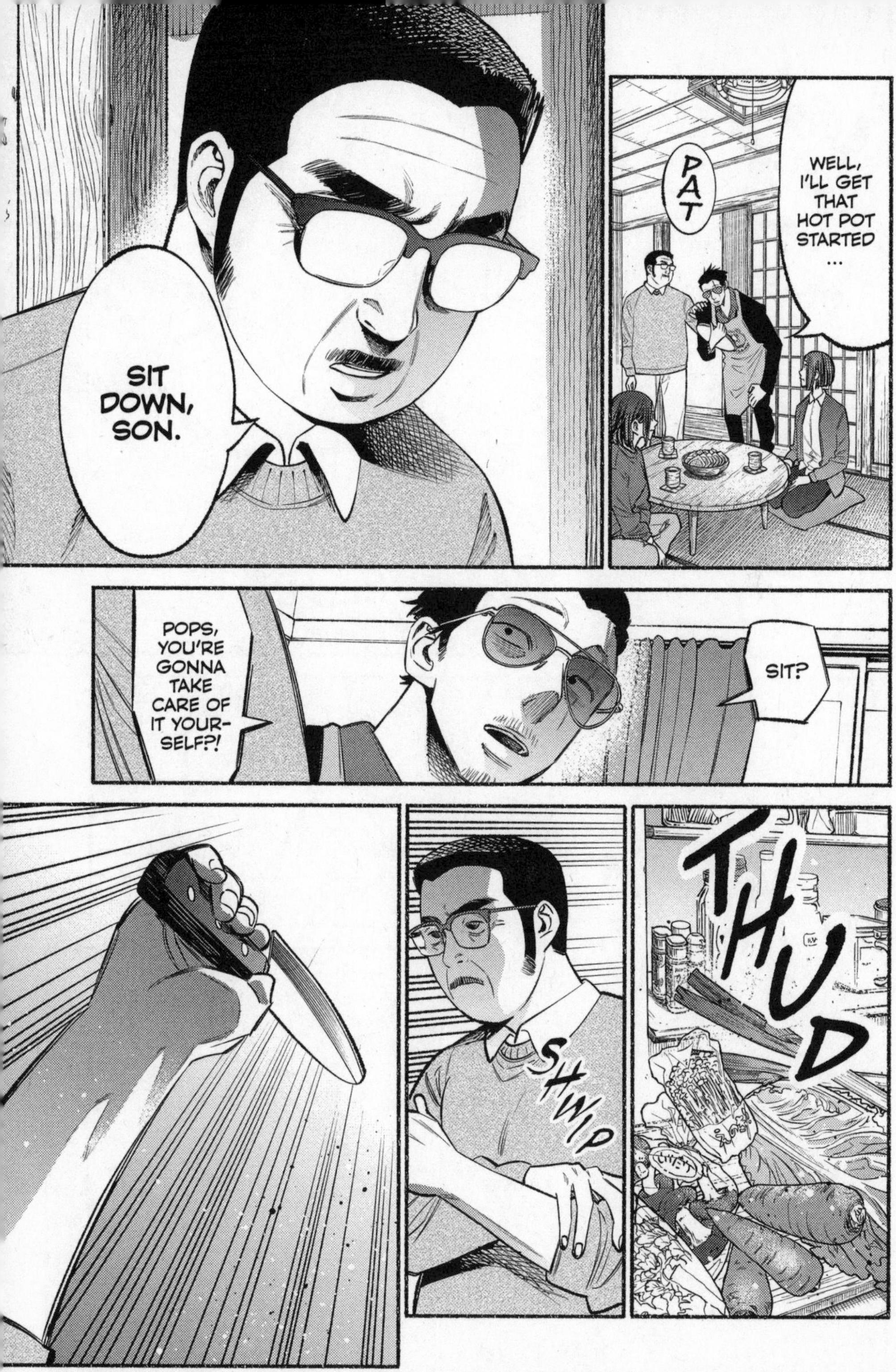
WELL, I'LL GET THAT HOT POT STARTED ...
PAT
SIT DOWN, SON.
SIT?
POPS, YOU'RE GONNA TAKE CARE OF IT YOUR-SELF?!
THUD
SHWIP

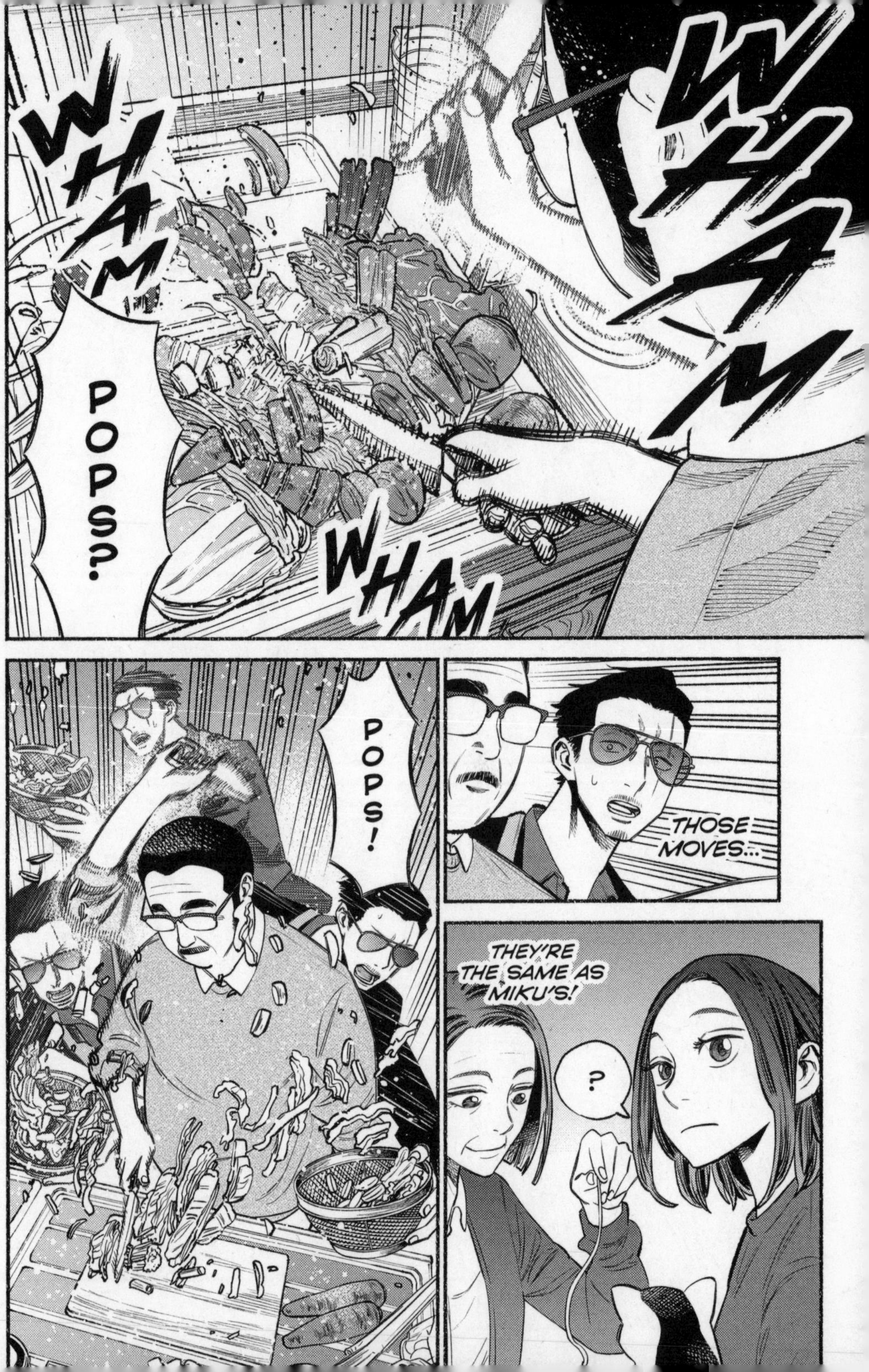
WHAM
WHAM
POPS?
WHAM
THOSE MOVES...
THEY'RE THE SAME AS MIKU'S!
?
POPS!

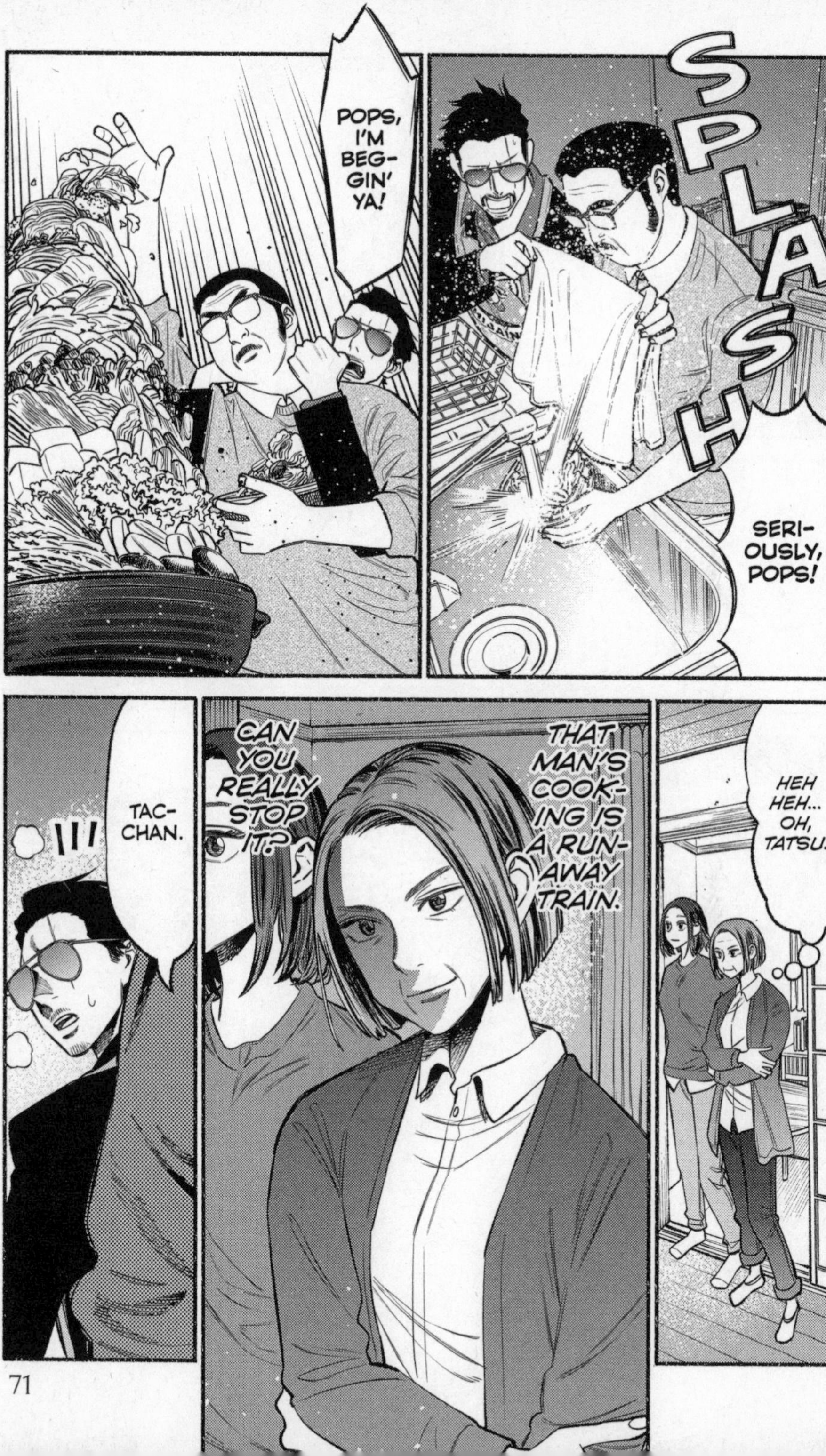
SPLASH
SERIOUSLY, POPS!
POPS, I'M BEGGIN' YA!
HEH HEH... OH, TATSU.
THAT MAN'S COOKING IS A RUNAWAY TRAIN.
CAN YOU REALLY STOP IT?
TAC-CHAN.

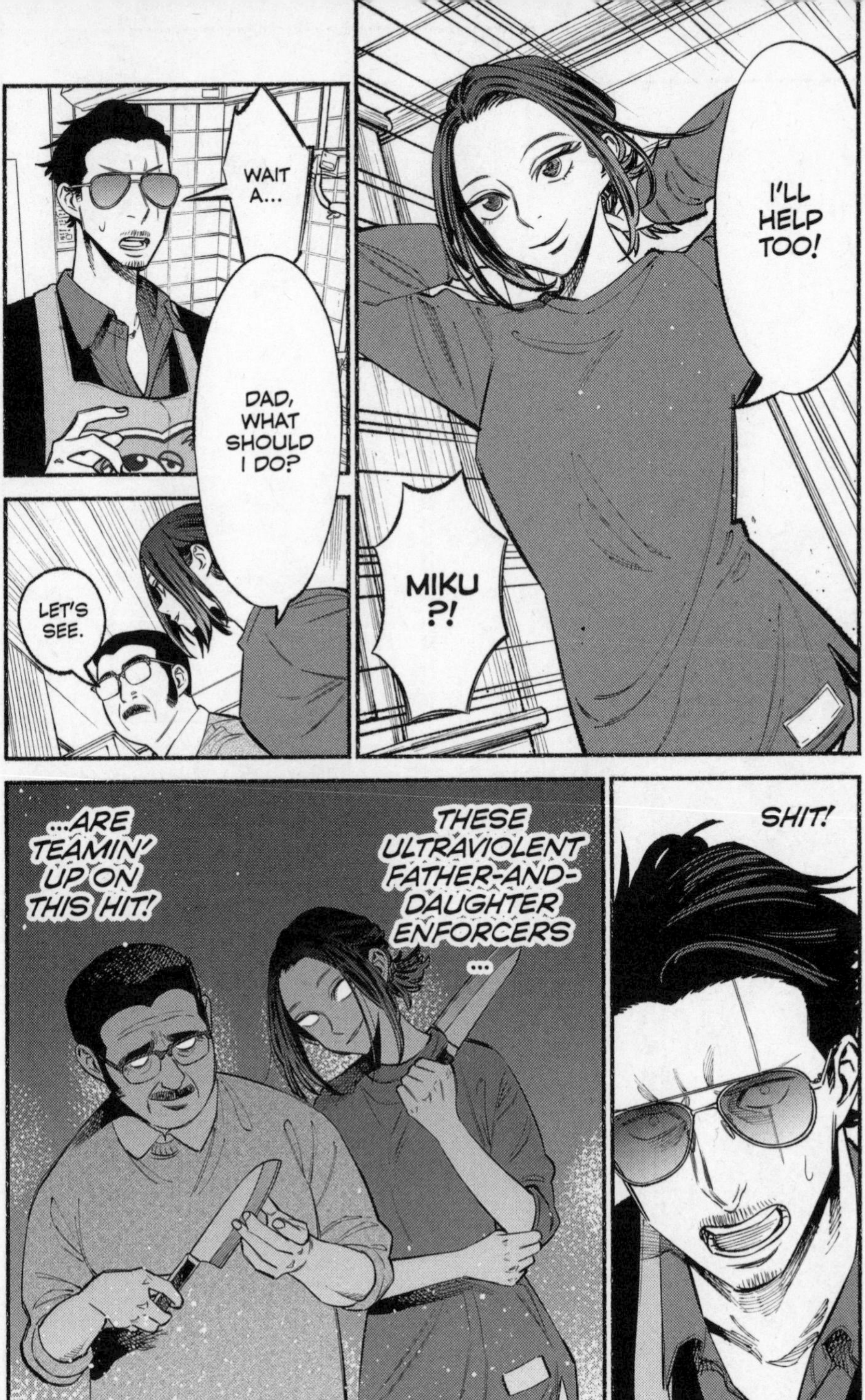
I'LL HELP TOO!
MIKU ?!
WAIT A...
DAD, WHAT SHOULD I DO?
LET'S SEE.
SHIT!
THESE ULTRAVIOLENT FATHER-AND-DAUGHTER ENFORCERS ...
...ARE TEAMIN' UP ON THIS HIT!

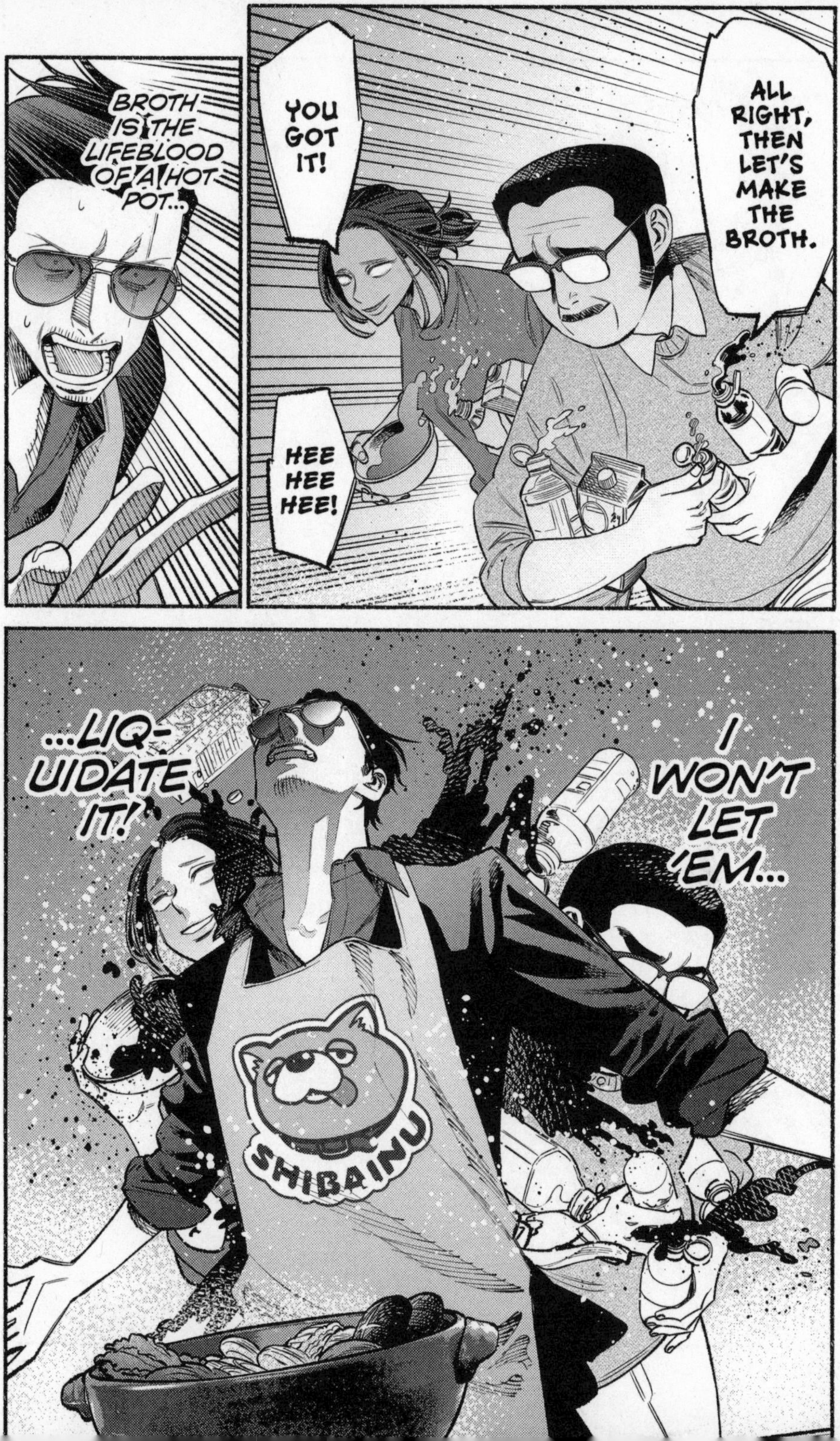
ALL RIGHT, THEN LET'S MAKE THE BROTH.
YOU GOT IT!
HEE HEE HEE!
BROTH IS THE LIFEBLOOD OF A HOT POT...
I WON'T LET 'EM...
...LIQ-UIDATE IT!
SHIBAINU

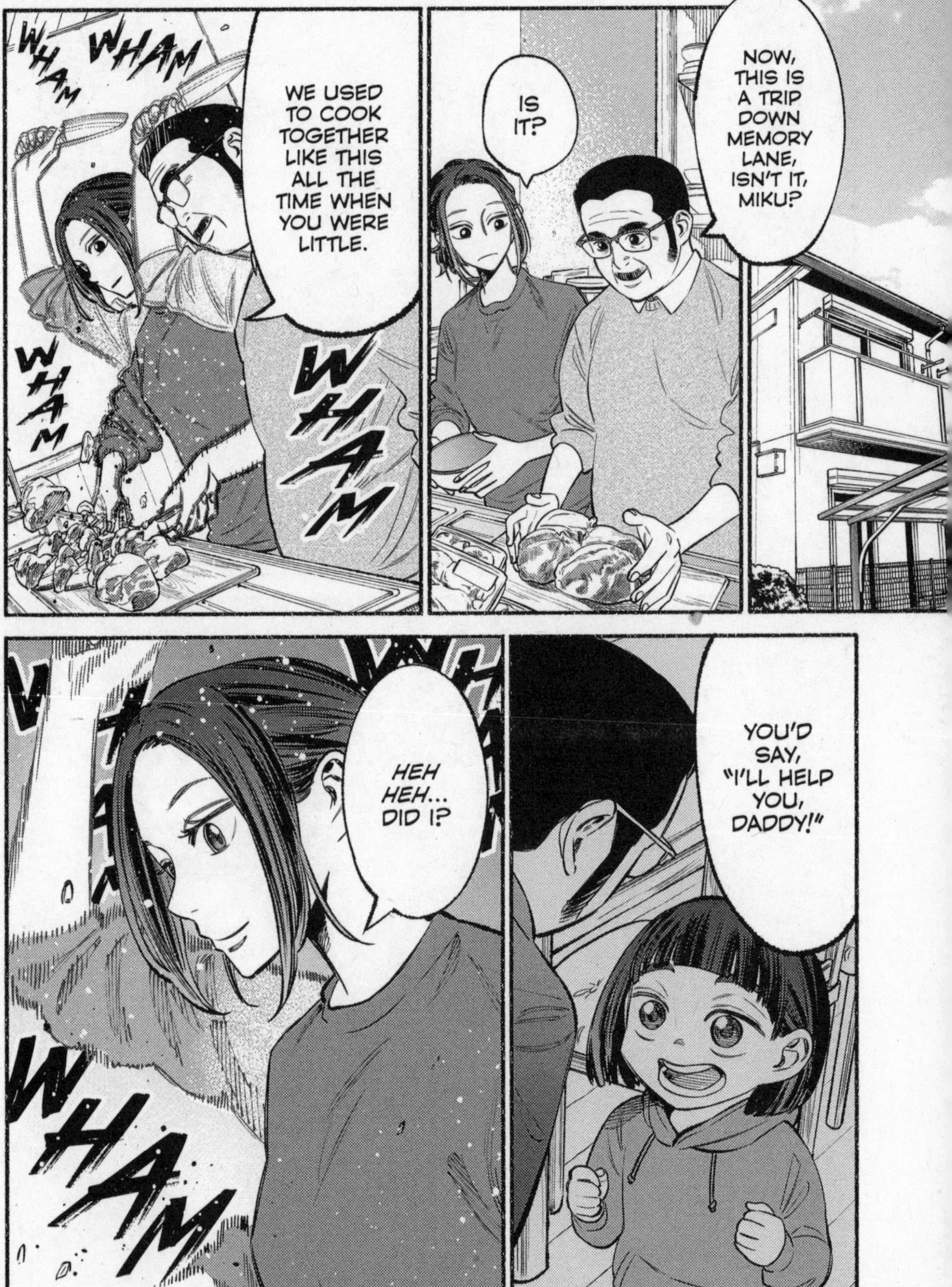
NOW, THIS IS A TRIP DOWN MEMORY LANE, ISN'T IT, MIKU?
IS IT?
WHAM
WHAM
WE USED TO COOK TOGETHER LIKE THIS ALL THE TIME WHEN YOU WERE LITTLE.
WHAM
WHAM
YOU'D SAY, "I'LL HELP YOU, DADDY!"
HEH HEH... DID I?
WHAM

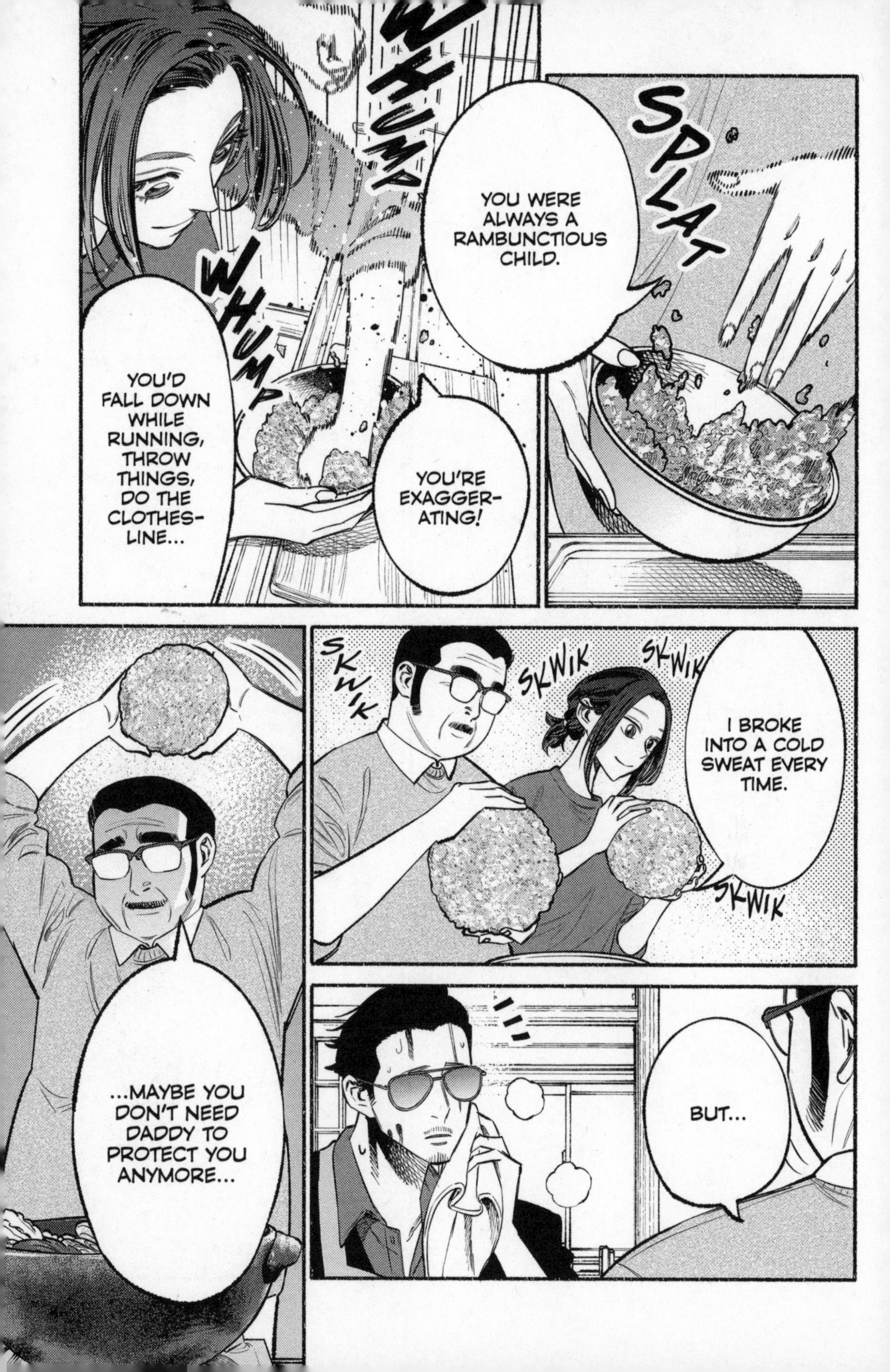
SPLAT
YOU WERE ALWAYS A RAMBUNCTIOUS CHILD.
WHUMP
WHUMP
YOU'D FALL DOWN WHILE RUNNING, THROW THINGS, DO THE CLOTHES-LINE...
YOU'RE EXAGGER-ATING!
SKWIK
SKWIK
SKWIK
I BROKE INTO A COLD SWEAT EVERY TIME.
SKWIK
BUT...
...MAYBE YOU DON'T NEED DADDY TO PROTECT YOU ANYMORE...

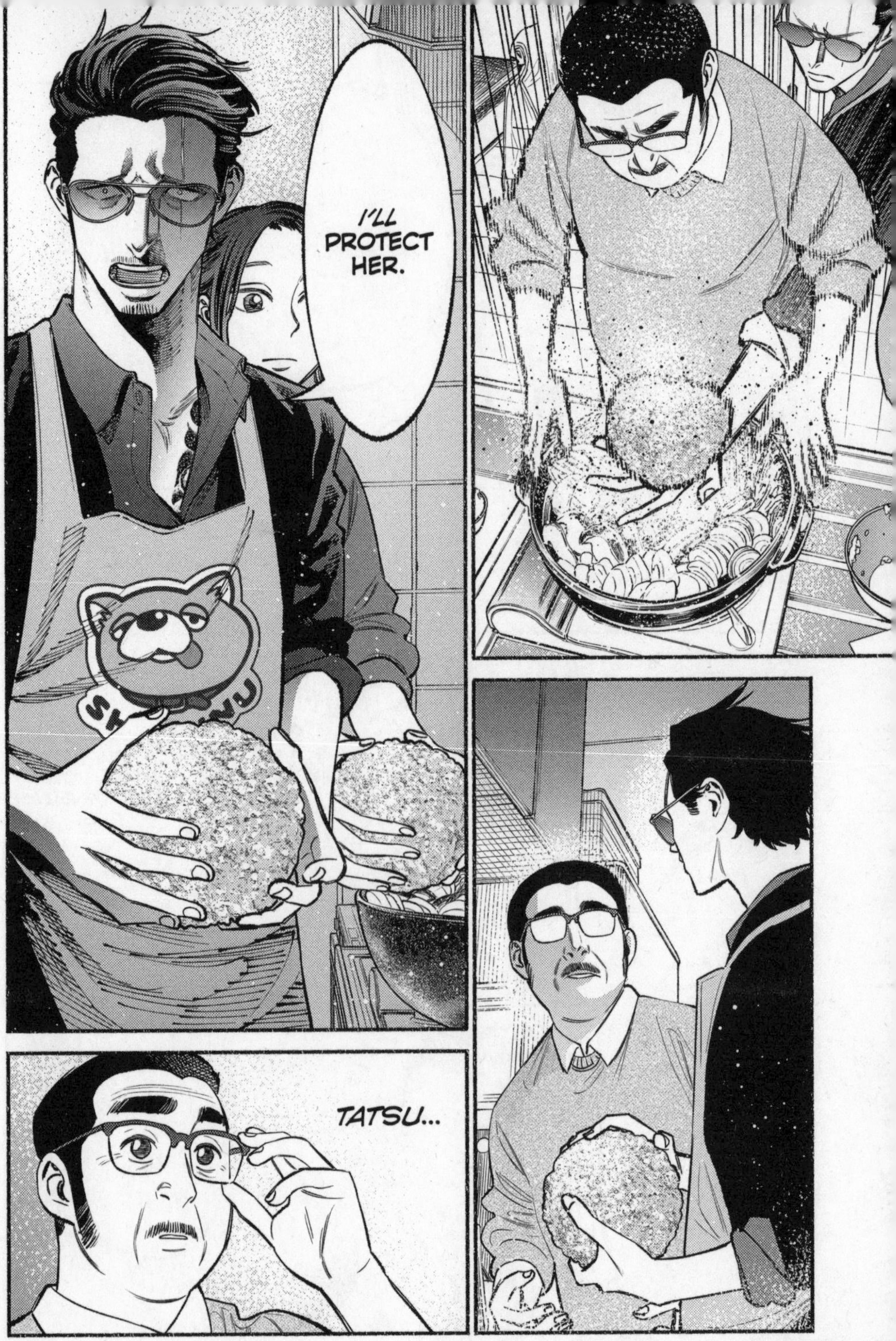
I'LL PROTECT HER.
TATSU...

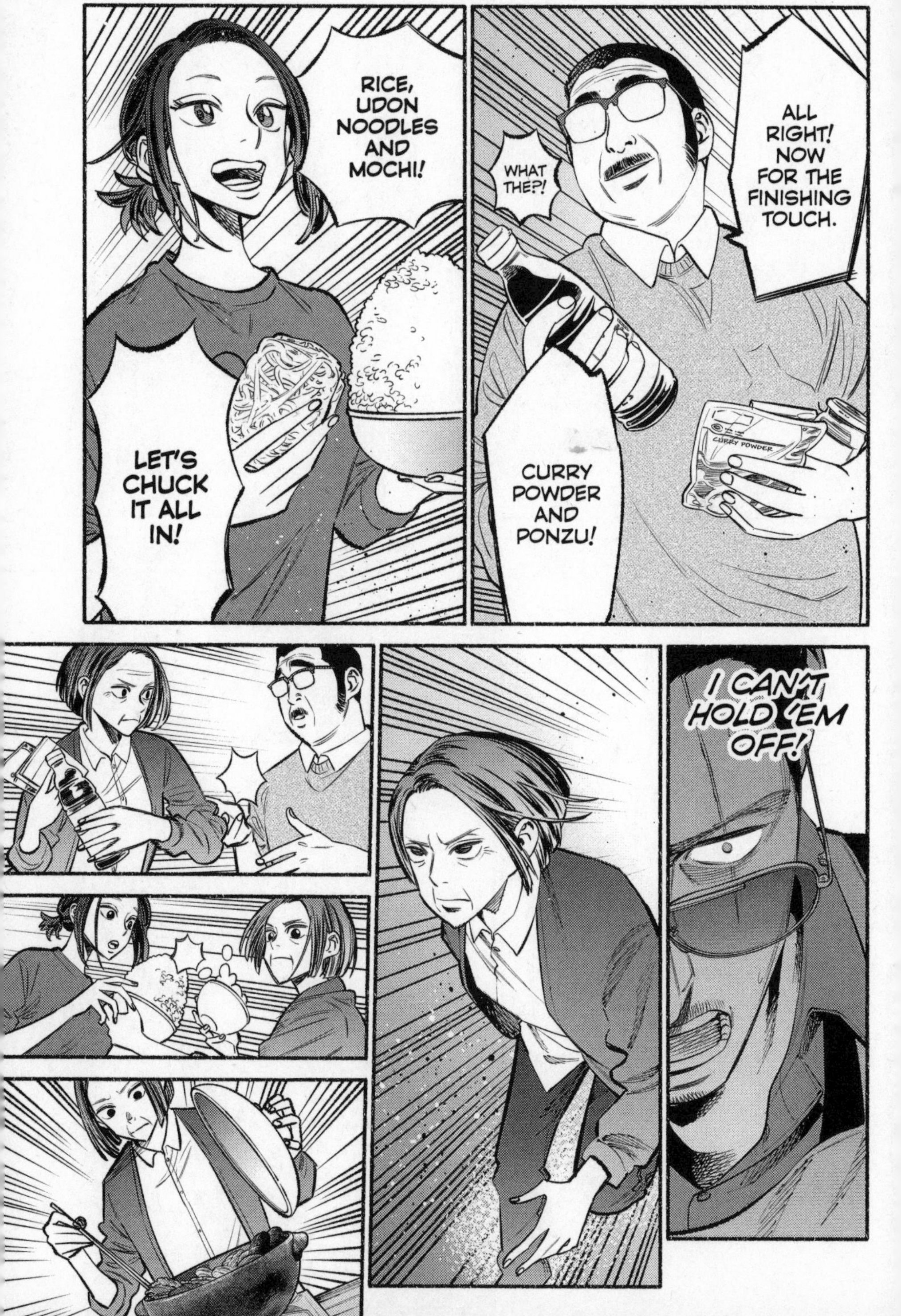
ALL RIGHT! NOW FOR THE FINISHING TOUCH.
WHAT THE?!
CURRY POWDER
CURRY POWDER AND PONZU!
RICE, UDON NOODLES AND MOCHI!
LET'S CHUCK IT ALL IN!
I CAN'T HOLD 'EM OFF!

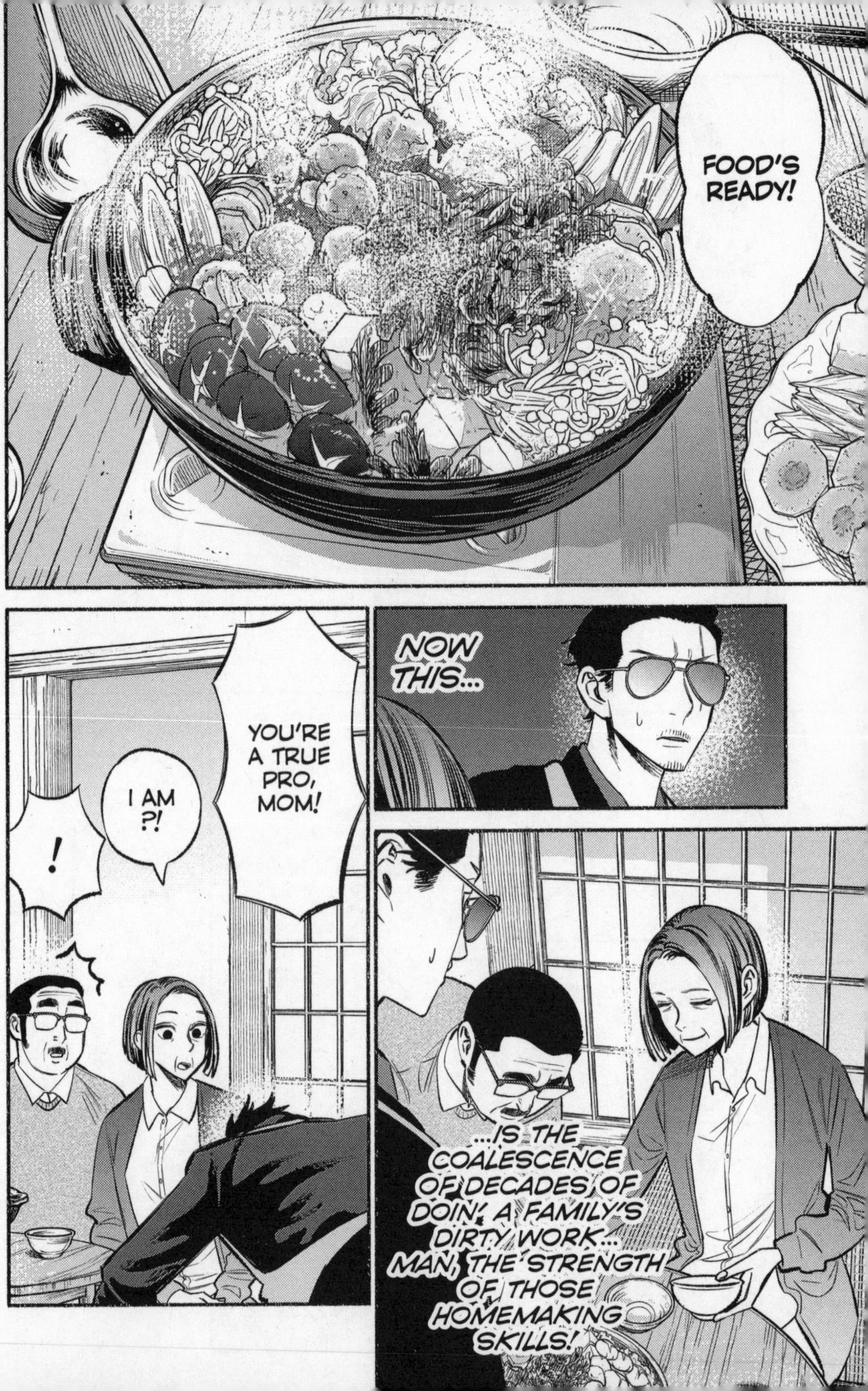
FOOD'S READY!
NOW THIS...
...IS THE COALESCENCE OF DECADES OF DOIN' A FAMILY'S DIRTY WORK... MAN, THE STRENGTH OF THOSE HOMEMAKING SKILLS!
YOU'RE A TRUE PRO, MOM!
I AM ?!
!

CHICKEN MEATBALL

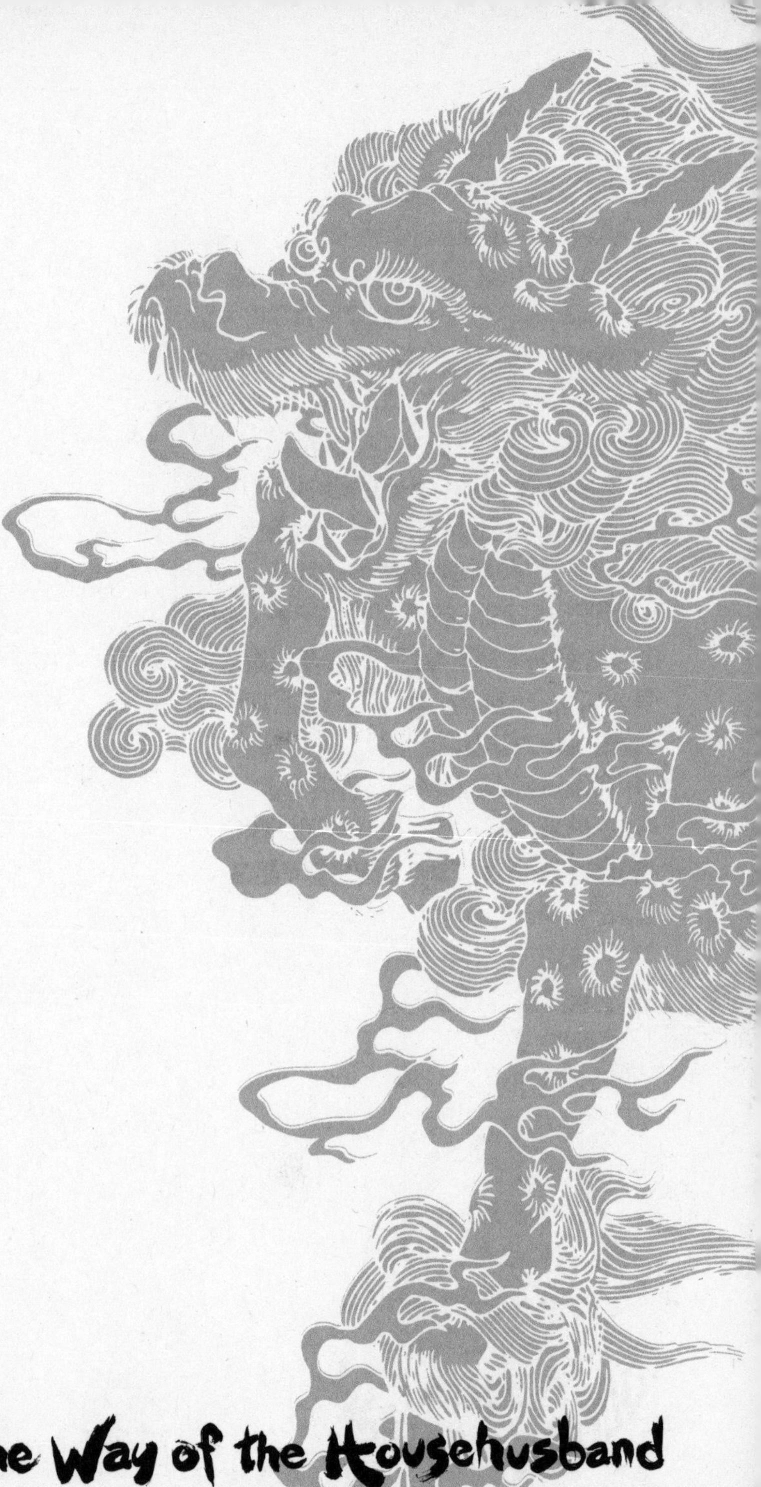

The Way of the Househusband

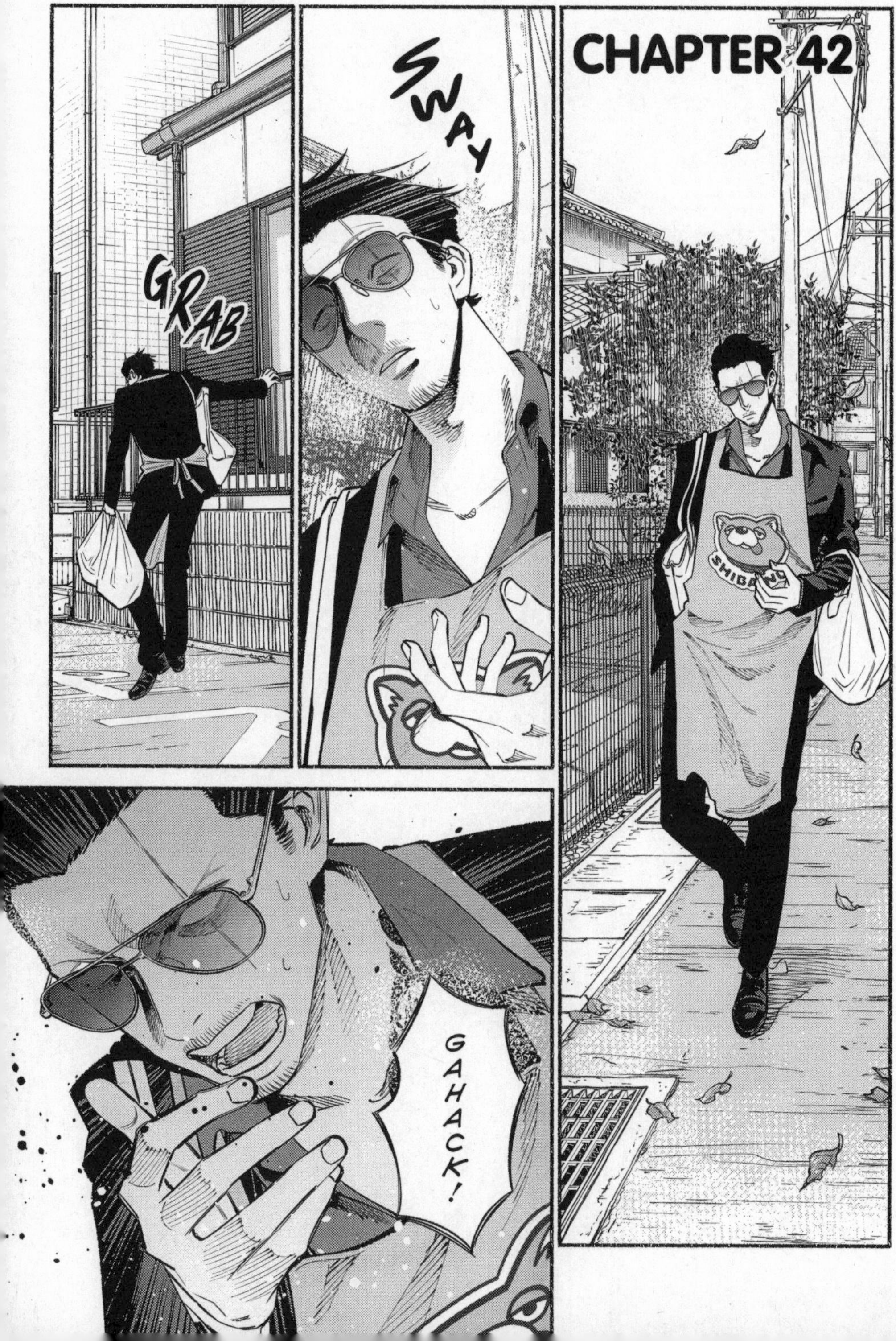
CHAPTER 42
SWAY
GRAB
GAHACK!

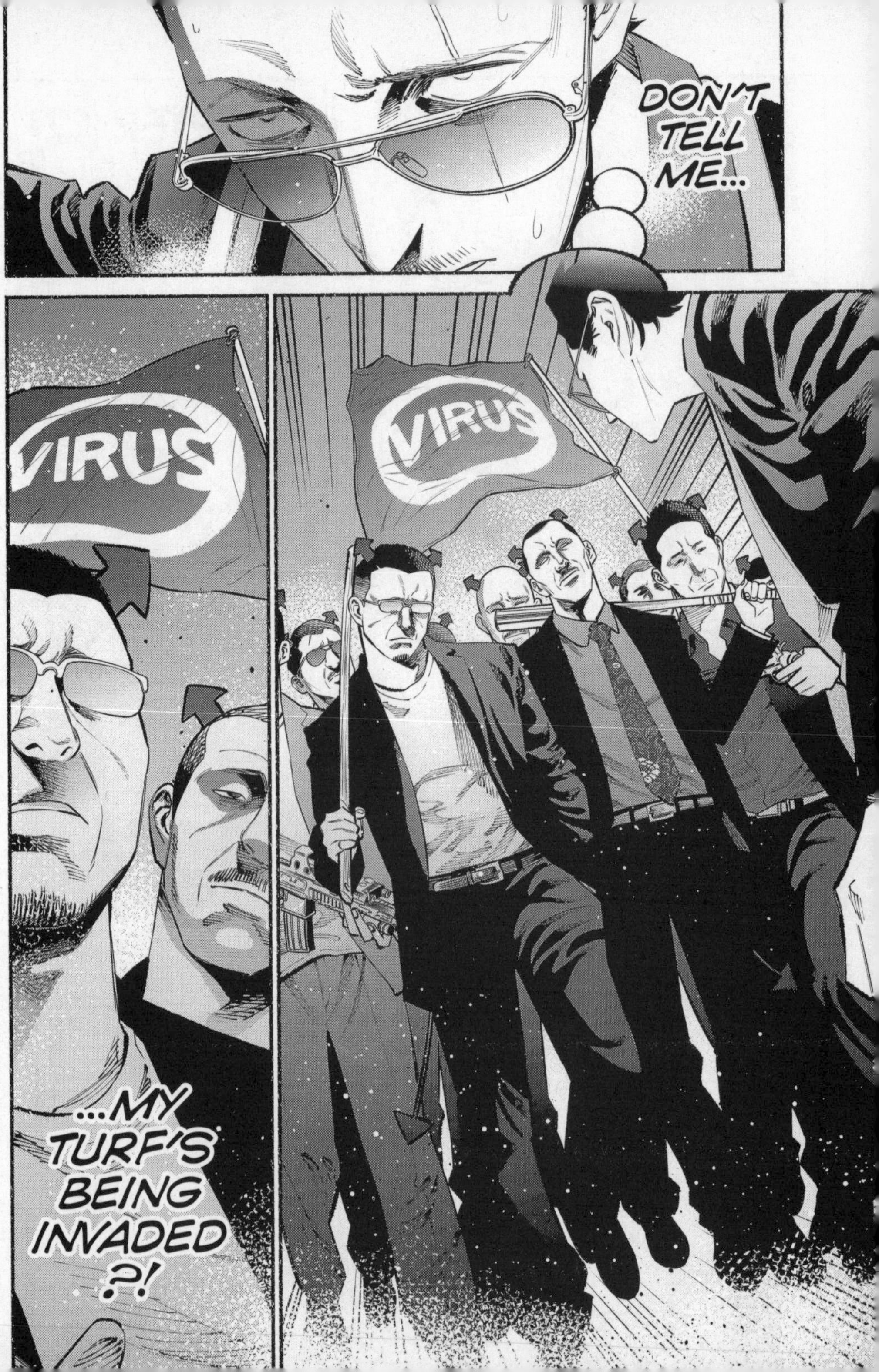
DON'T TELL ME...
VIRUS
VIRUS
...MY TURF'S BEING INVADED ?!

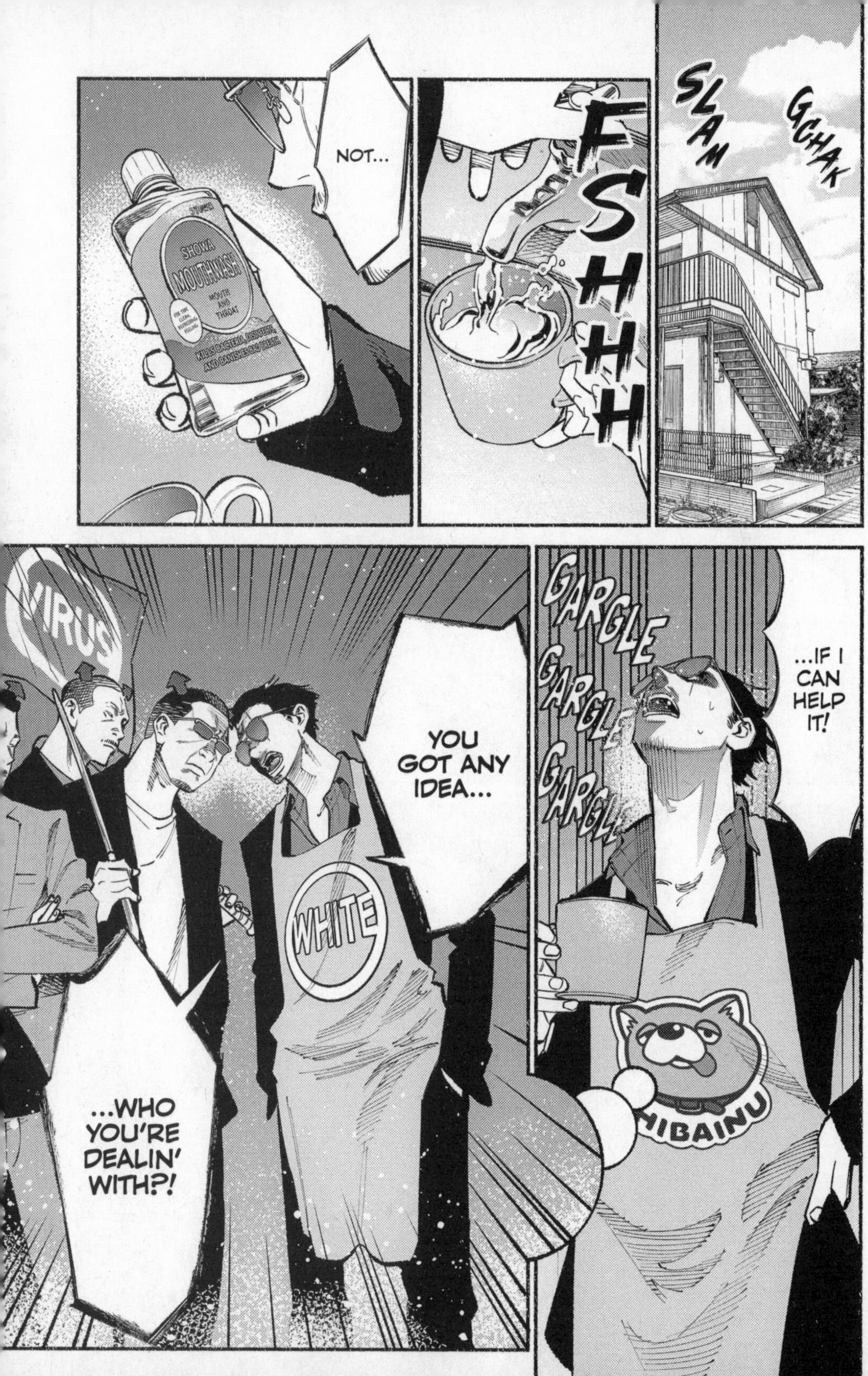
SLAM
GCHAK
FSHHHH
NOT...
SHOWA
MOUTHWASH
MOUTH AND THROAT
KILLS BACTERIA, DISINFECTS, AND BANISHES BAD BREATH
GARGLE
GARGLE
GARGLE
GARGLE
...IF I CAN HELP IT!
HIBAINU
IRUS
WHITE
YOU GOT ANY IDEA...
...WHO YOU'RE DEALIN' WITH?!

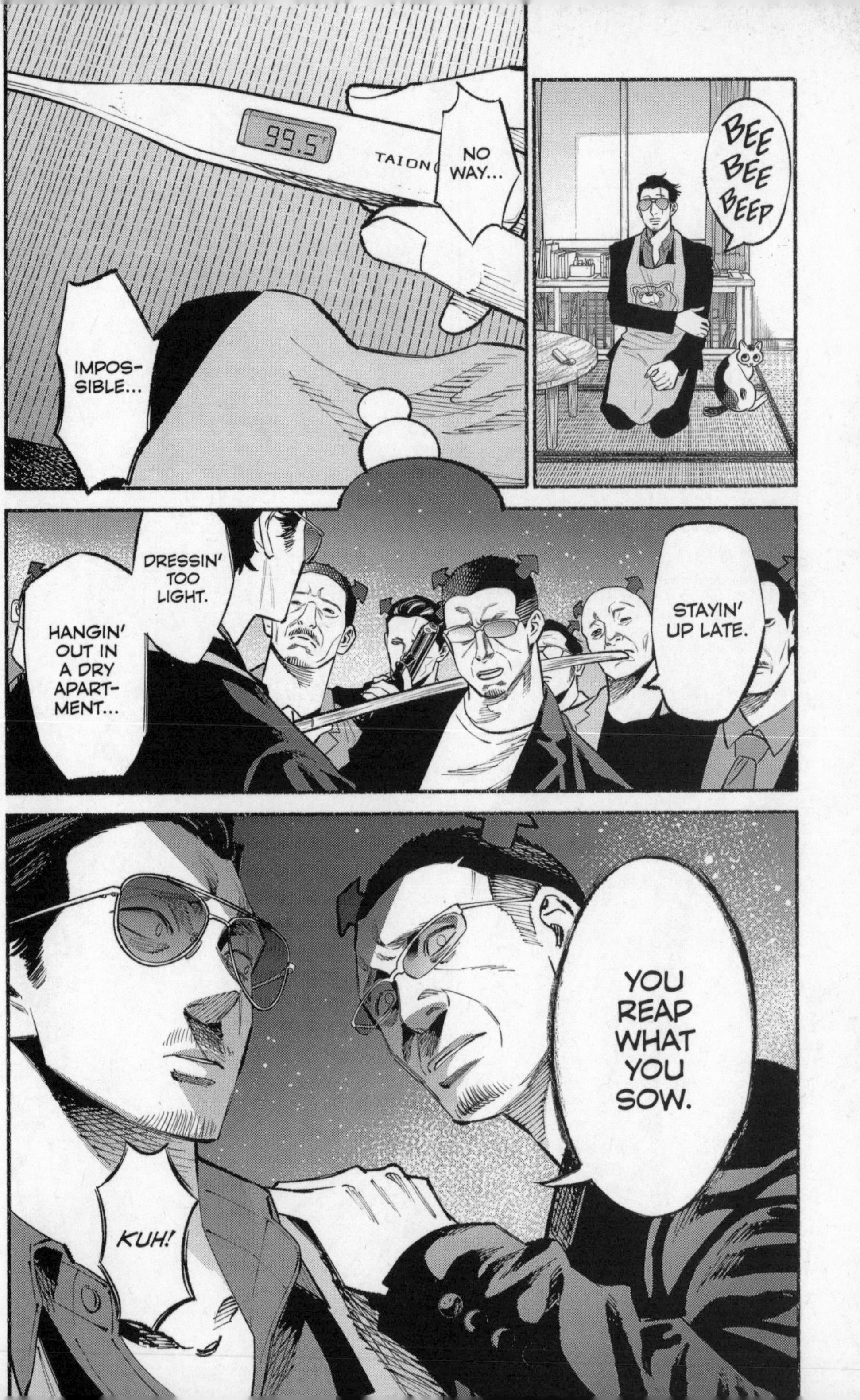
BEE BEE BEEP
99.5
NO WAY...
IMPOSSIBLE...
STAYIN' UP LATE.
DRESSIN' TOO LIGHT.
HANGIN' OUT IN A DRY APARTMENT...
YOU REAP WHAT YOU SOW.
KUH!

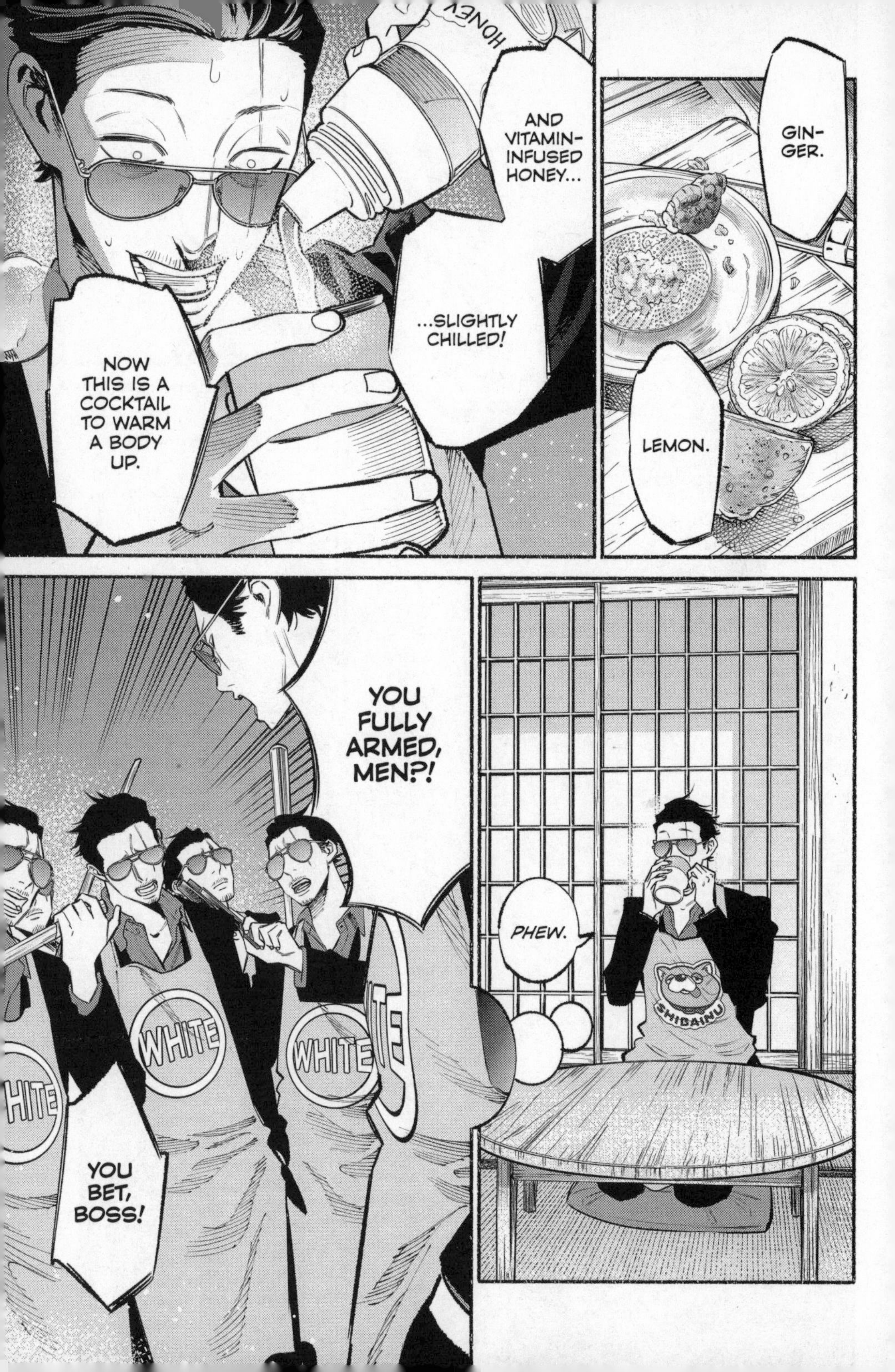
GIN-
GER.
LEMON.
HONEY
AND VITAMIN-INFUSED HONEY...
...SLIGHTLY CHILLED!
NOW THIS IS A COCKTAIL TO WARM A BODY UP.
PHEW.
SHIBAINU
YOU FULLY ARMED, MEN?!
WHITE
WHITE
HITE
YOU BET, BOSS!

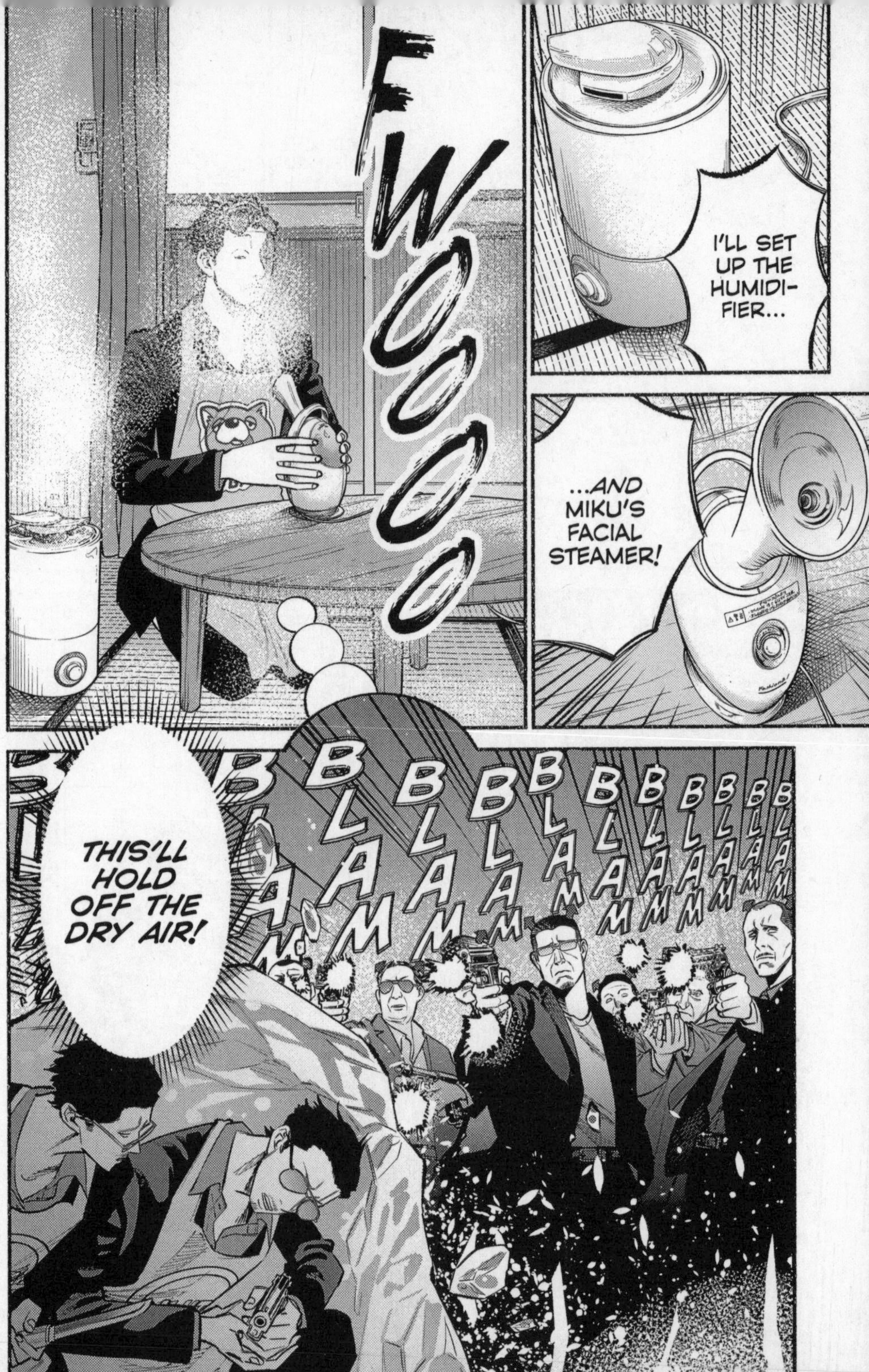
I'LL SET UP THE HUMIDI-FIER...
...AND MIKU'S FACIAL STEAMER!
FWOOOOO
BLAM BLAM BLAM BLAM BLAM BLAM BLAM BLAM BLAM BLAM BLAM
THIS'LL HOLD OFF THE DRY AIR!

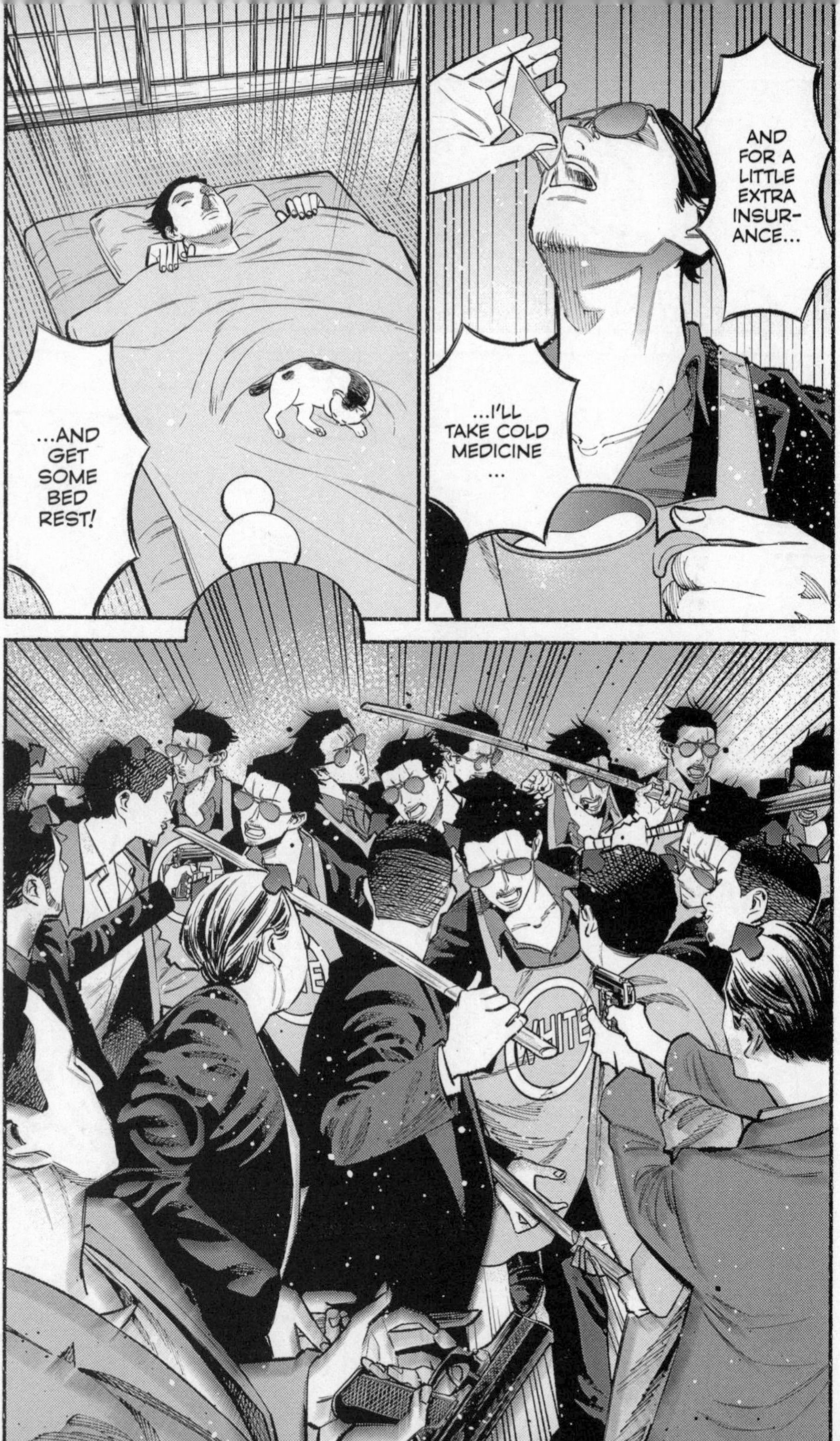
AND FOR A LITTLE EXTRA INSURANCE...
...I'LL TAKE COLD MEDICINE ...
...AND GET SOME BED REST!

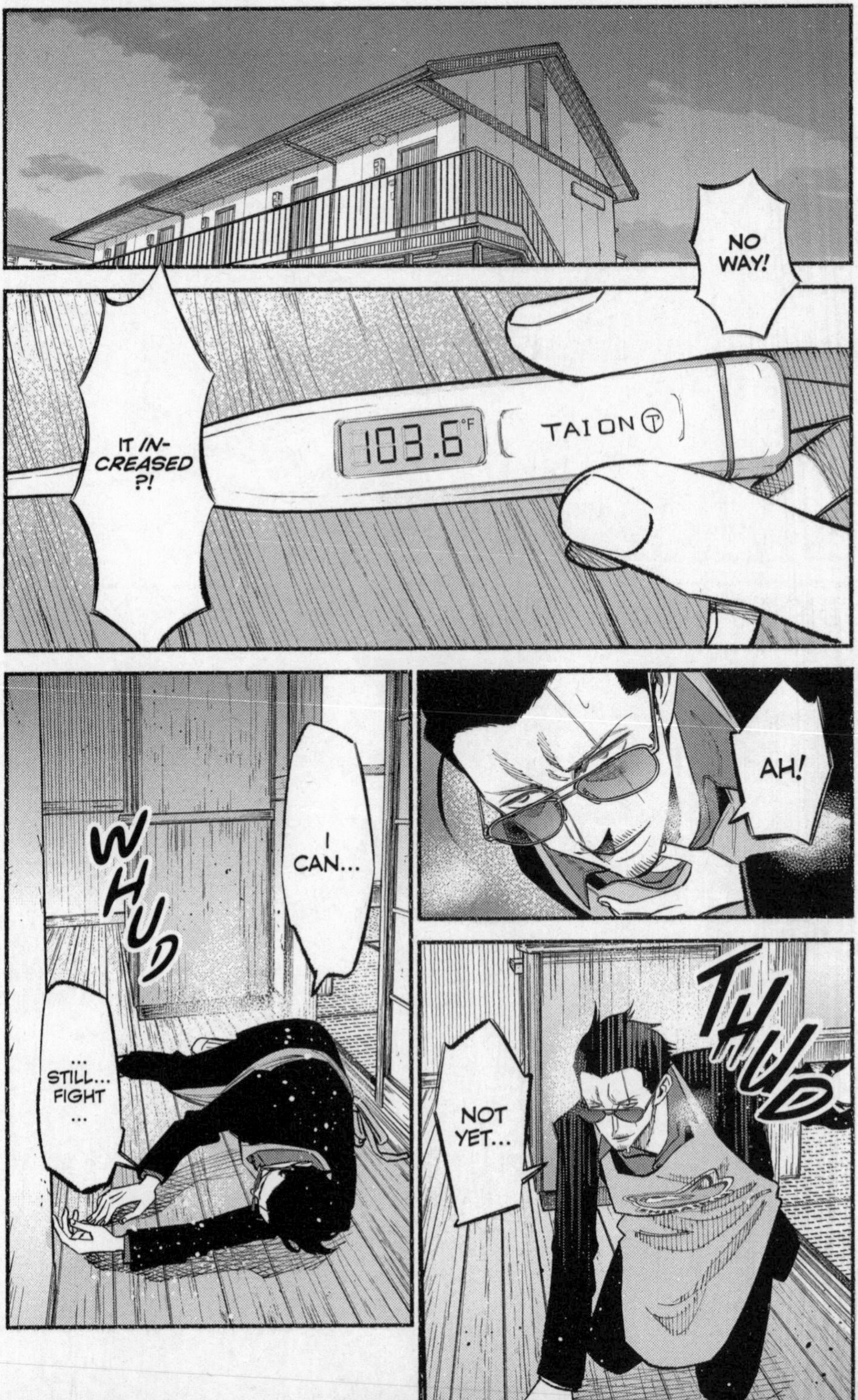
NO WAY!
103.6°F
TAION
IT IN-CREASED?!
AH!
THUD
NOT YET...
I CAN...
WHUD
...STILL...FIGHT...

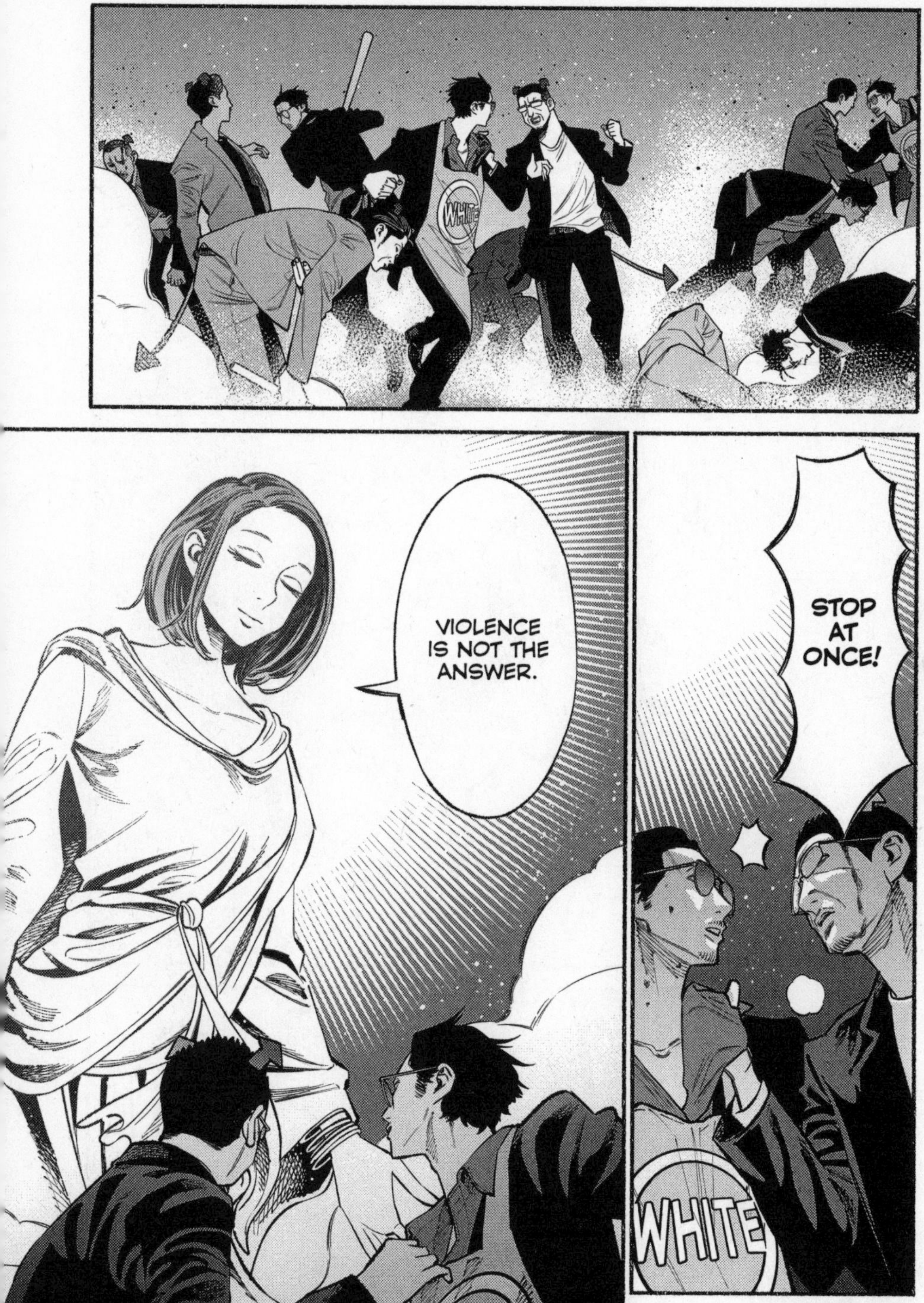
STOP AT ONCE!
VIOLENCE IS NOT THE ANSWER.

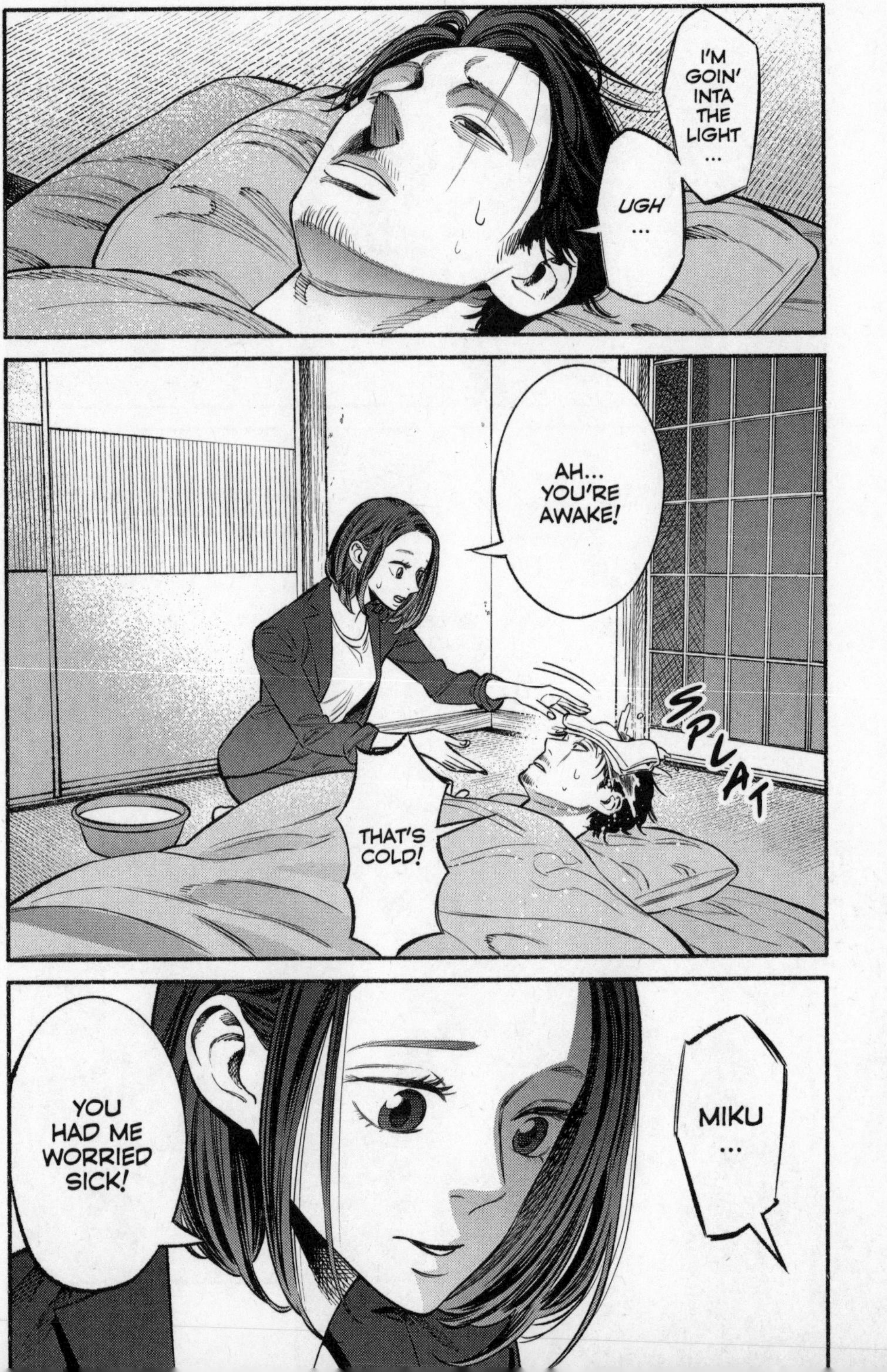
I'M GOIN' INTA THE LIGHT ...
UGH ...
AH... YOU'RE AWAKE!
SPLAT
THAT'S COLD!
MIKU ...
YOU HAD ME WORRIED SICK!

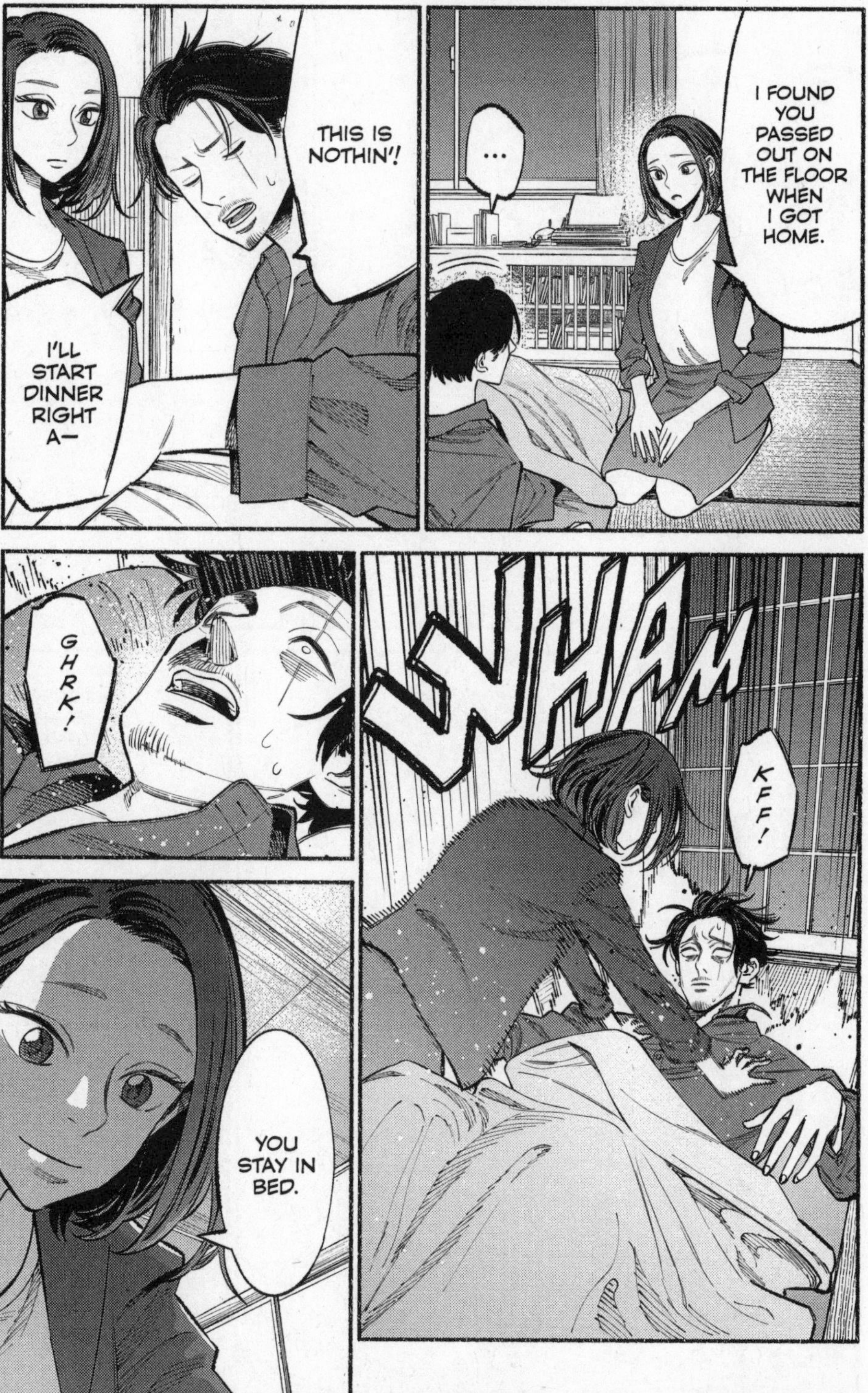
I FOUND YOU PASSED OUT ON THE FLOOR WHEN I GOT HOME.
...
THIS IS NOTHIN'!
I'LL START DINNER RIGHT A—
WHAM
KFF!
GHRK!
YOU STAY IN BED.

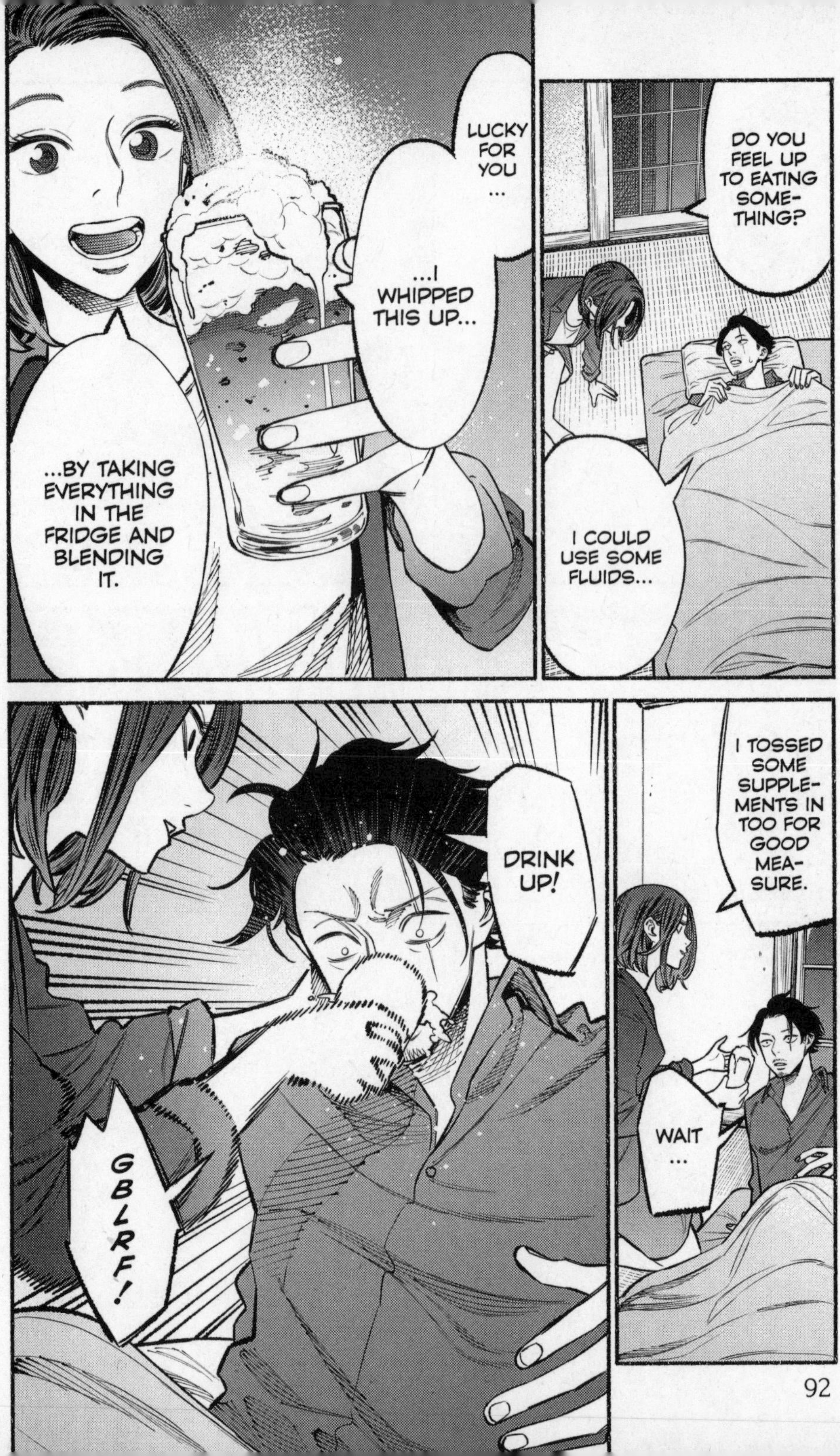
DO YOU FEEL UP TO EATING SOMETHING?
I COULD USE SOME FLUIDS...
LUCKY FOR YOU ...
...I WHIPPED THIS UP...
...BY TAKING EVERYTHING IN THE FRIDGE AND BLENDING IT.
I TOSSED SOME SUPPLEMENTS IN TOO FOR GOOD MEASURE.
WAIT ...
DRINK UP!
GBLRF!

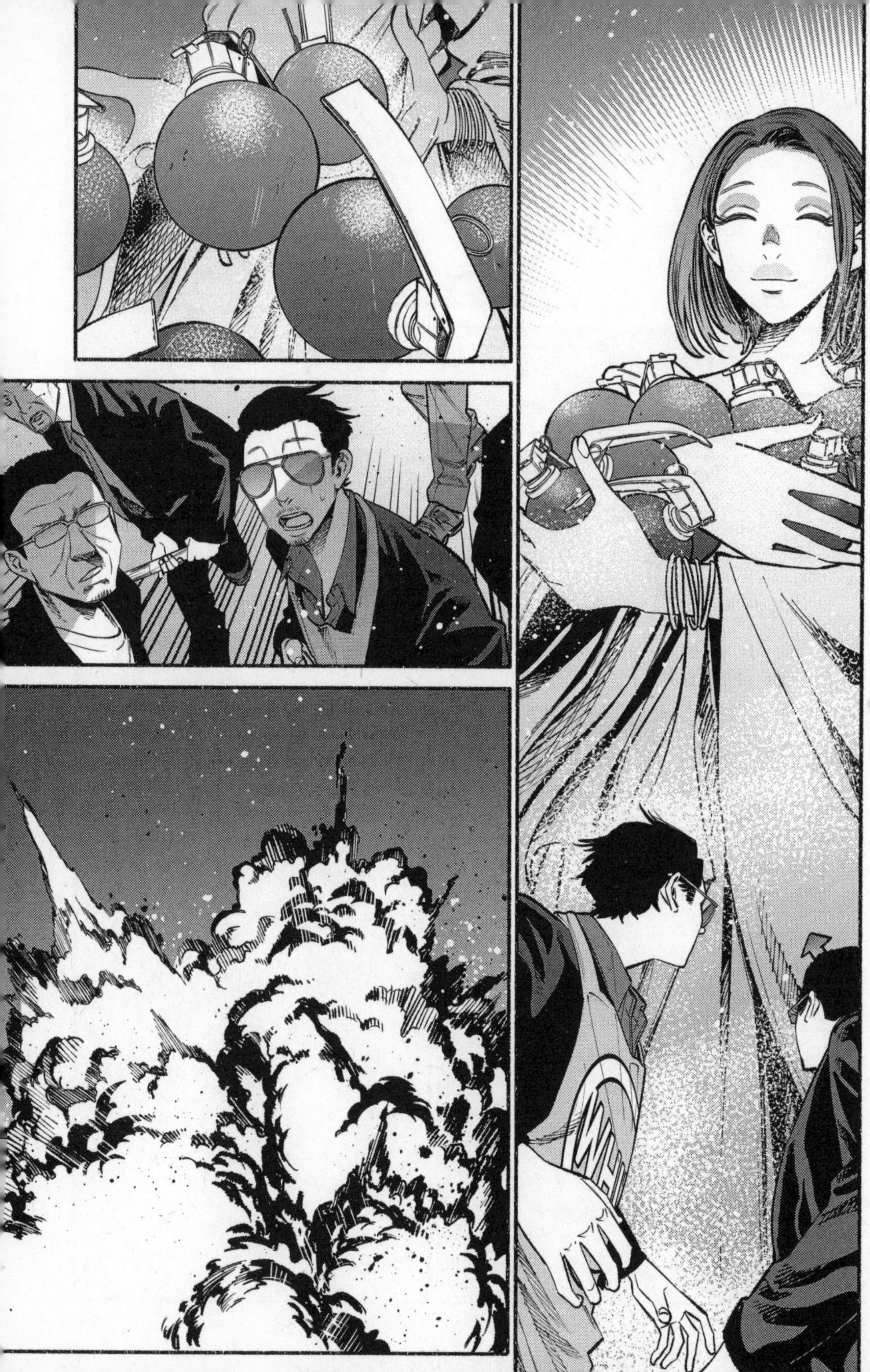

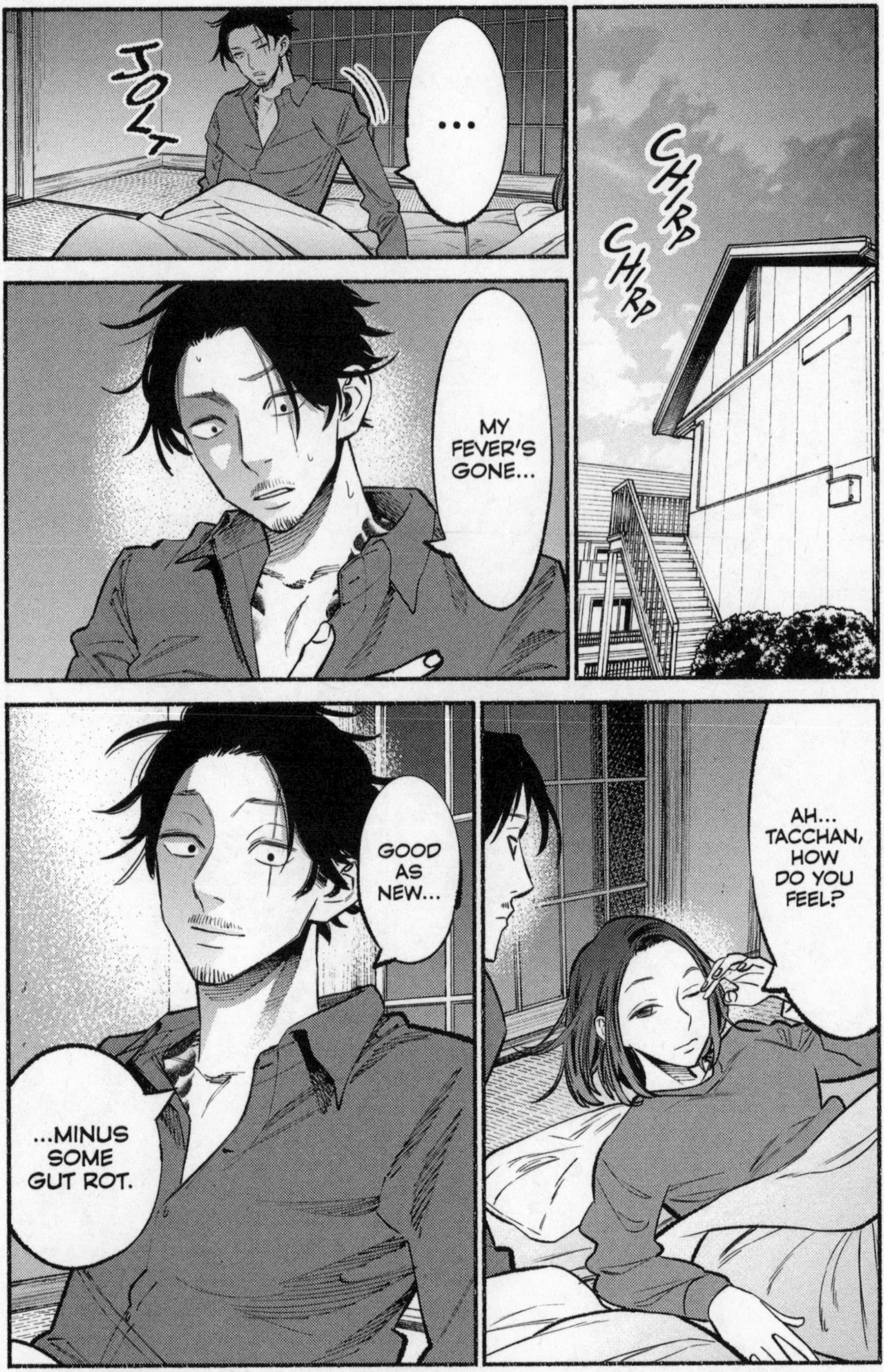

CHIRP CHIRP
JOLT
...
MY FEVER'S GONE...
AH... TACCHAN, HOW DO YOU FEEL?
GOOD AS NEW...
...MINUS SOME GUT ROT.

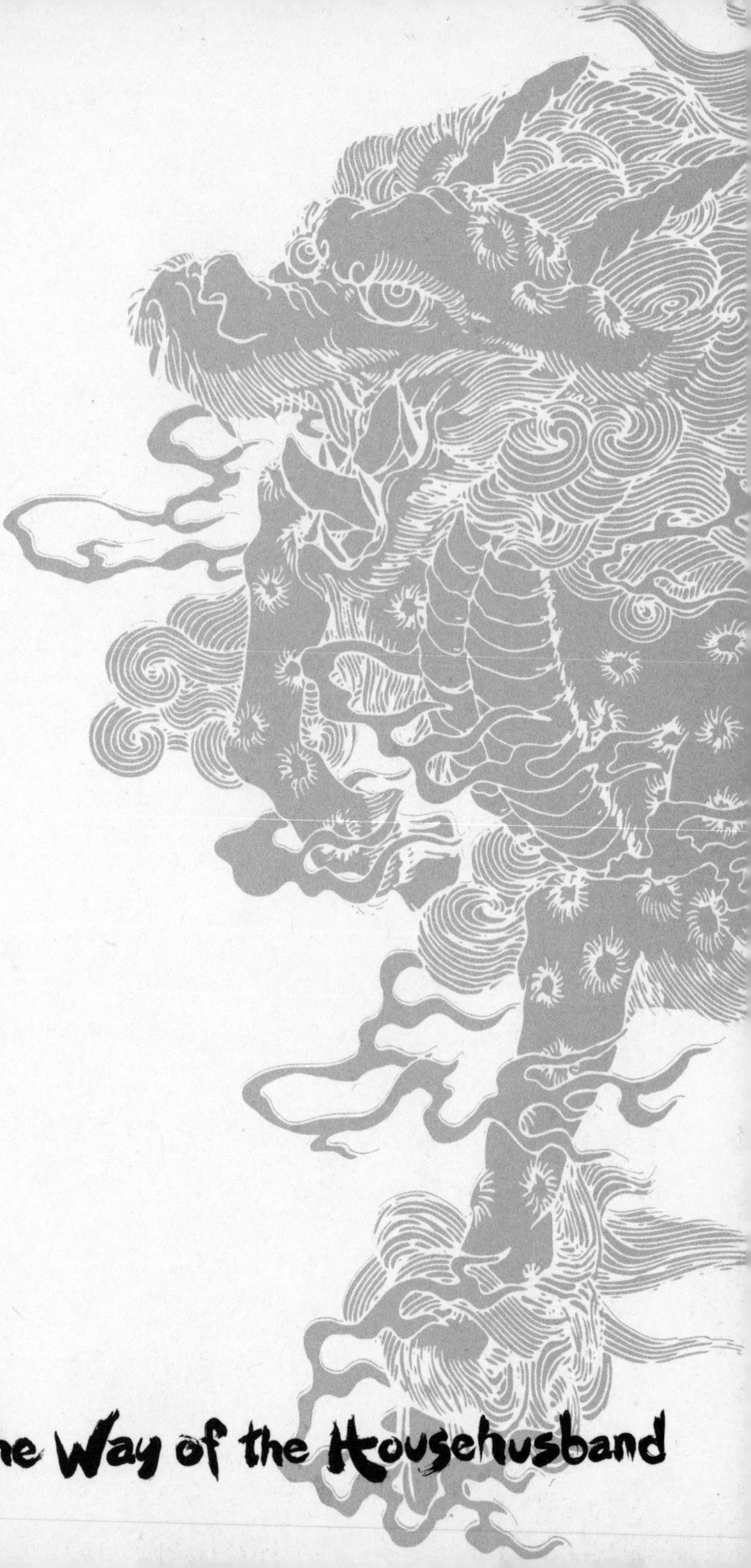

The Way of the Househusband

CHAPTER 43

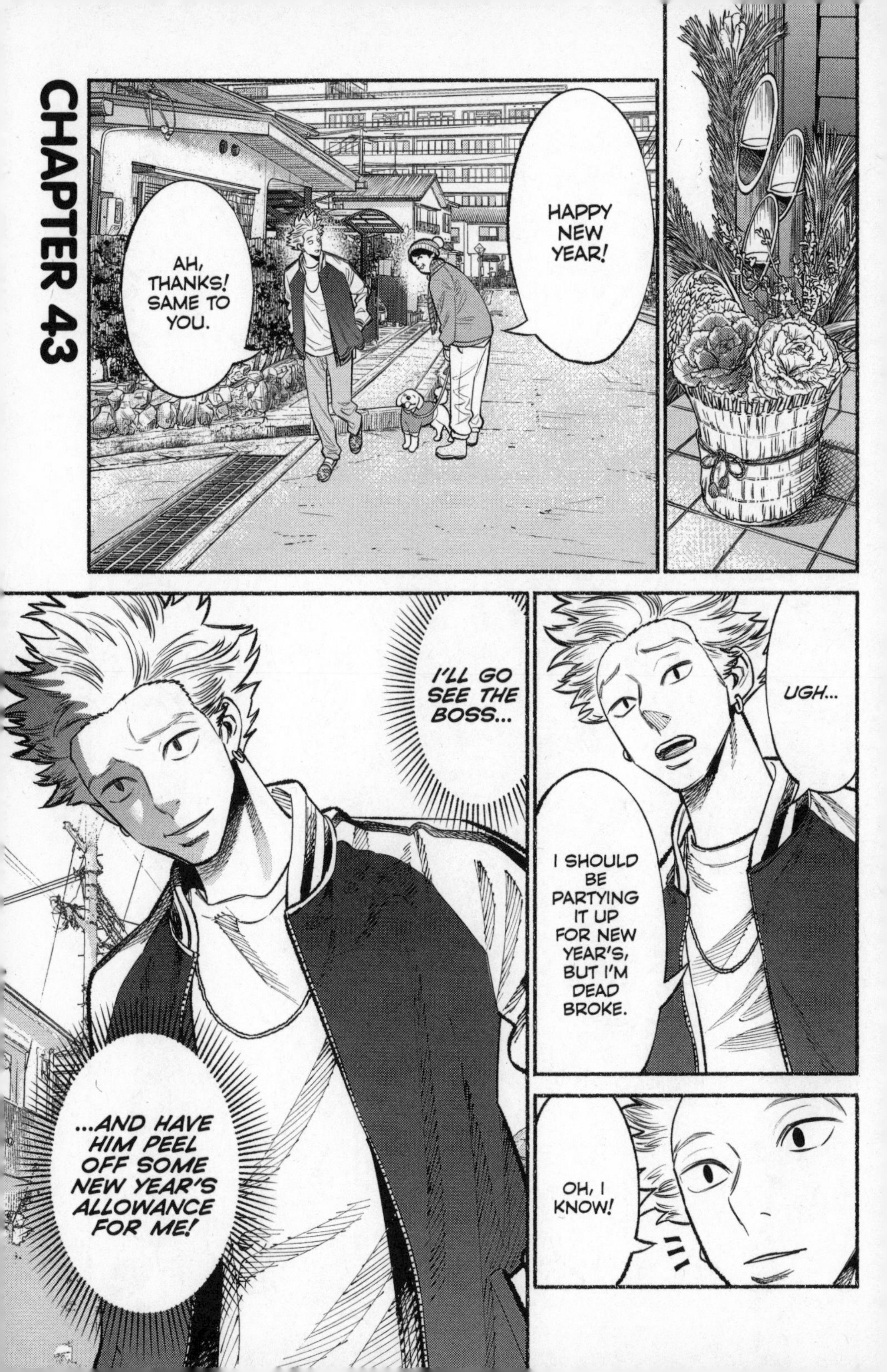
HAPPY NEW YEAR!
AH, THANKS! SAME TO YOU.
UGH...
I SHOULD BE PARTYING IT UP FOR NEW YEAR'S, BUT I'M DEAD BROKE.
OH, I KNOW!
I'LL GO SEE THE BOSS...
...AND HAVE HIM PEEL OFF SOME NEW YEAR'S ALLOWANCE FOR ME!

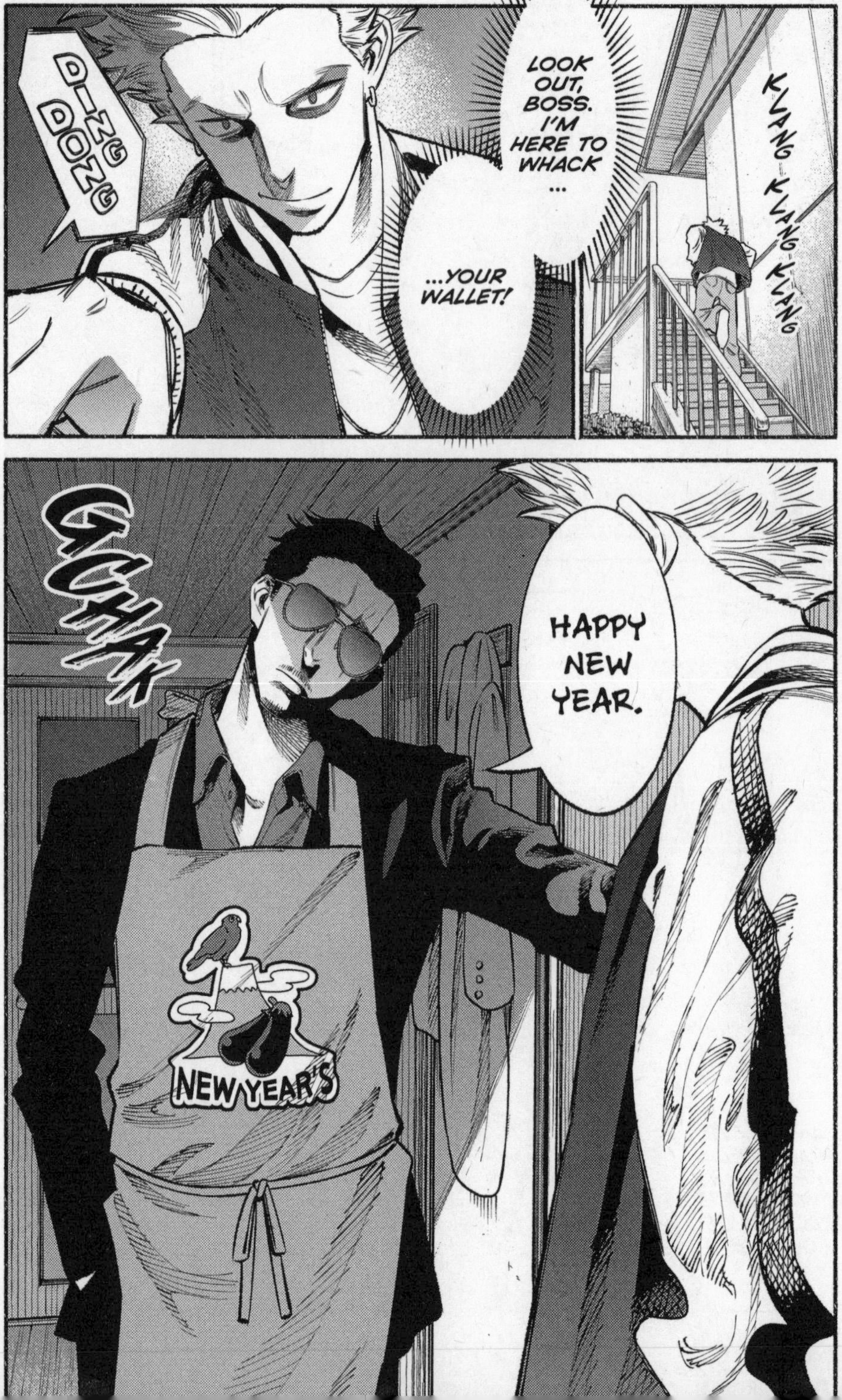
KLANG KLANG KLANG
LOOK OUT, BOSS. I'M HERE TO WHACK ...
...YOUR WALLET!
DING DONG
HAPPY NEW YEAR.
GACHAK
NEW YEAR'S

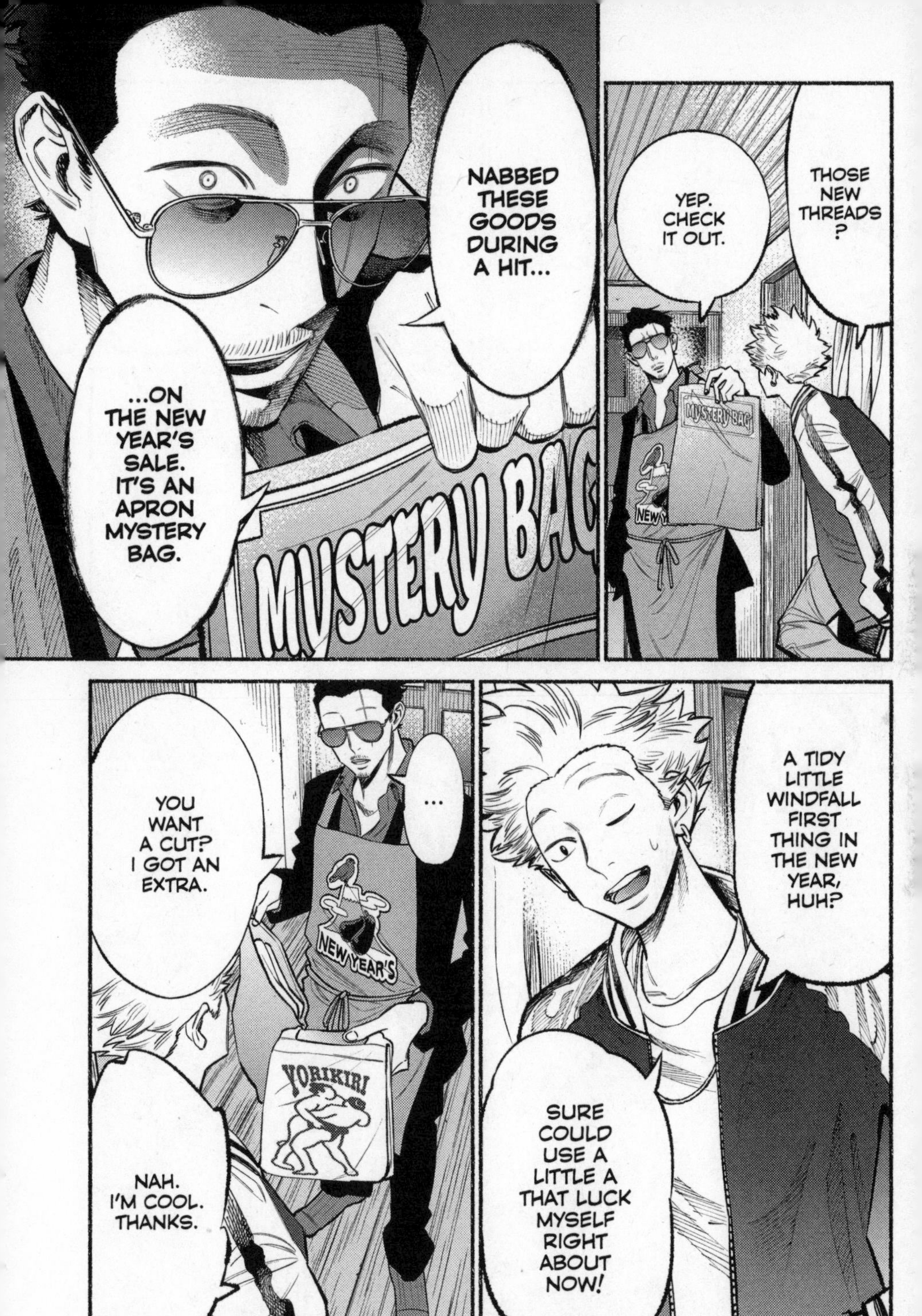
THOSE NEW THREADS ?
YEP. CHECK IT OUT.
MYSTERY BAG
NEW Y
NABBED THESE GOODS DURING A HIT...
...ON THE NEW YEAR'S SALE. IT'S AN APRON MYSTERY BAG.
MYSTERY BAG
A TIDY LITTLE WINDFALL FIRST THING IN THE NEW YEAR, HUH?
SURE COULD USE A LITTLE A THAT LUCK MYSELF RIGHT ABOUT NOW!
...
YOU WANT A CUT? I GOT AN EXTRA.
NEW YEAR'S
YORIKIRI
NAH. I'M COOL. THANKS.

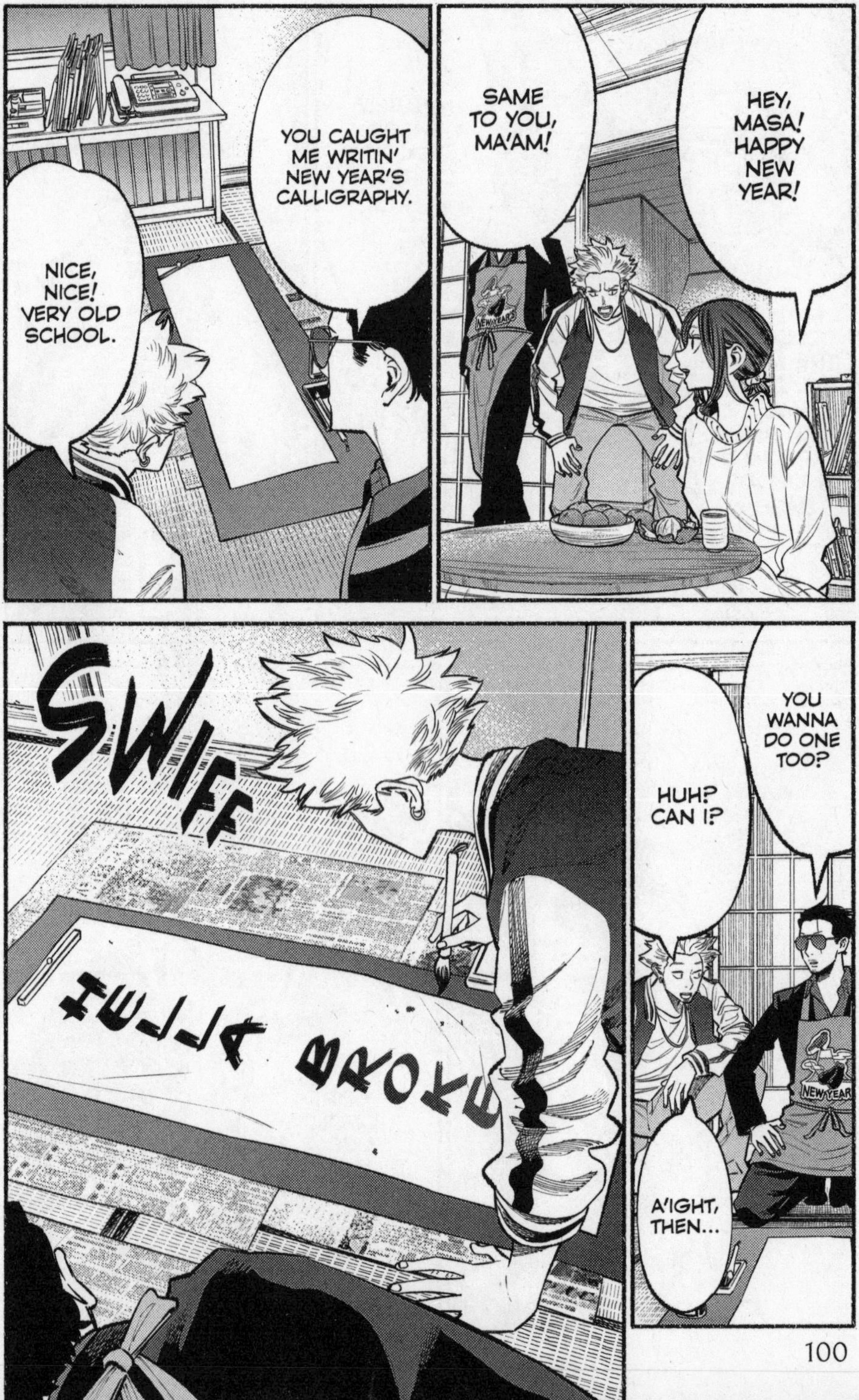
HEY, MASA! HAPPY NEW YEAR!
SAME TO YOU, MA'AM!
YOU CAUGHT ME WRITIN' NEW YEAR'S CALLIGRAPHY.
NICE, NICE! VERY OLD SCHOOL.
YOU WANNA DO ONE TOO?
HUH? CAN I?
A'IGHT, THEN...
SWIFF
HELLA BROKE

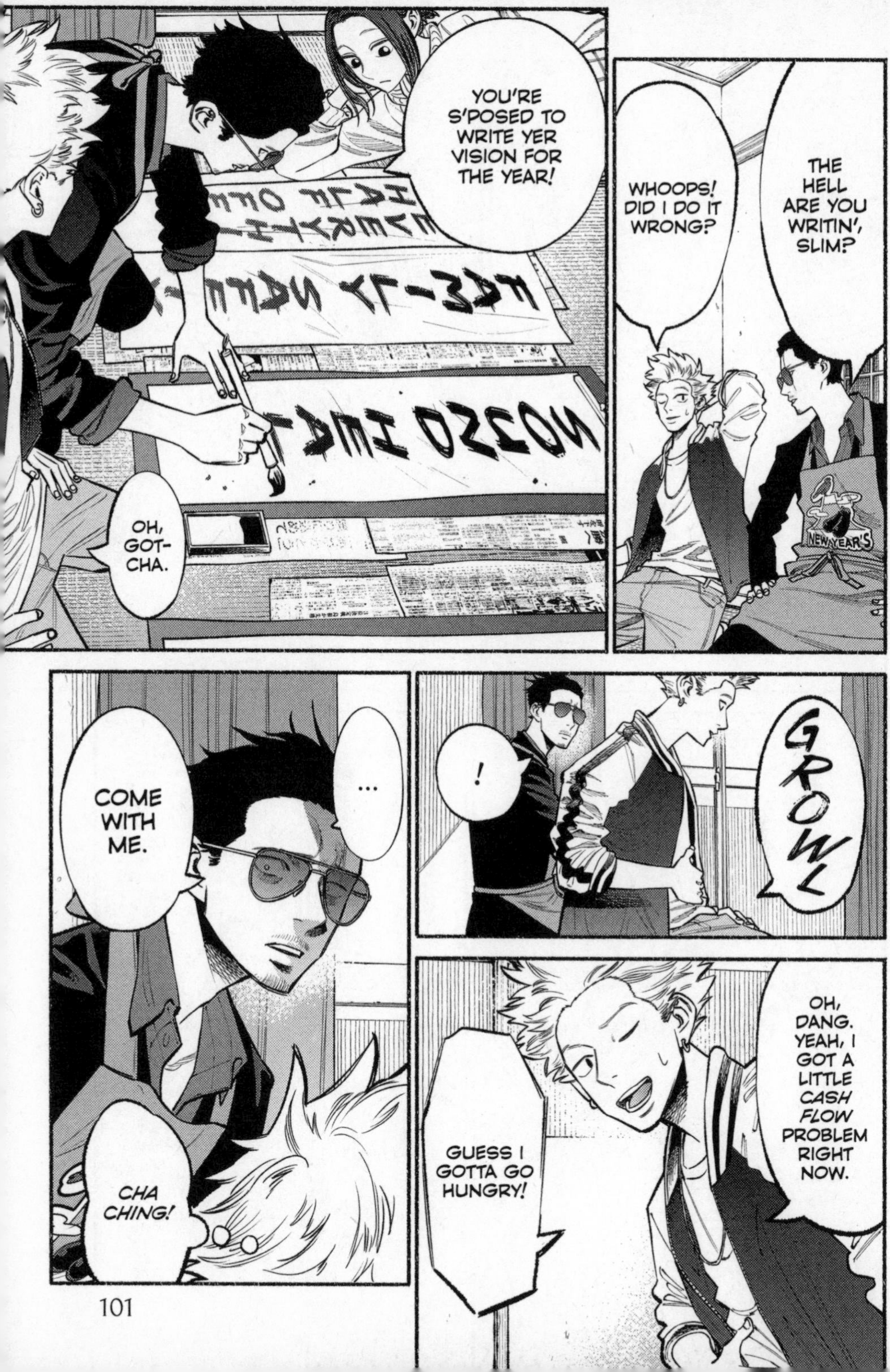
THE HELL ARE YOU WRITIN', SLIM?
WHOOPS! DID I DO IT WRONG?
NEW YEAR'S
YOU'RE S'POSED TO WRITE YER VISION FOR THE YEAR!
OH, GOT-CHA.
GROWL
!
OH, DANG. YEAH, I GOT A LITTLE *CASH FLOW* PROBLEM RIGHT NOW.
GUESS I GOTTA GO HUNGRY!
...
COME WITH ME.
CHA CHING!

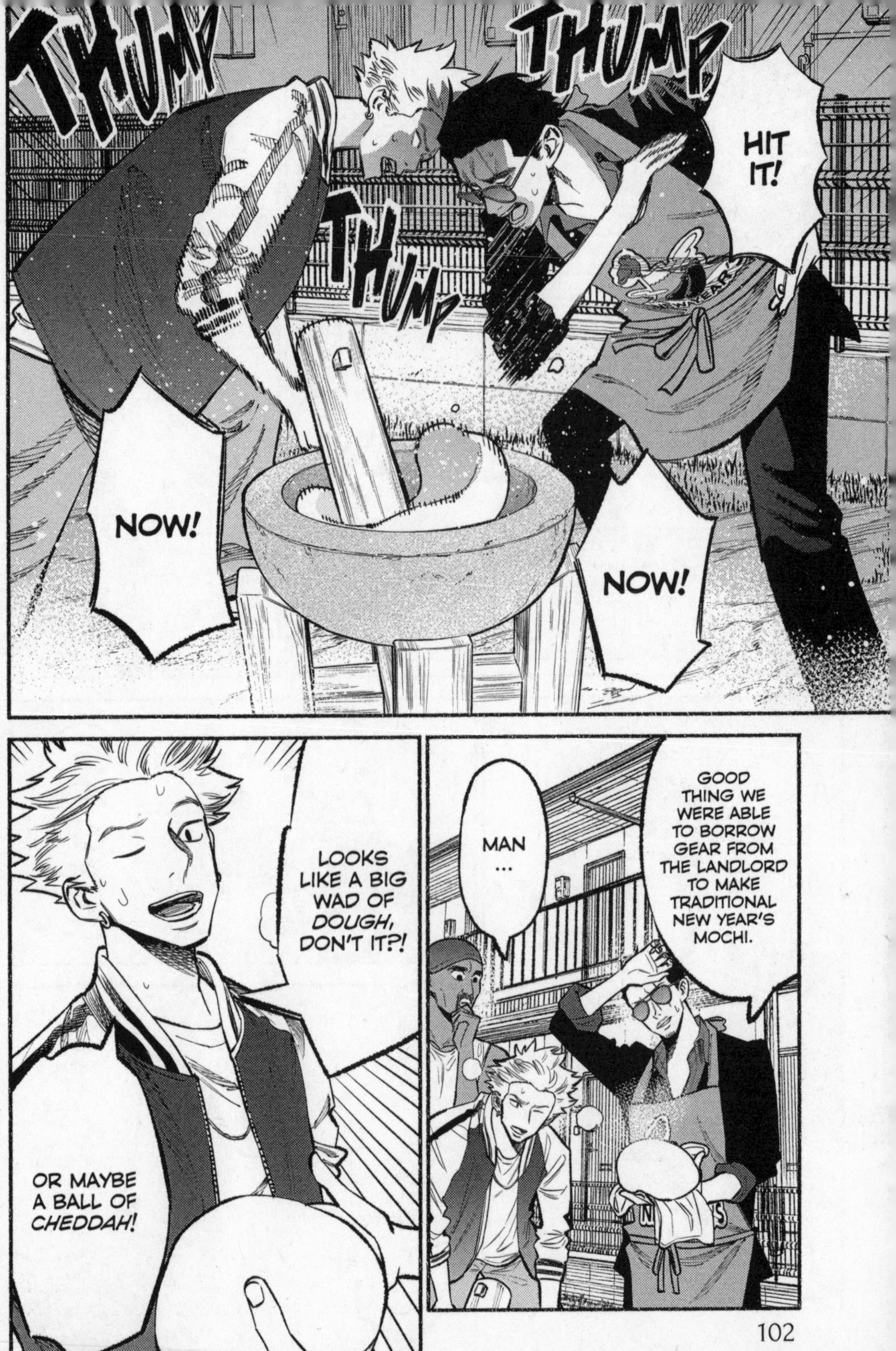
THUMP
HIT IT!
THUMP
THUMP THUMP
NOW!
NOW!
GOOD THING WE WERE ABLE TO BORROW GEAR FROM THE LANDLORD TO MAKE TRADITIONAL NEW YEAR'S MOCHI.
MAN ...
LOOKS LIKE A BIG WAD OF *DOUGH*, DON'T IT?!
OR MAYBE A BALL OF *CHEDDAH*!

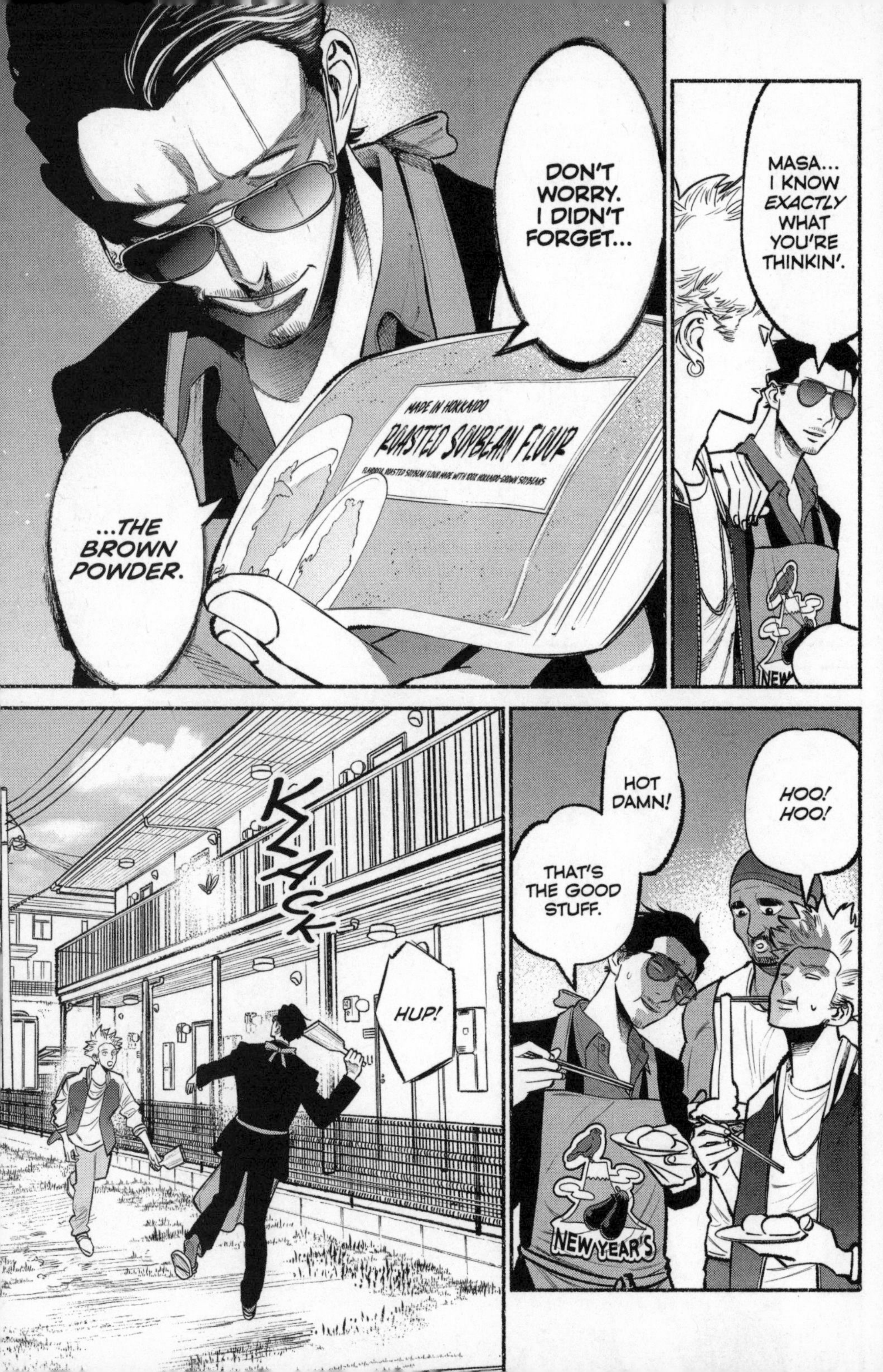
MASA... I KNOW *EXACTLY* WHAT YOU'RE THINKIN'.
DON'T WORRY. I DIDN'T FORGET...
...THE BROWN POWDER.
MADE IN HOKKAIDO
ROASTED SOYBEAN FLOUR
FLAVORFUL ROASTED SOYBEAN FLOUR MADE WITH 100% HOKKAIDO-GROWN SOYBEANS
HOO! HOO!
HOT DAMN!
THAT'S THE GOOD STUFF.
NEW YEAR'S
KLACK
HUP!

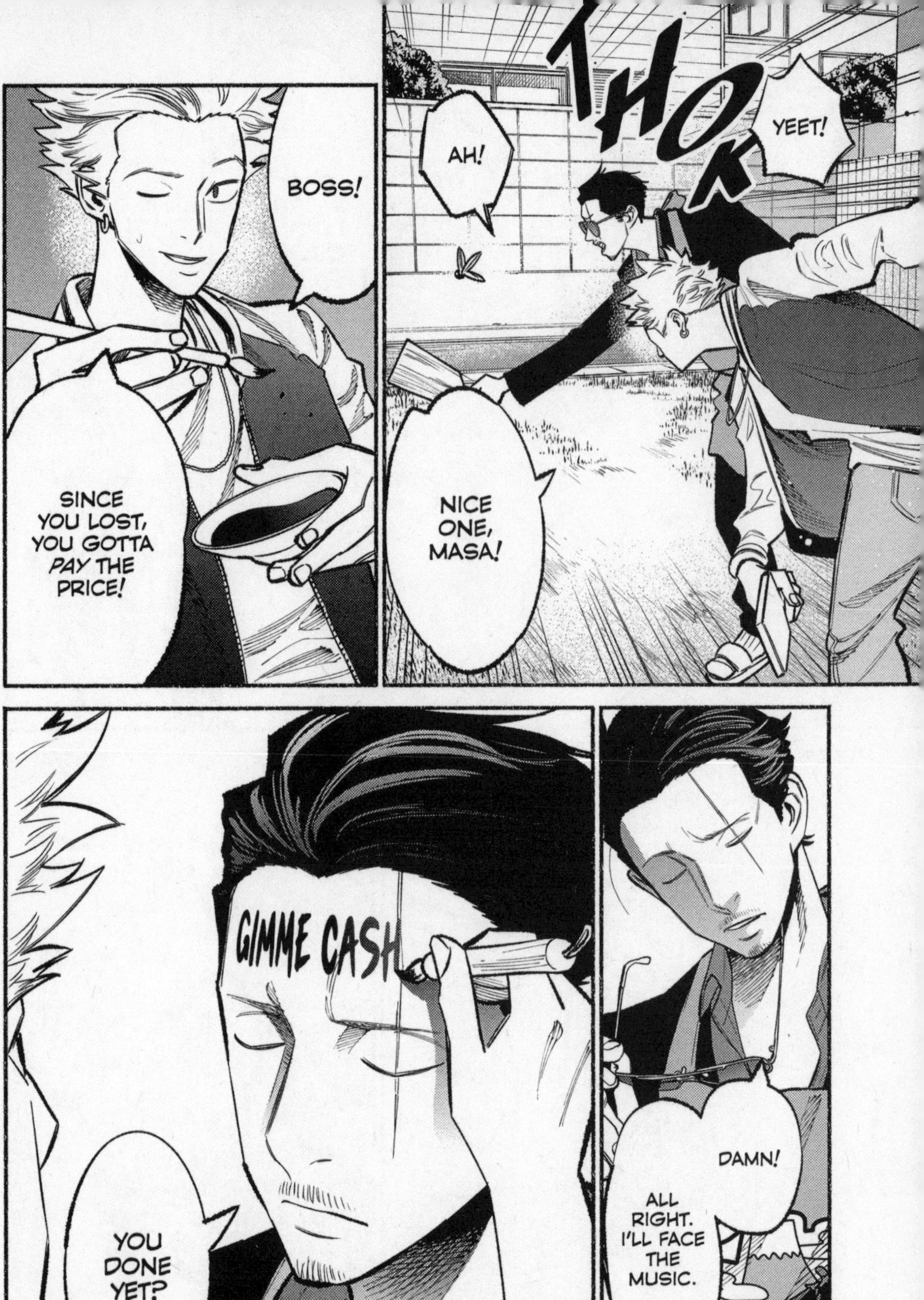
YEET!
THOK
AH!
NICE ONE, MASA!
BOSS!
SINCE YOU LOST, YOU GOTTA *PAY* THE PRICE!
DAMN!
ALL RIGHT. I'LL FACE THE MUSIC.
GIMME CASH
YOU DONE YET?

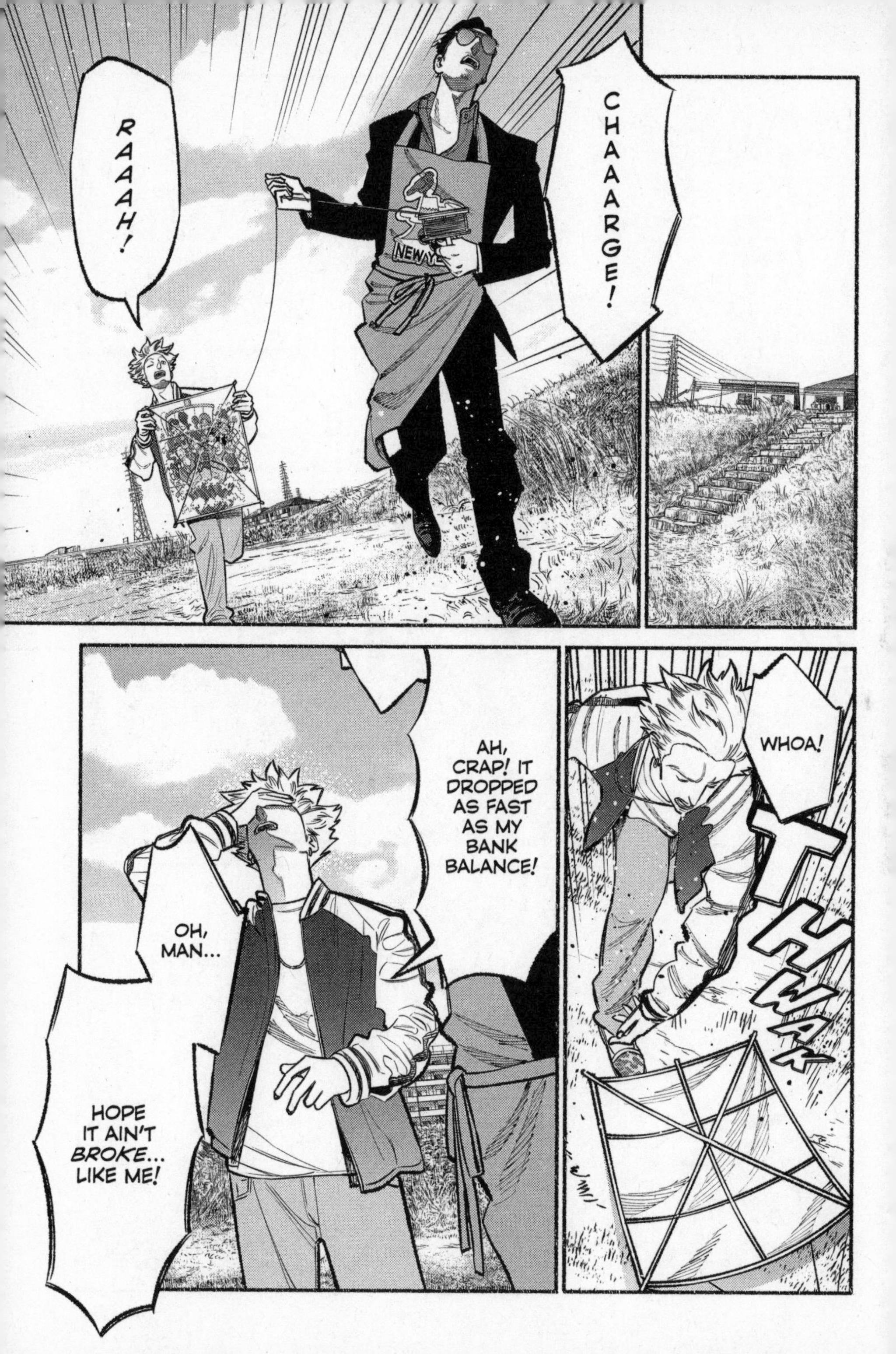
CHAAARGE!
RAAAH!
WHOA!
THWAK
AH, CRAP! IT DROPPED AS FAST AS MY BANK BALANCE!
OH, MAN...
HOPE IT AIN'T *BROKE*... LIKE ME!

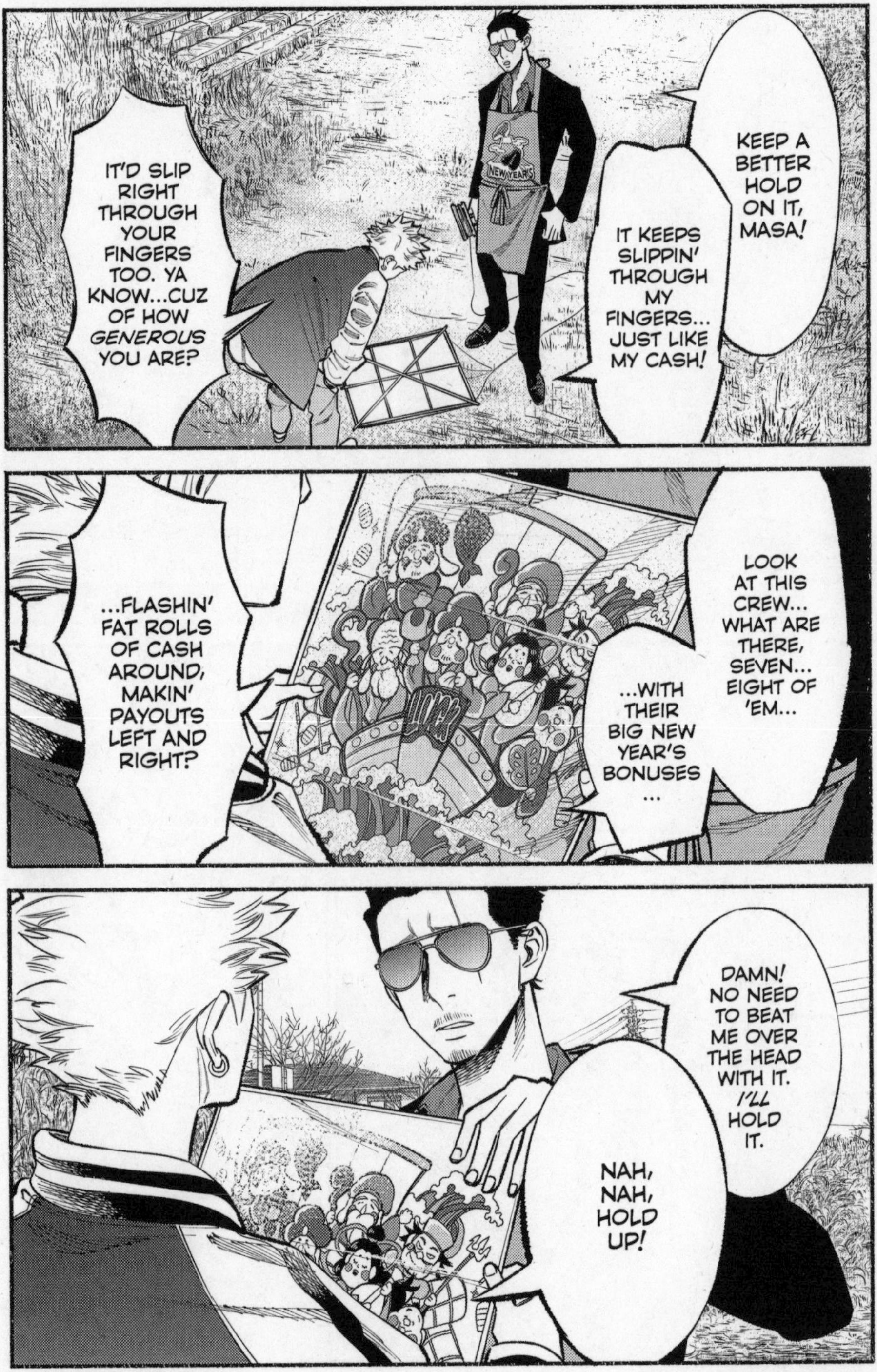
KEEP A BETTER HOLD ON IT, MASA!
IT KEEPS SLIPPIN' THROUGH MY FINGERS... JUST LIKE MY CASH!
NEW YEAR'S
IT'D SLIP RIGHT THROUGH YOUR FINGERS TOO. YA KNOW...CUZ OF HOW *GENEROUS* YOU ARE?
LOOK AT THIS CREW... WHAT ARE THERE, SEVEN... EIGHT OF 'EM...
...WITH THEIR BIG NEW YEAR'S BONUSES...
...FLASHIN' FAT ROLLS OF CASH AROUND, MAKIN' PAYOUTS LEFT AND RIGHT?
DAMN! NO NEED TO BEAT ME OVER THE HEAD WITH IT. *I'LL* HOLD IT.
NAH, NAH, HOLD UP!

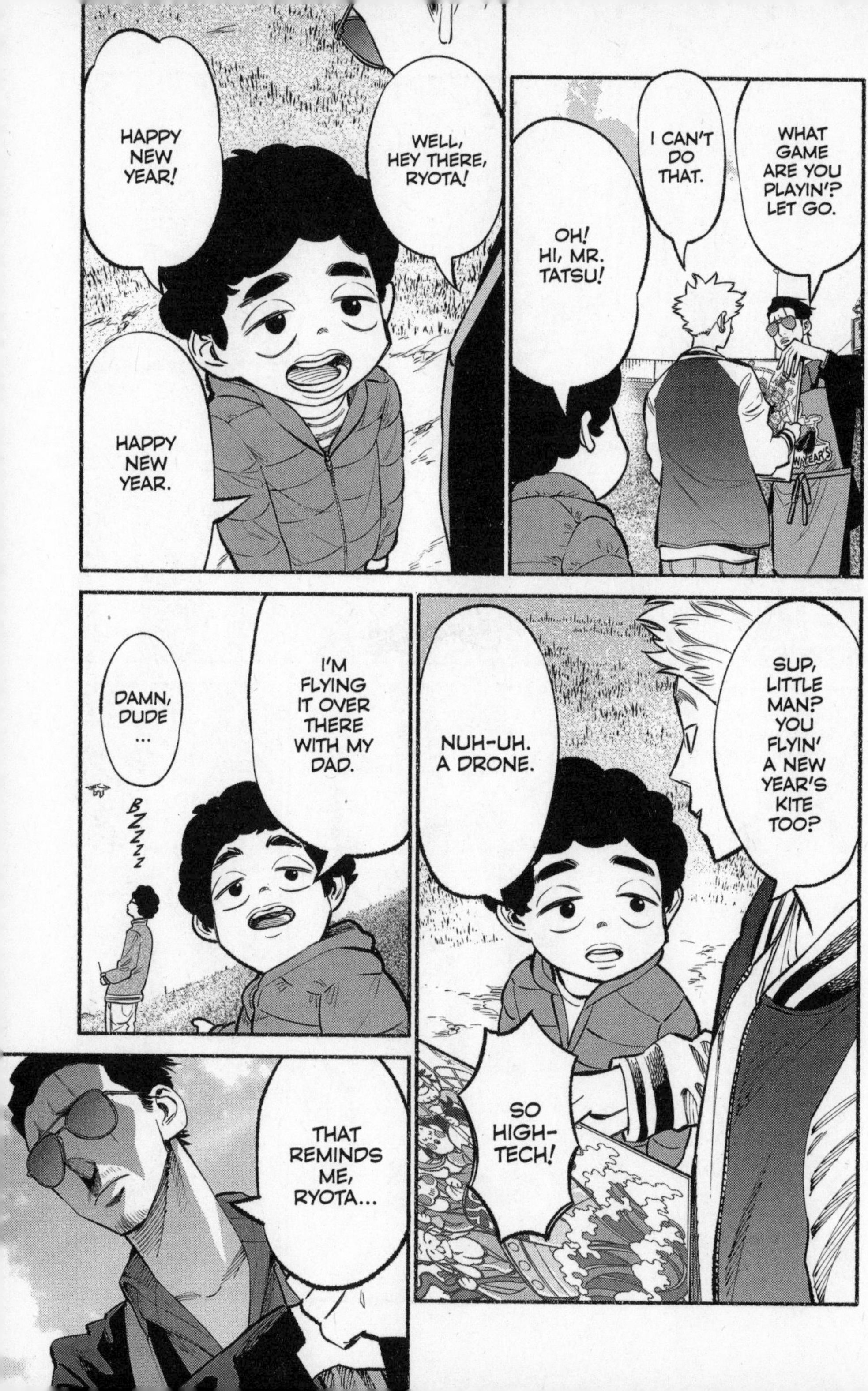
WHAT GAME ARE YOU PLAYIN'? LET GO.
I CAN'T DO THAT.
OH! HI, MR. TATSU!
WELL, HEY THERE, RYOTA!
HAPPY NEW YEAR!
HAPPY NEW YEAR.
SUP, LITTLE MAN? YOU FLYIN' A NEW YEAR'S KITE TOO?
NUH-UH. A DRONE.
SO HIGH-TECH!
I'M FLYING IT OVER THERE WITH MY DAD.
DAMN, DUDE...
BZZZZ
THAT REMINDS ME, RYOTA...

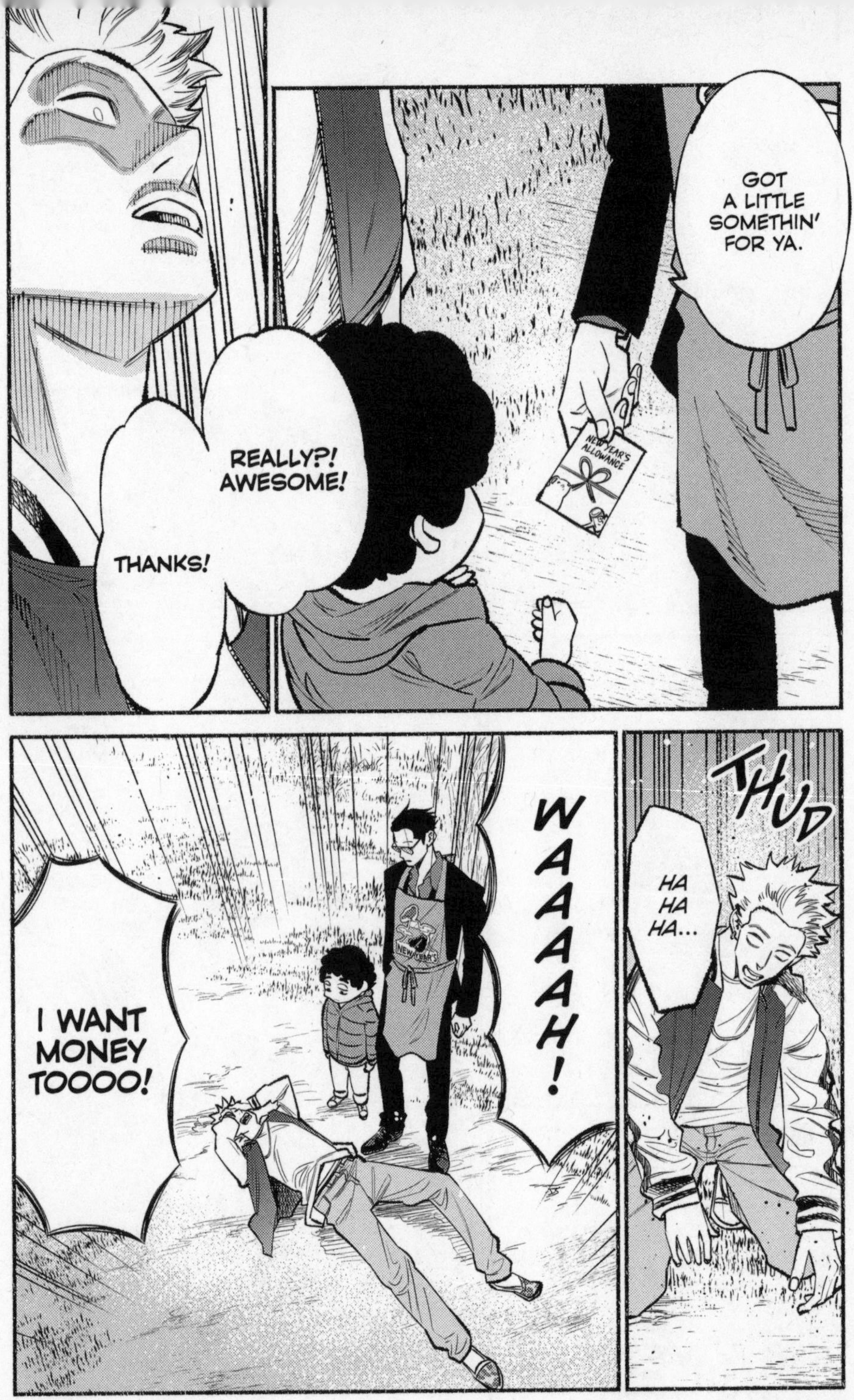
GOT A LITTLE SOMETHIN' FOR YA.
NEW YEAR'S ALLOWANCE
REALLY?! AWESOME!
THANKS!
THUD
HA HA HA...
WAAAAAH!
NEW YEAR'S
I WANT MONEY TOOOO!

NEW YEAR'S

*MT. FUJI, A HAWK AND AN EGGPLANT ARE AUSPICIOUS
SYMBOLS IN THE FIRST DREAM OF THE YEAR.

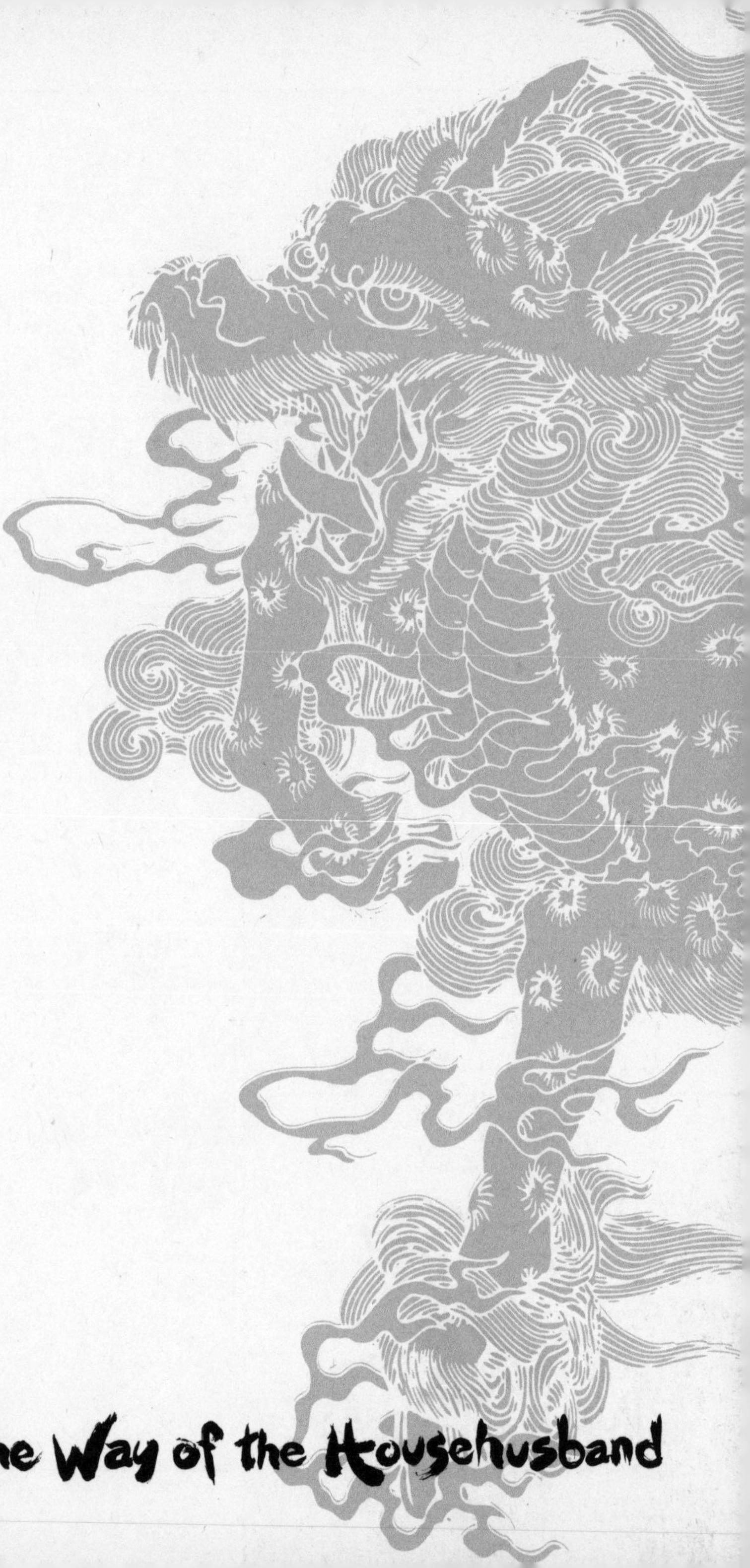

The Way of the Househusband

CHAPTER 44

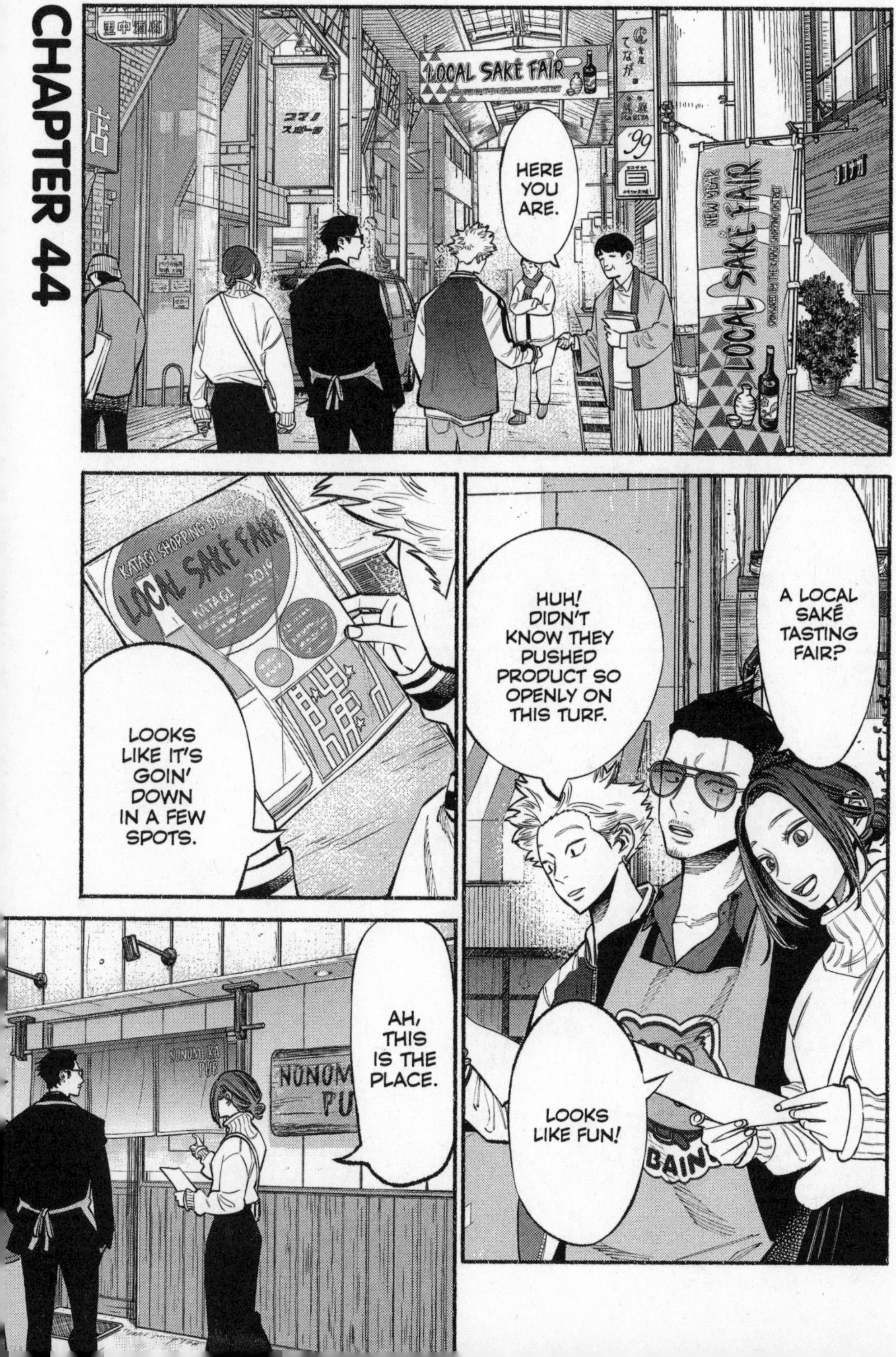
LOCAL SAKÉ FAIR
NEW YEAR
LOCAL SAKÉ FAIR
HERE YOU ARE.
A LOCAL SAKÉ TASTING FAIR?
HUH! DIDN'T KNOW THEY PUSHED PRODUCT SO OPENLY ON THIS TURF.
LOOKS LIKE FUN!
KATAGI SHOPPING DISTRICT
LOCAL SAKÉ FAIR
LOOKS LIKE IT'S GOIN' DOWN IN A FEW SPOTS.
AH, THIS IS THE PLACE.
NUNOMURA PUB

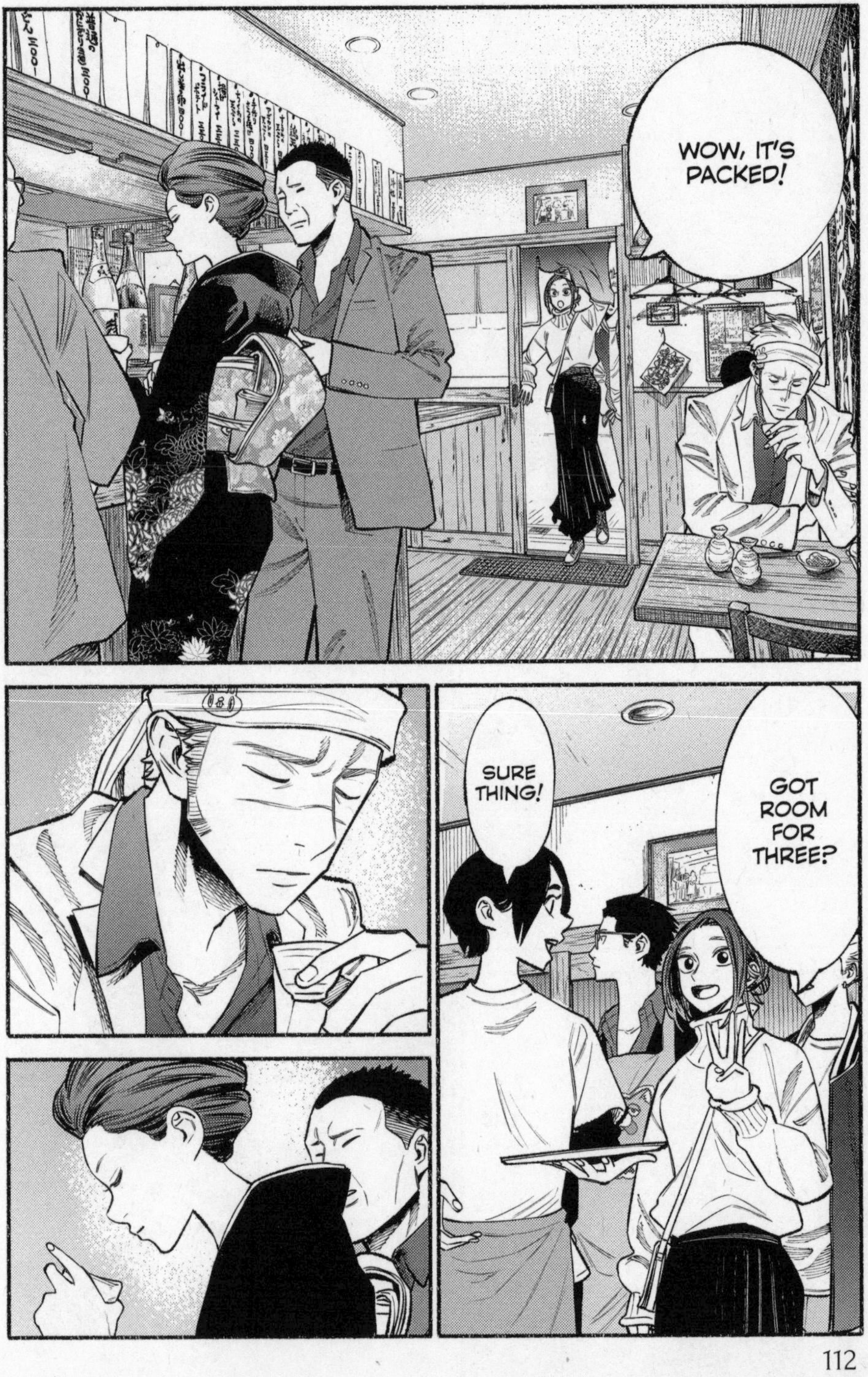
WOW, IT'S PACKED!
GOT ROOM FOR THREE?
SURE THING!

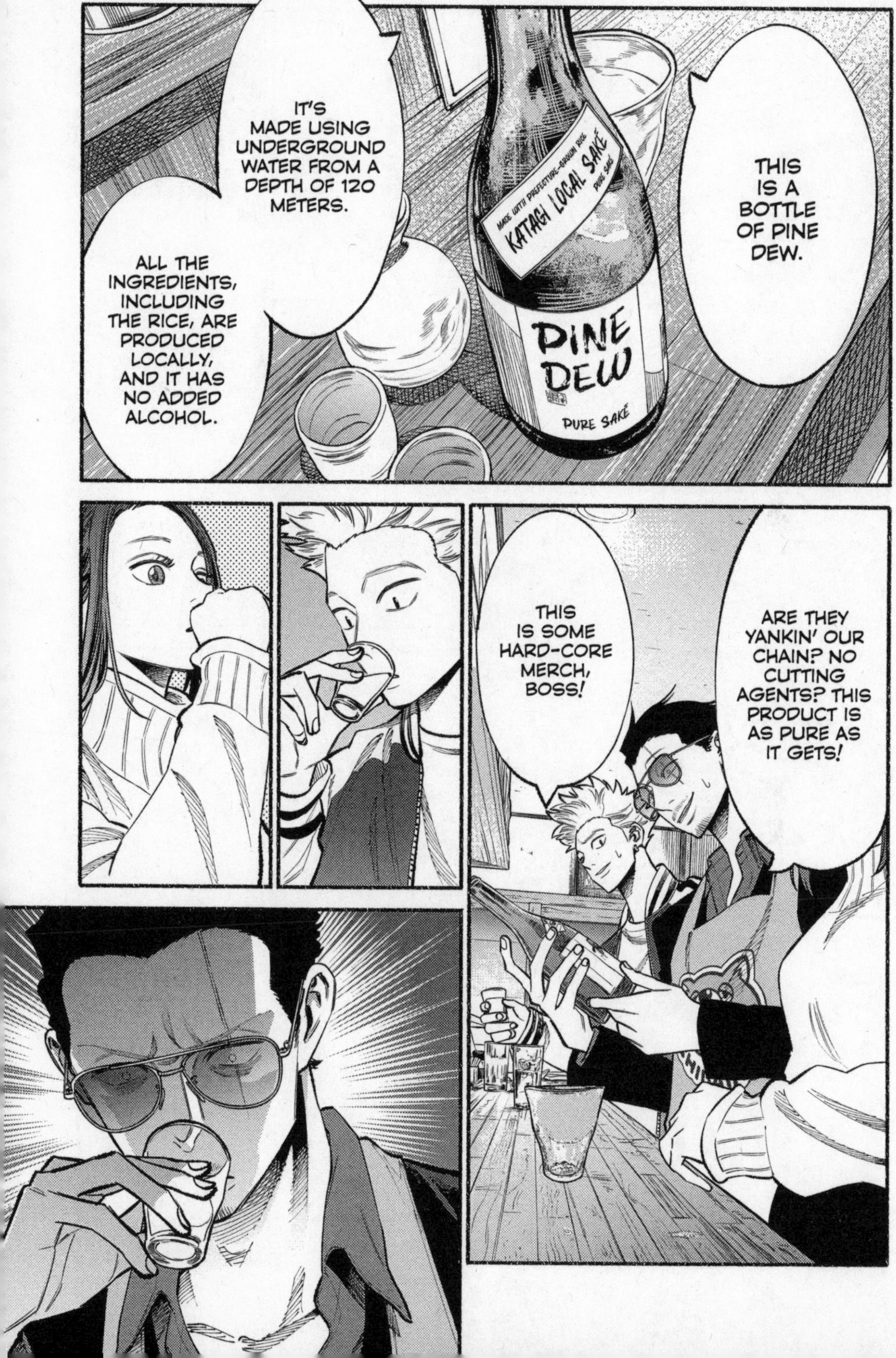
THIS IS A BOTTLE OF PINE DEW.
MADE WITH PREFECTURE-GROWN RICE
KATAGI LOCAL SAKÉ
PURE SAKÉ
PINE DEW
PURE SAKÉ
IT'S MADE USING UNDERGROUND WATER FROM A DEPTH OF 120 METERS.
ALL THE INGREDIENTS, INCLUDING THE RICE, ARE PRODUCED LOCALLY, AND IT HAS NO ADDED ALCOHOL.
ARE THEY YANKIN' OUR CHAIN? NO CUTTING AGENTS? THIS PRODUCT IS AS PURE AS IT GETS!
THIS IS SOME HARD-CORE MERCH, BOSS!

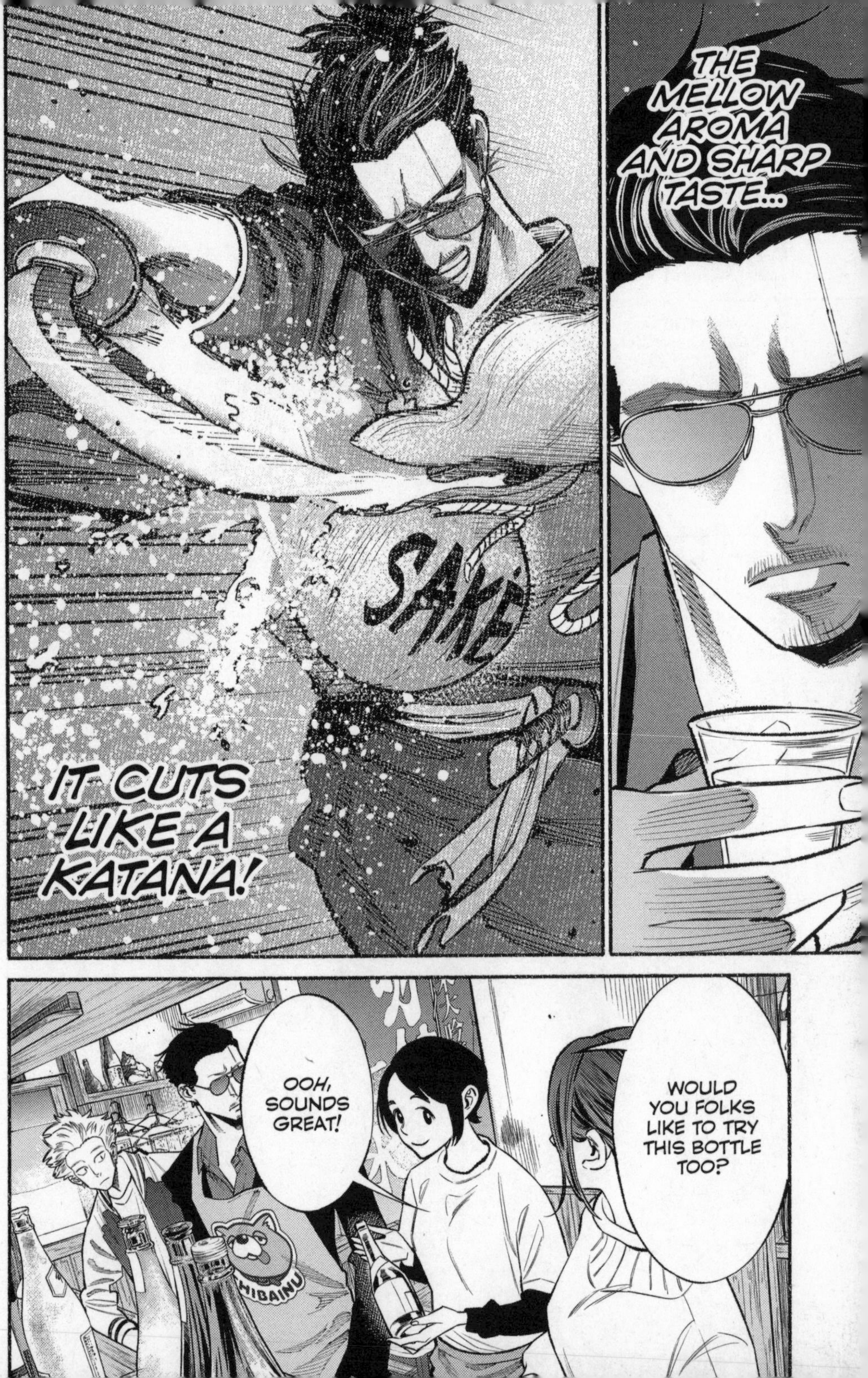
THE MELLOW AROMA AND SHARP TASTE...
SAKE
IT CUTS LIKE A KATANA!
WOULD YOU FOLKS LIKE TO TRY THIS BOTTLE TOO?
OOH, SOUNDS GREAT!

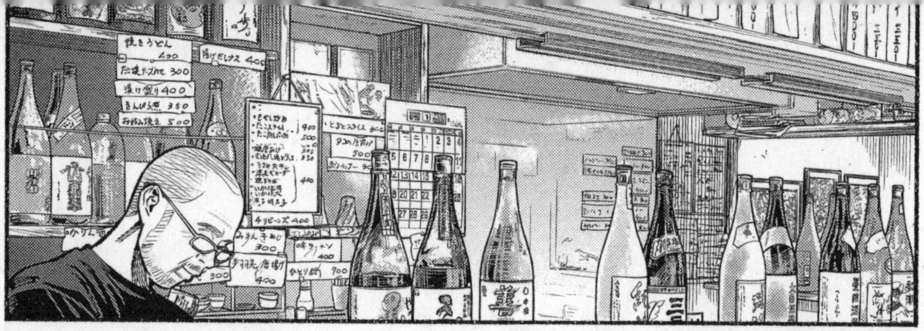
焼きうどん 400
揚げだしナス 400
たこ焼チーズのせ 300
漬け盛り 400
きんぴら煮 350
お好み焼き 500
みりん干あじ 300
手羽先唐揚げ 400
ひとり鍋 700
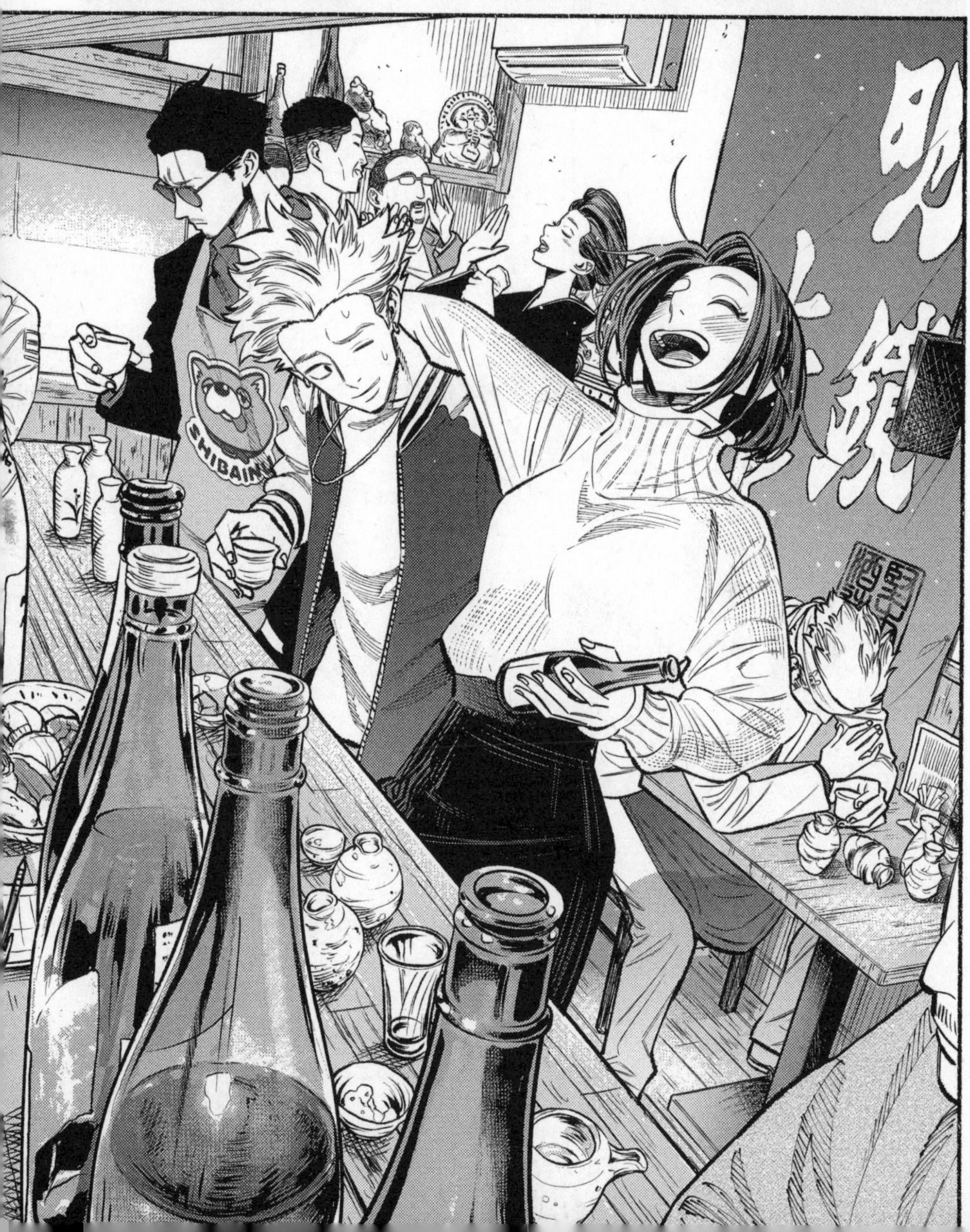
SHIBAINU

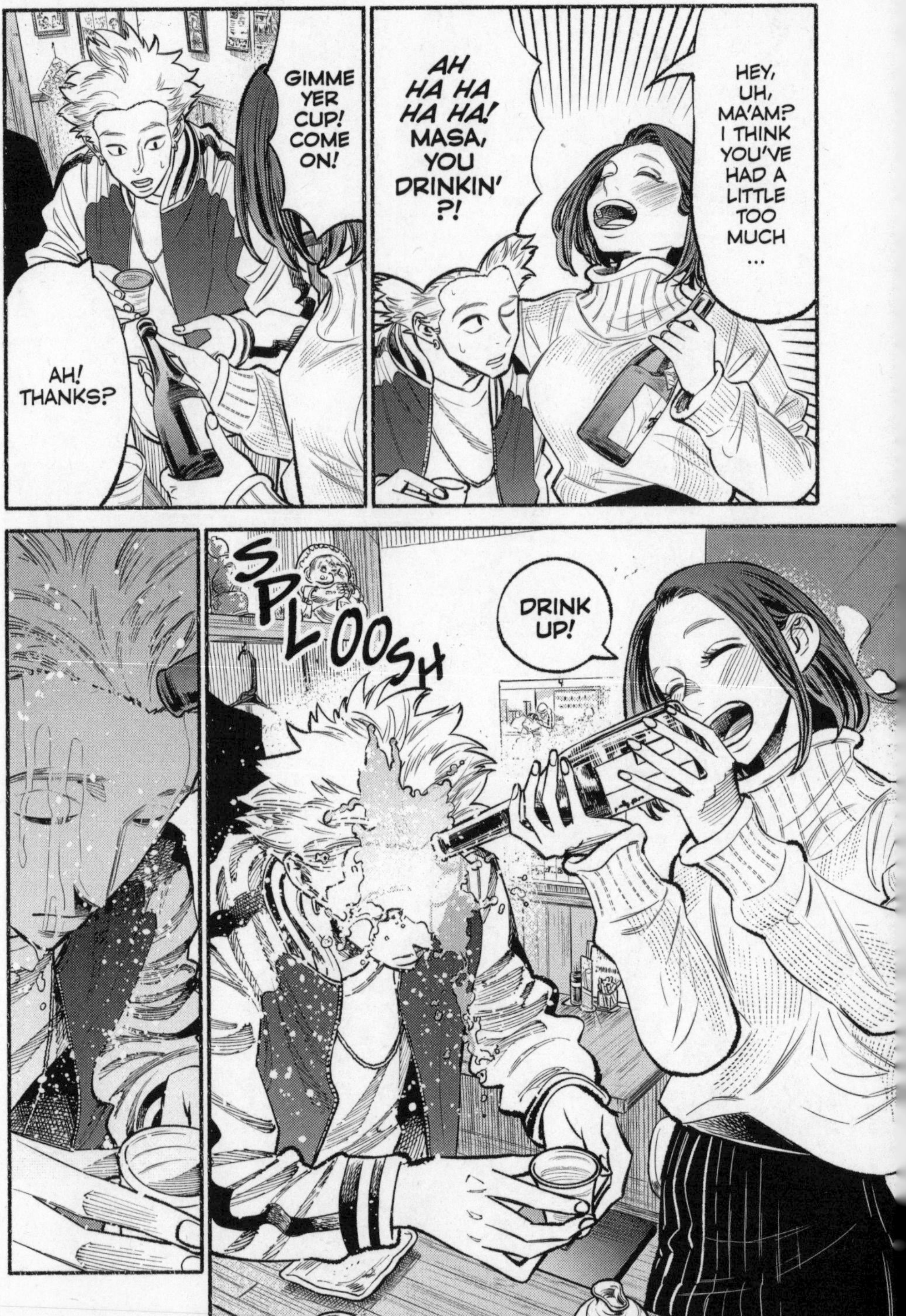
HEY, UH, MA'AM? I THINK YOU'VE HAD A LITTLE TOO MUCH...
AH HA HA HA HA! MASA, YOU DRINKIN'?!
GIMME YER CUP! COME ON!
AH! THANKS?
DRINK UP!
SPLOOSH

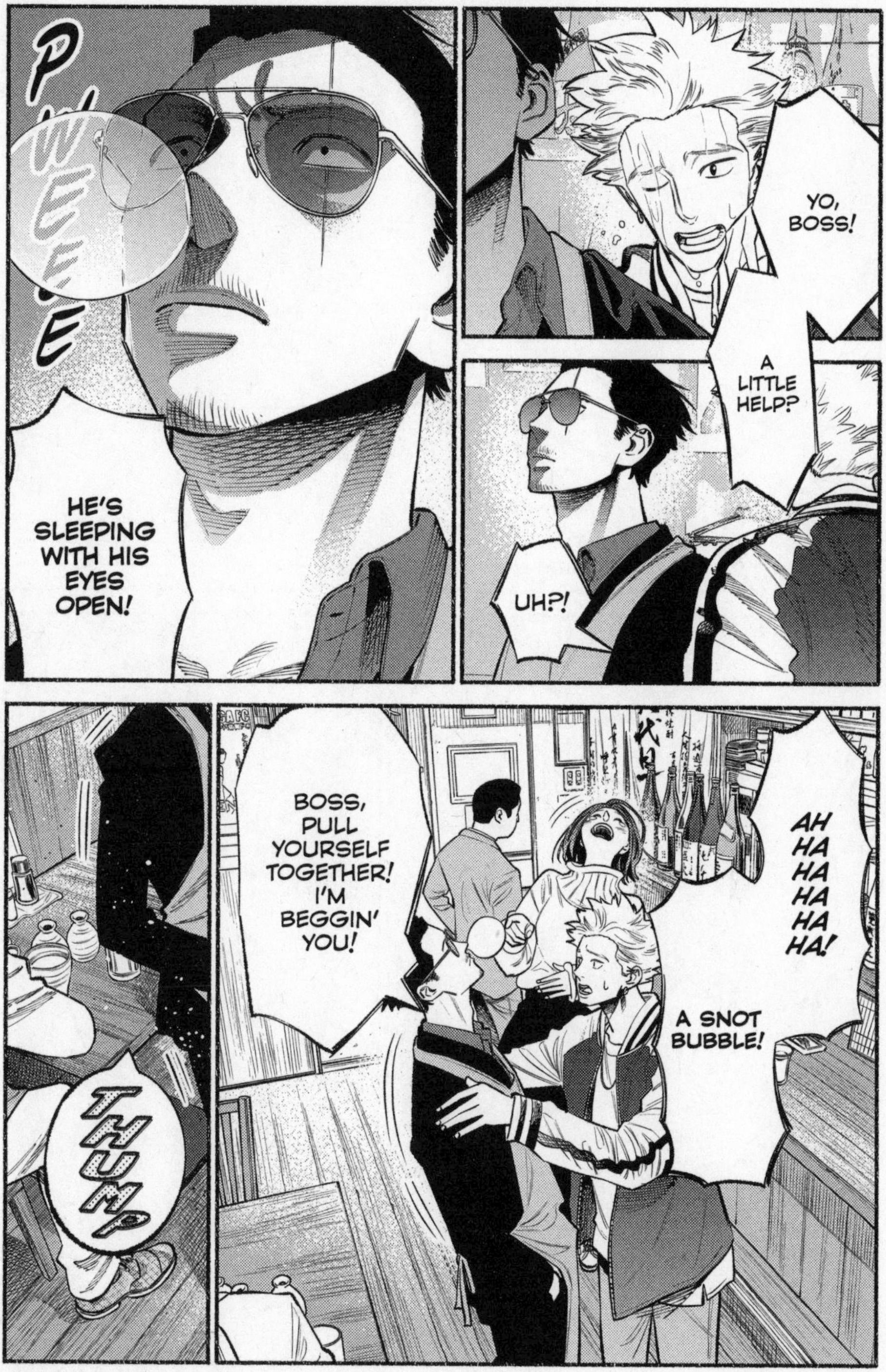
YO, BOSS!
A LITTLE HELP?
UH?!
PWEEEE
HE'S SLEEPING WITH HIS EYES OPEN!
AH HA HA HA HA HA HA!
A SNOT BUBBLE!
BOSS, PULL YOURSELF TOGETHER! I'M BEGGIN' YOU!
THUMP

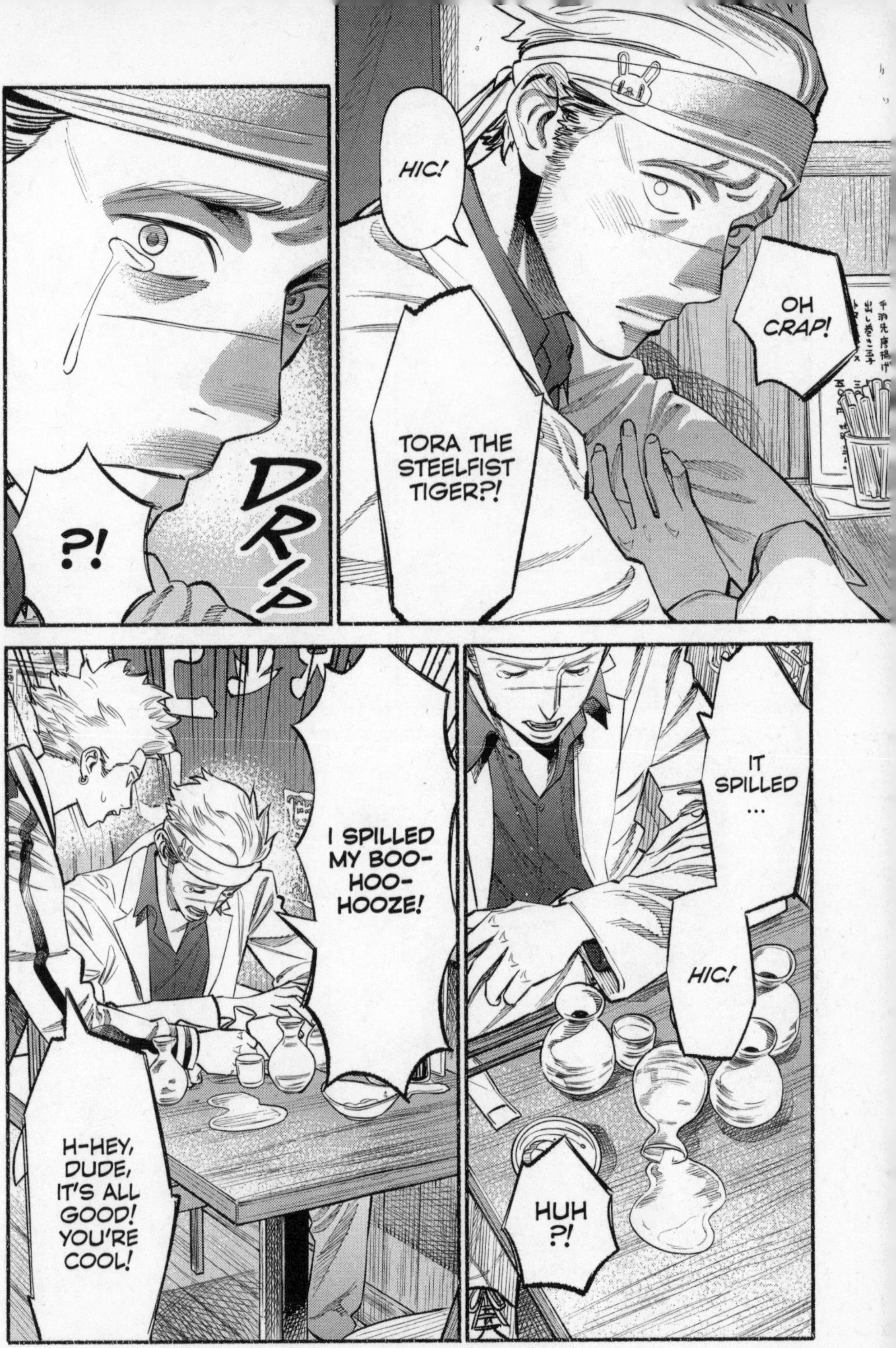
HIC!
OH CRAP!
TORA THE STEELFIST TIGER?!
?!
DRIP
IT SPILLED...
HIC!
HUH?!
I SPILLED MY BOO-HOO-HOOZE!
H-HEY, DUDE, IT'S ALL GOOD! YOU'RE COOL!

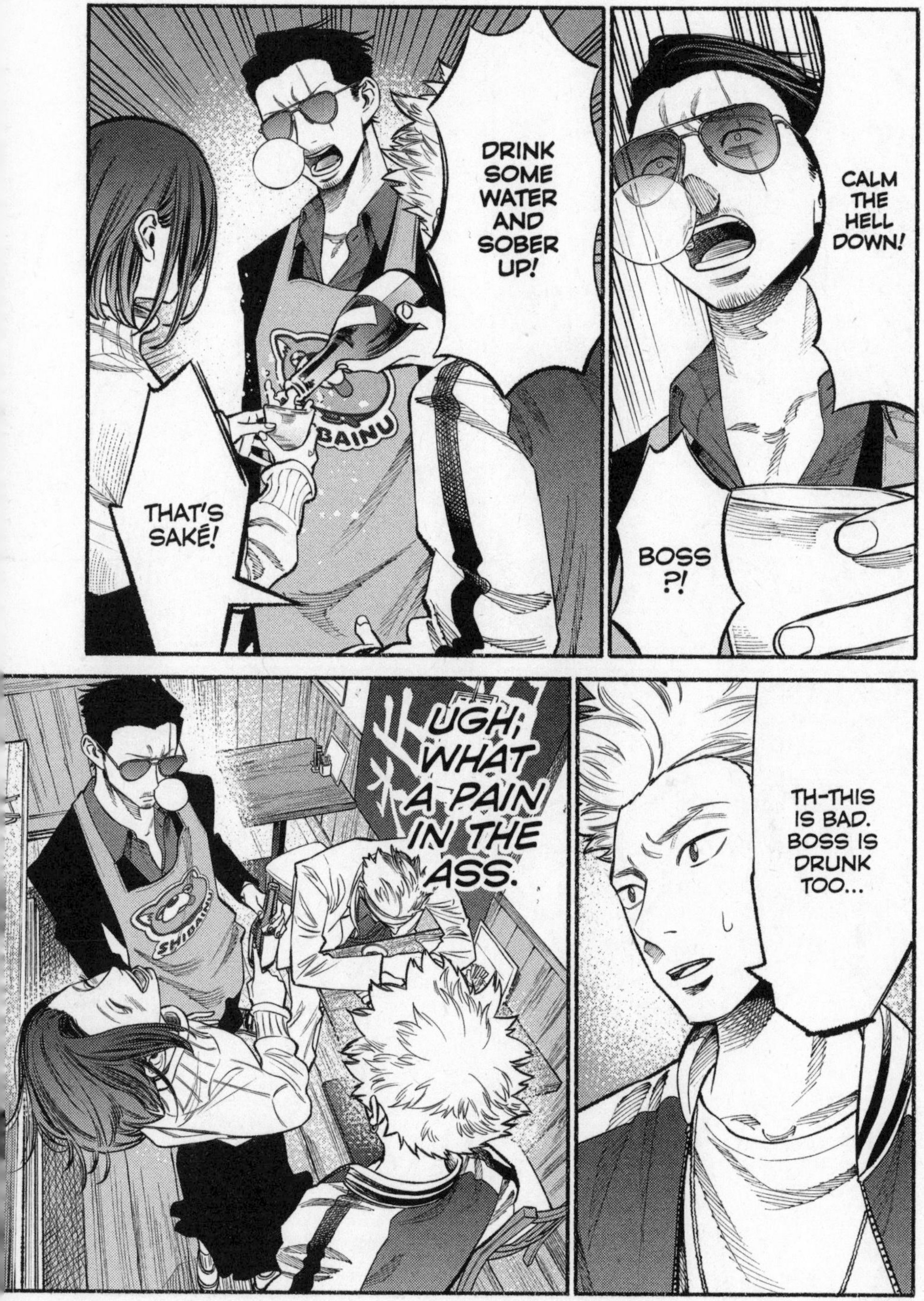

CALM THE HELL DOWN!
BOSS ?!
DRINK SOME WATER AND SOBER UP!
THAT'S SAKÉ!
TH-THIS IS BAD. BOSS IS DRUNK TOO...
UGH, WHAT A PAIN IN THE ASS.

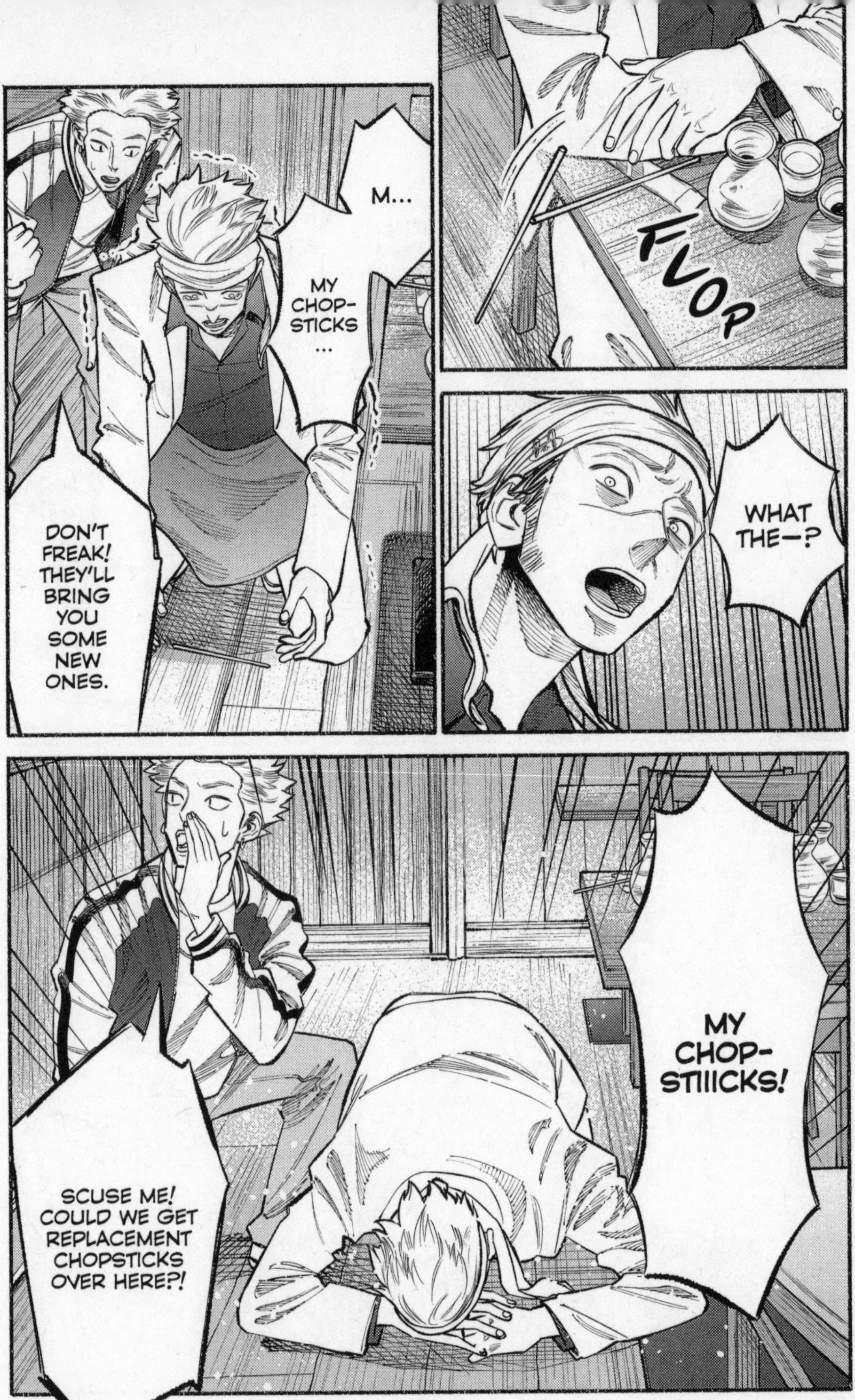
FLOP
WHAT THE—?
M...
MY CHOP-STICKS ...
DON'T FREAK! THEY'LL BRING YOU SOME NEW ONES.
MY CHOP-STIIICKS!
SCUSE ME! COULD WE GET REPLACEMENT CHOPSTICKS OVER HERE?!

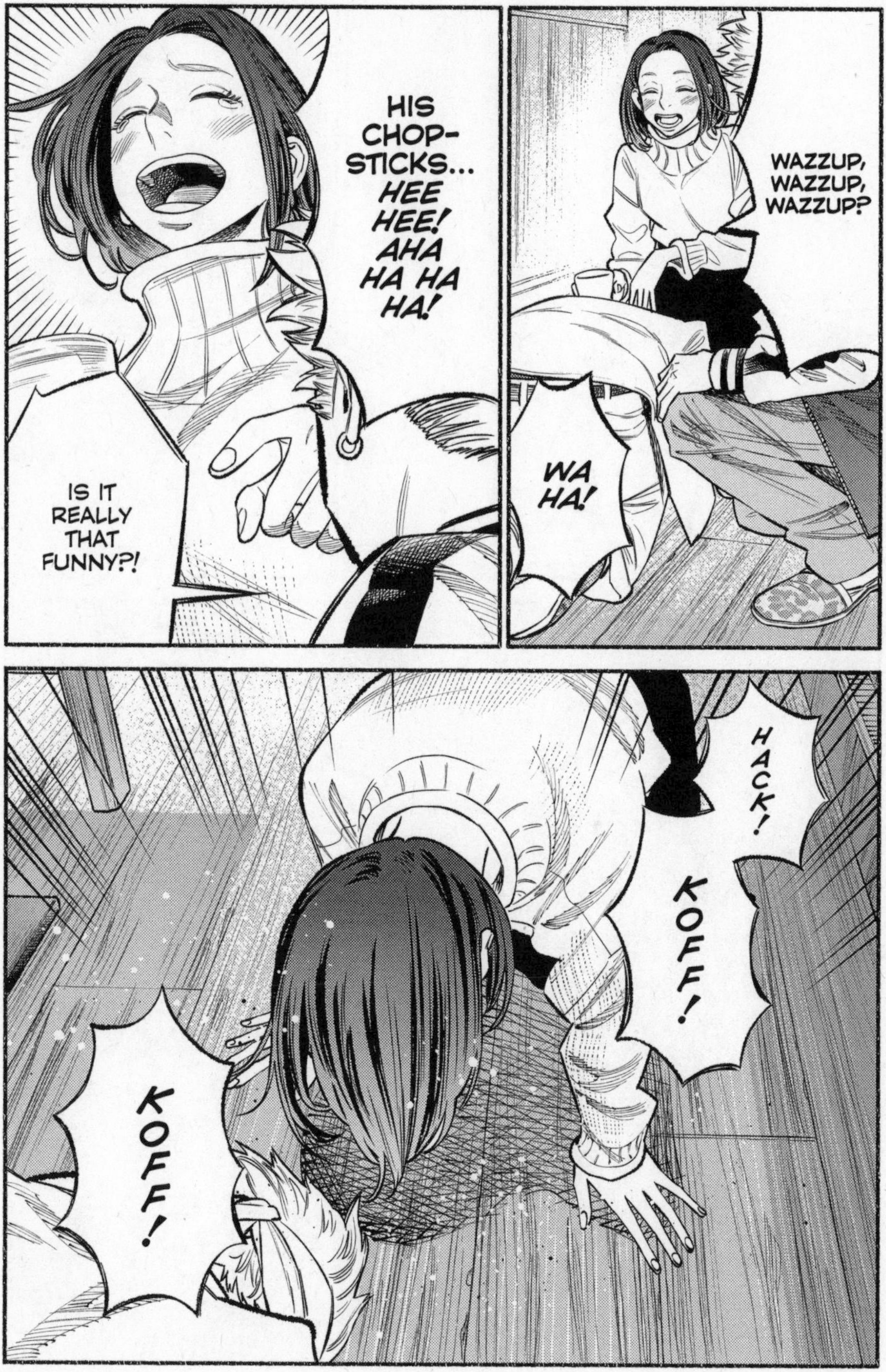
WAZZUP, WAZZUP, WAZZUP?
WA HA!
HIS CHOP-STICKS... HEE HEE! AHA HA HA HA!
IS IT REALLY THAT FUNNY?!
HACK!
KOFF!
KOFF!

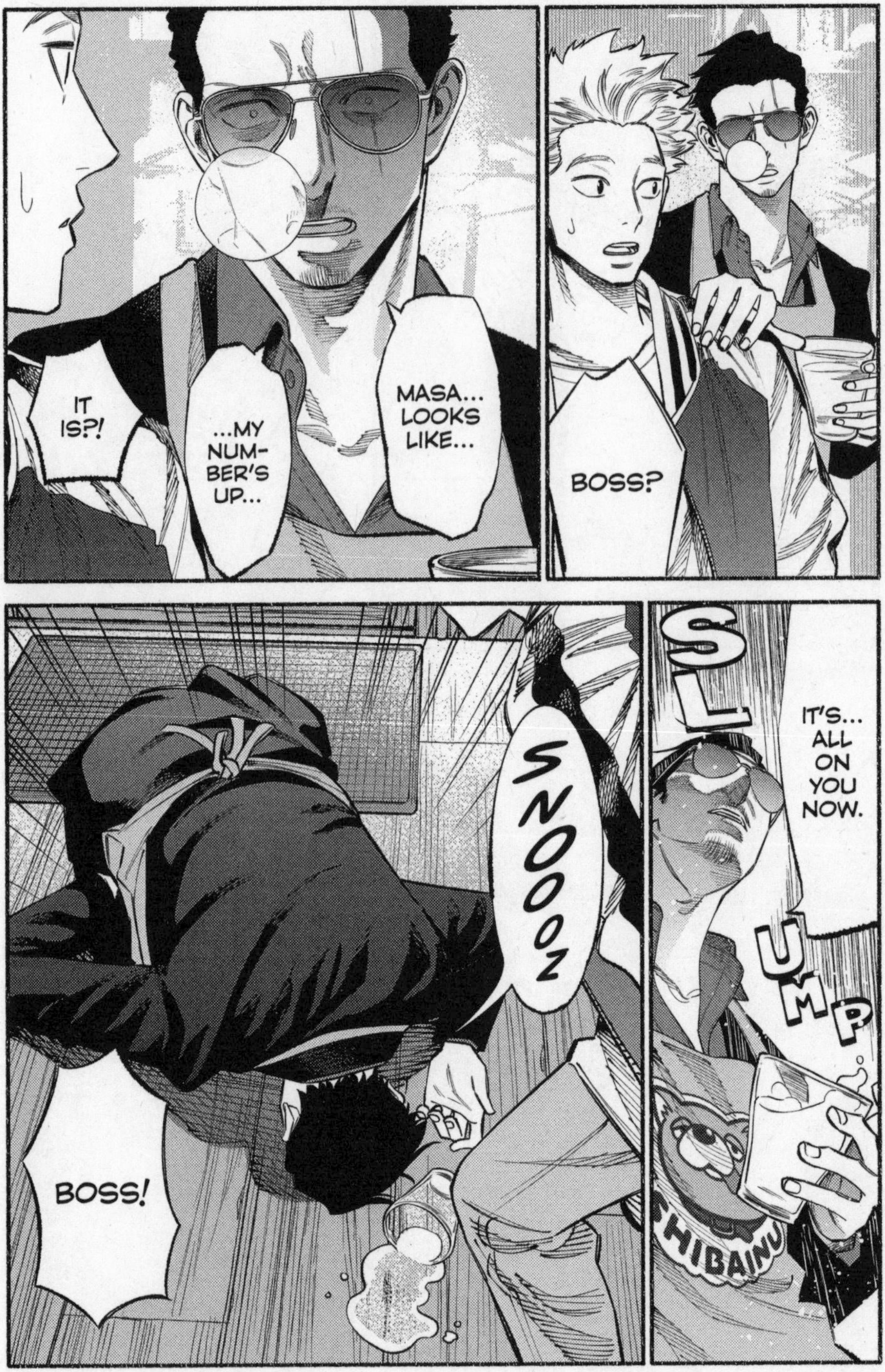
BOSS?
MASA... LOOKS LIKE...
...MY NUMBER'S UP...
IT IS?!
SLUMP
IT'S... ALL ON YOU NOW.
SHIBAINU
SNOOOOZ
BOSS!

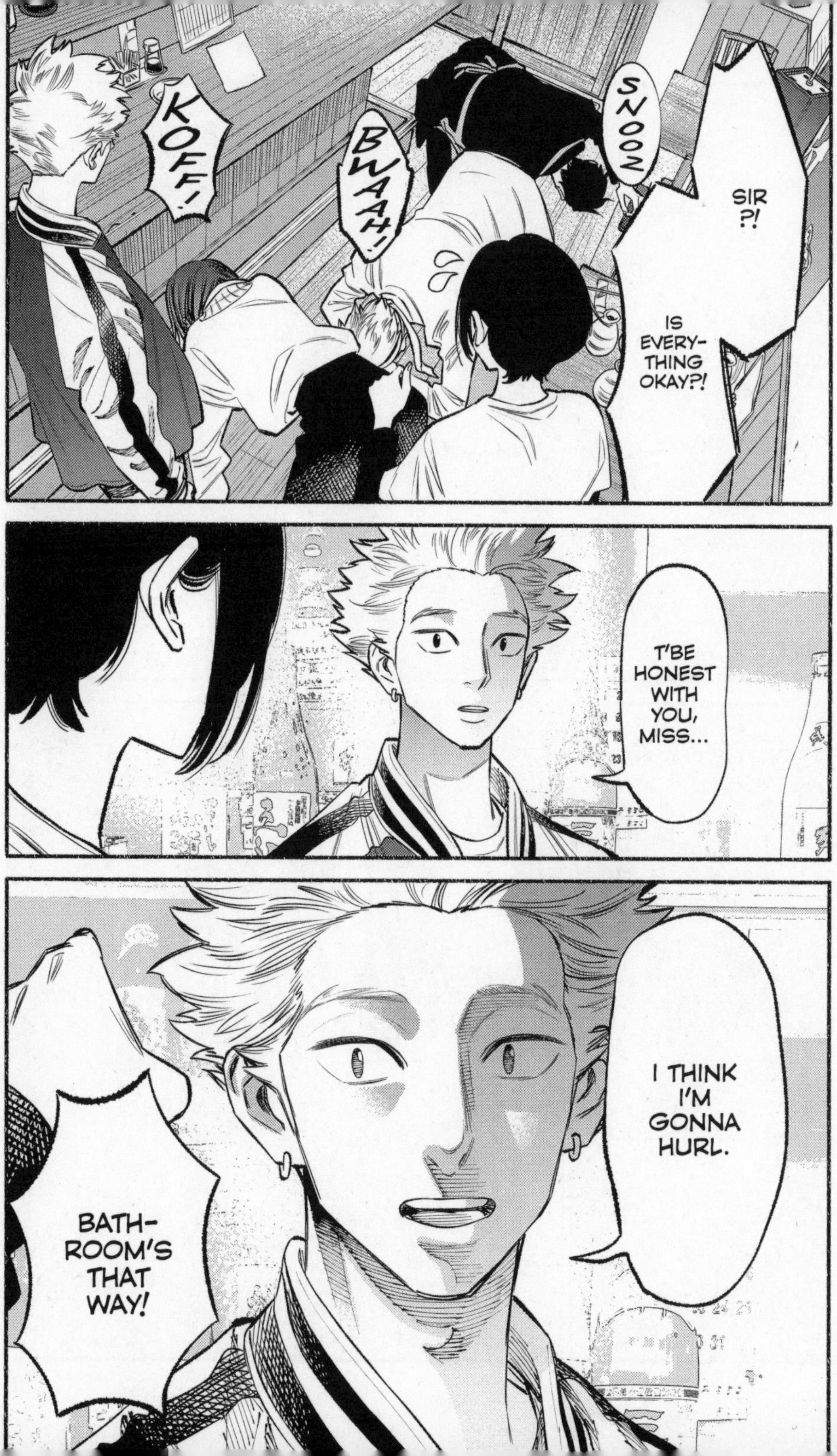
SIR?!
IS EVERY-THING OKAY?!
SNOOZ
BWAAH!
KOFF!
T'BE HONEST WITH YOU, MISS...
I THINK I'M GONNA HURL.
BATH-ROOM'S THAT WAY!

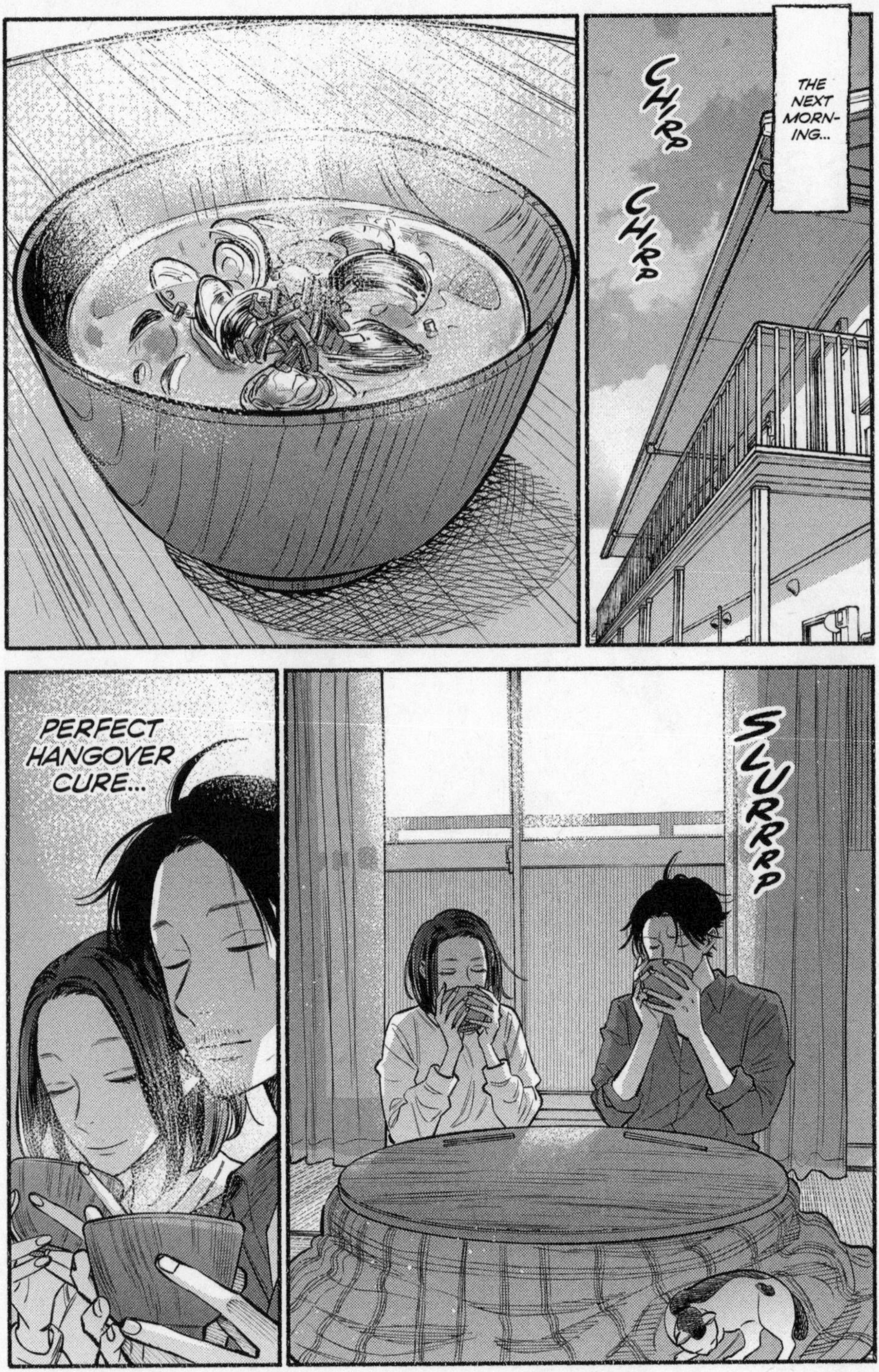

THE NEXT MORNING...
CHIRP
CHIRP
SLURRRP
PERFECT HANGOVER CURE...

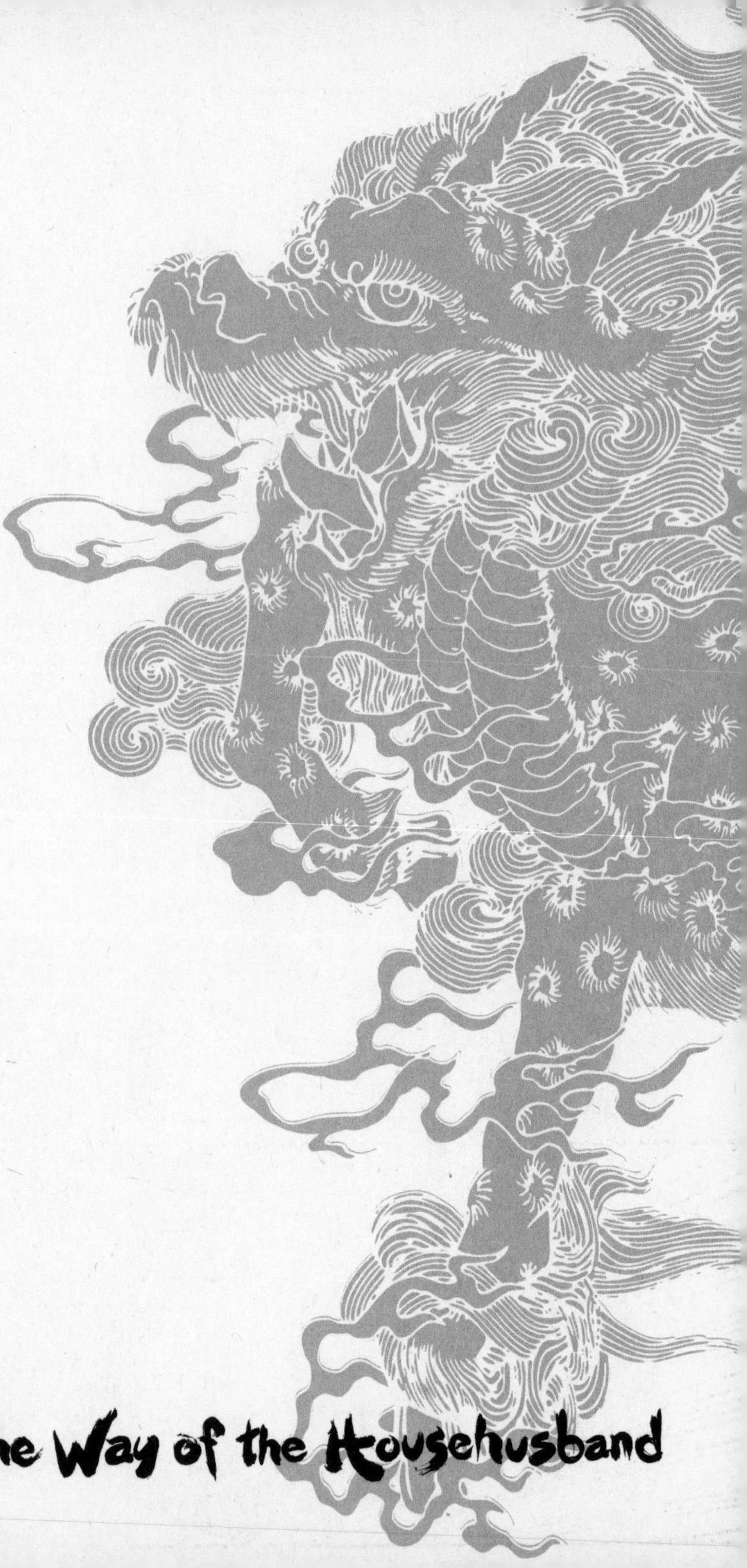

The Way of the Househusband

CHAPTER 45

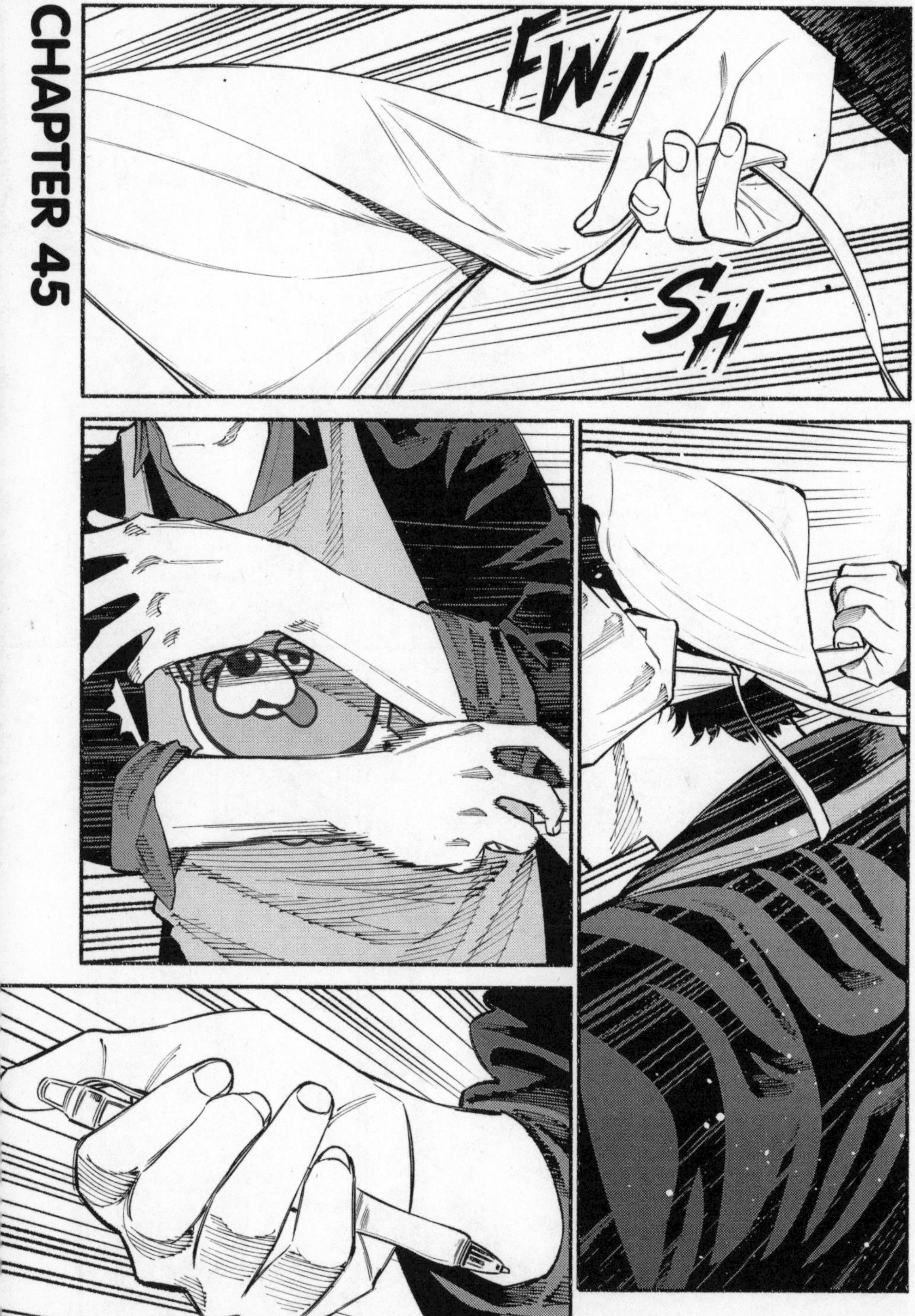
FWISH

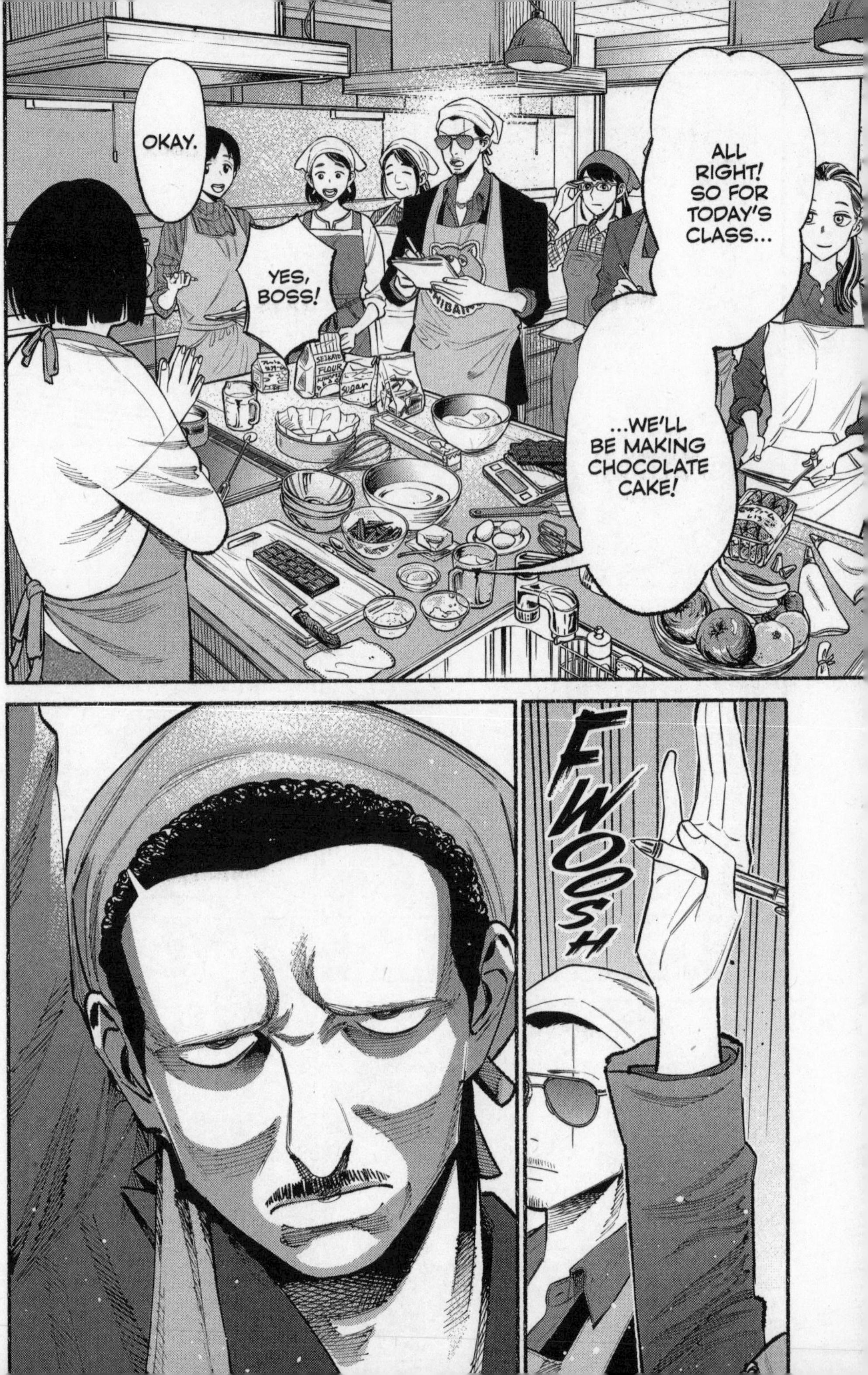
ALL RIGHT! SO FOR TODAY'S CLASS...
...WE'LL BE MAKING CHOCOLATE CAKE!
YES, BOSS!
OKAY.
FWOOSH

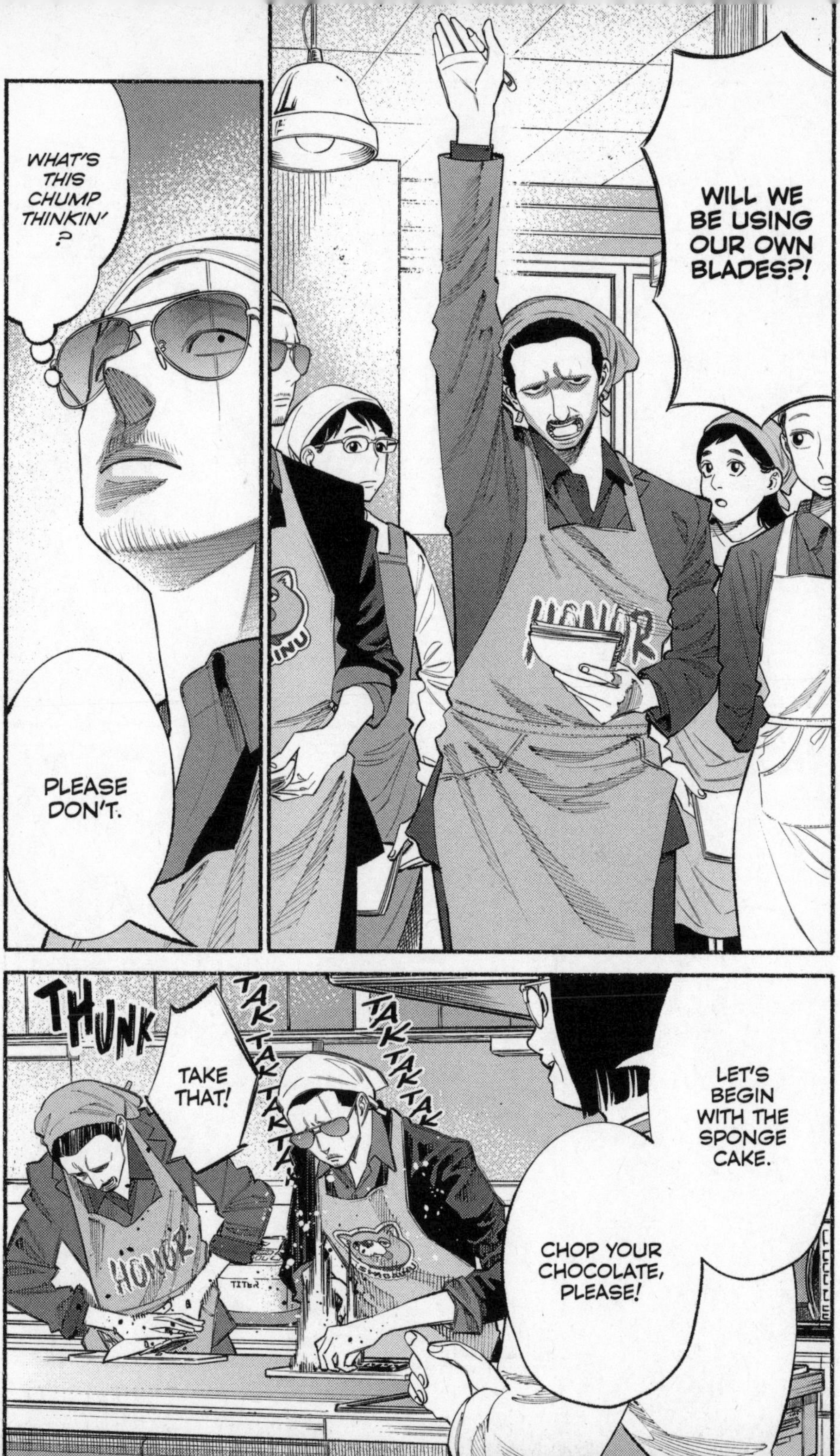
WILL WE BE USING OUR OWN BLADES?!
WHAT'S THIS CHUMP THINKIN'?
PLEASE DON'T.
LET'S BEGIN WITH THE SPONGE CAKE.
CHOP YOUR CHOCOLATE, PLEASE!
TAK TAK TAK TAK
TAK TAK TAK TAK
TAKE THAT!
THUNK

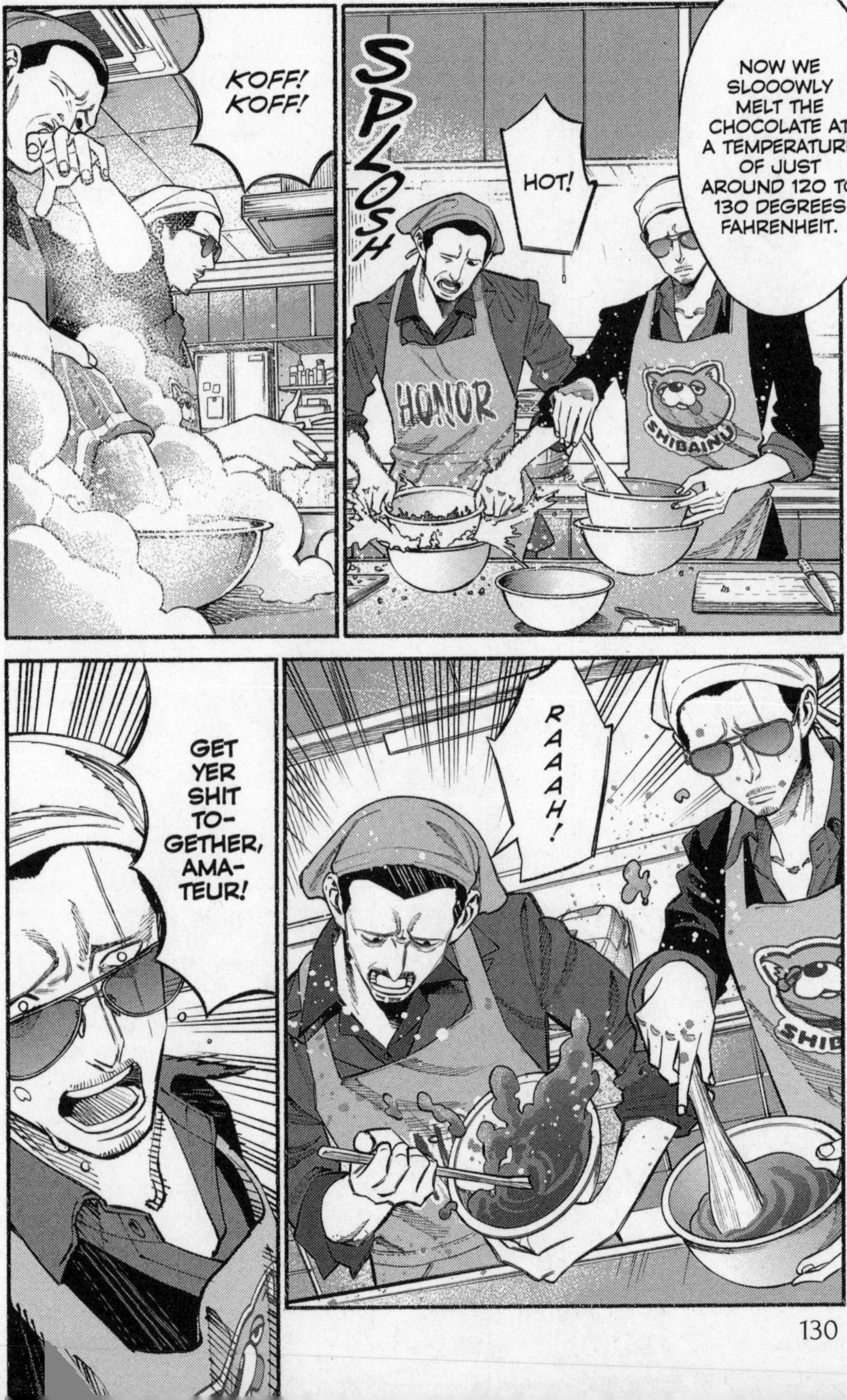
NOW WE SLOOOWLY MELT THE CHOCOLATE AT A TEMPERATURE OF JUST AROUND 120 TO 130 DEGREES FAHRENHEIT.
HOT!
SPLOSH
KOFF! KOFF!
RAAAH!
GET YER SHIT TO-GETHER, AMA-TEUR!

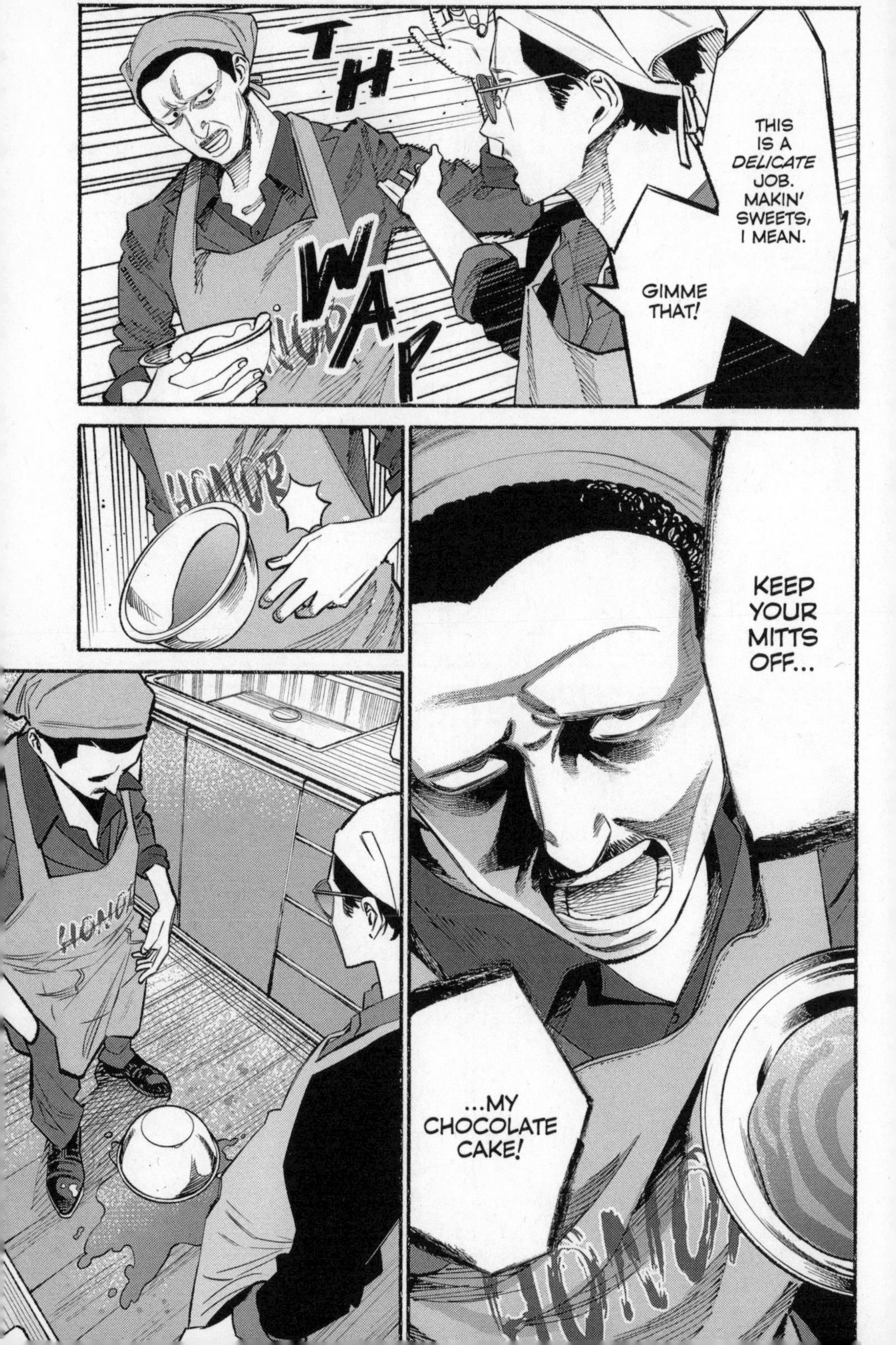
THIS IS A DELICATE JOB. MAKIN' SWEETS, I MEAN.
GIMME THAT!
THWAP
KEEP YOUR MITTS OFF...
...MY CHOCOLATE CAKE!

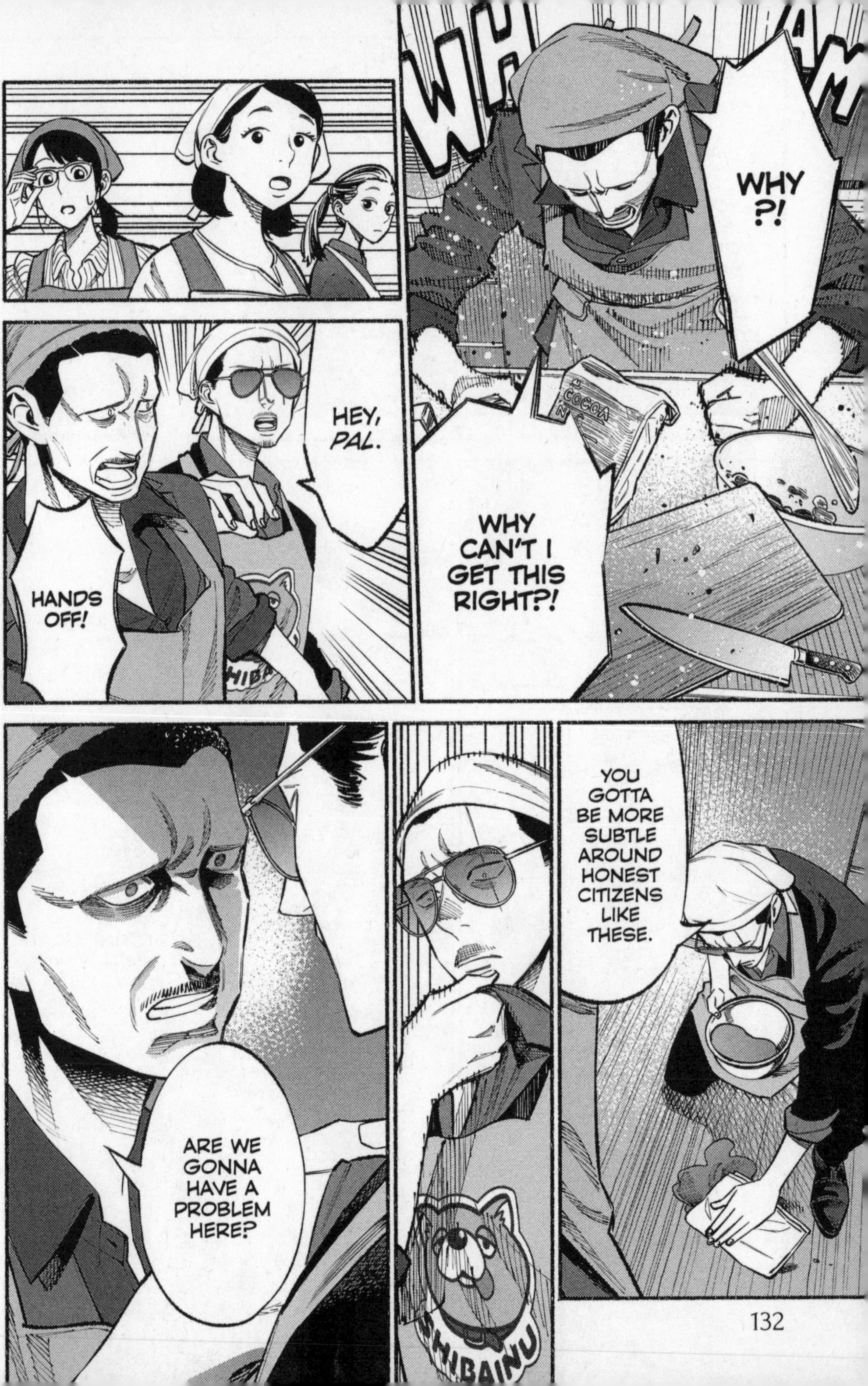

WHY?!
COCOA
WHY CAN'T I GET THIS RIGHT?!
HEY, *PAL*.
HANDS OFF!
YOU GOTTA BE MORE SUBTLE AROUND HONEST CITIZENS LIKE THESE.
SHIBAINU
ARE WE GONNA HAVE A PROBLEM HERE?

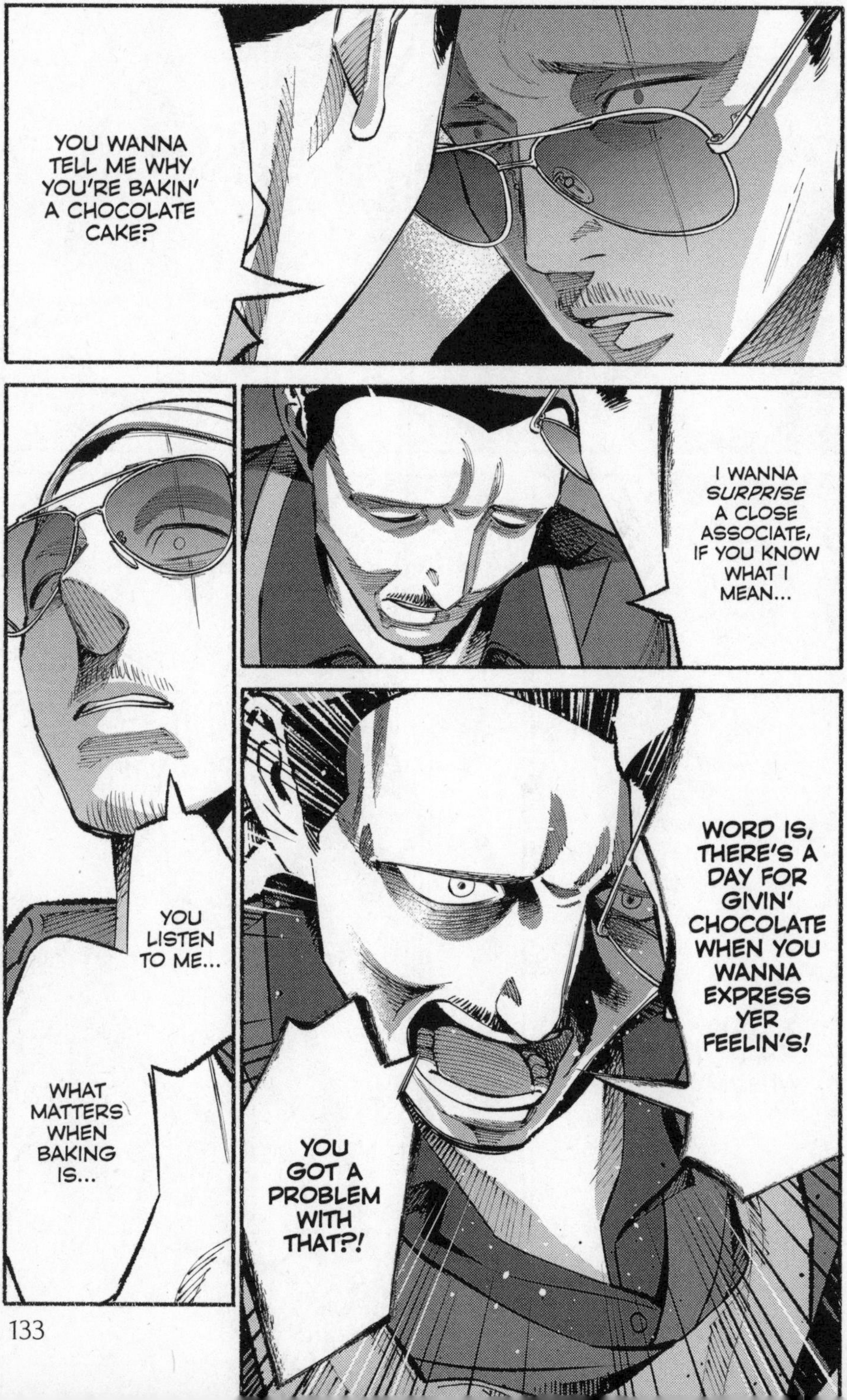
YOU WANNA TELL ME WHY YOU'RE BAKIN' A CHOCOLATE CAKE?
I WANNA *SURPRISE* A CLOSE ASSOCIATE, IF YOU KNOW WHAT I MEAN...
WORD IS, THERE'S A DAY FOR GIVIN' CHOCOLATE WHEN YOU WANNA EXPRESS YER FEELIN'S!
YOU GOT A PROBLEM WITH THAT?!
YOU LISTEN TO ME...
WHAT MATTERS WHEN BAKING IS...

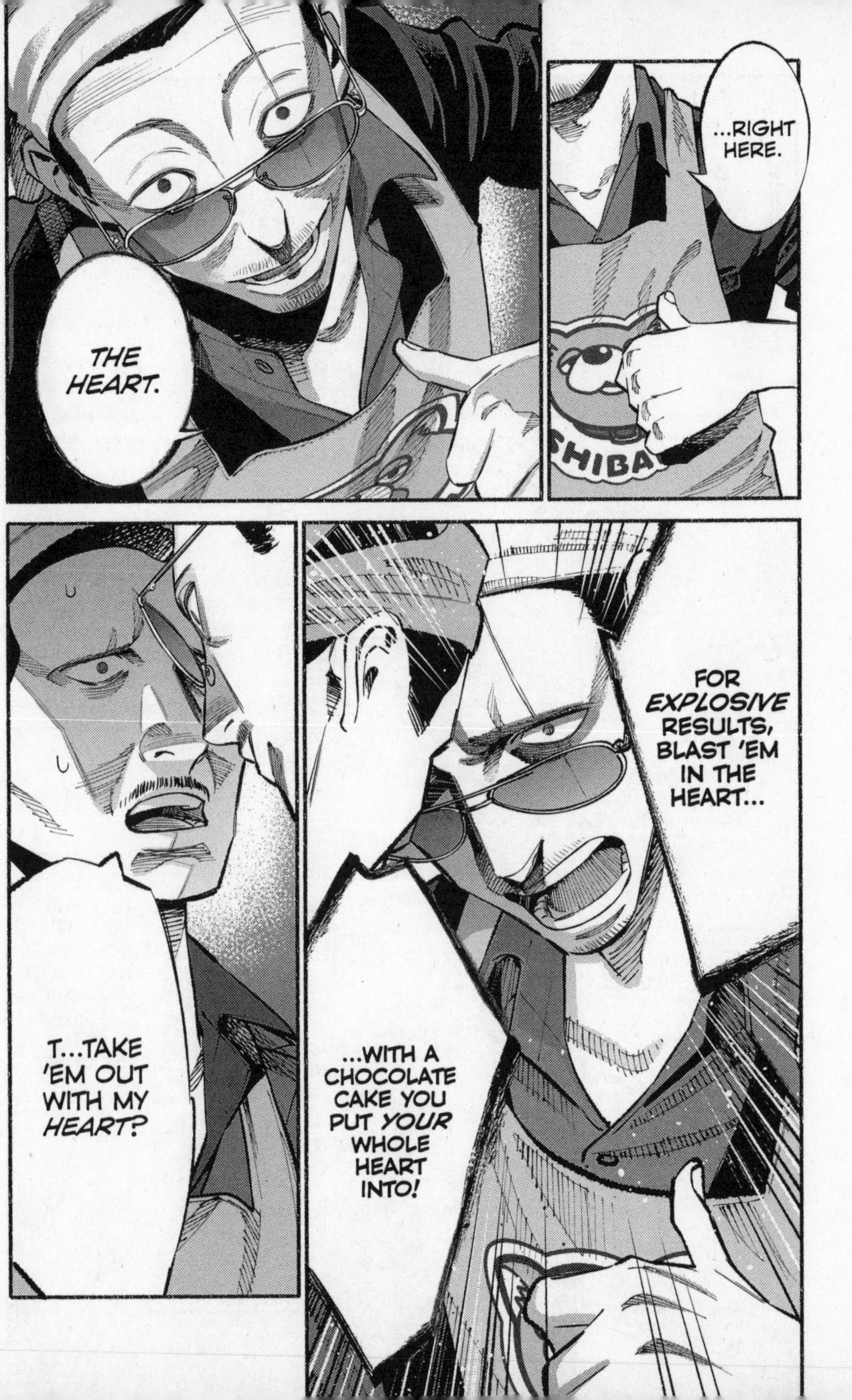
...RIGHT HERE.
SHIBA
THE HEART.
FOR EXPLOSIVE RESULTS, BLAST 'EM IN THE HEART...
...WITH A CHOCOLATE CAKE YOU PUT YOUR WHOLE HEART INTO!
T...TAKE 'EM OUT WITH MY HEART?

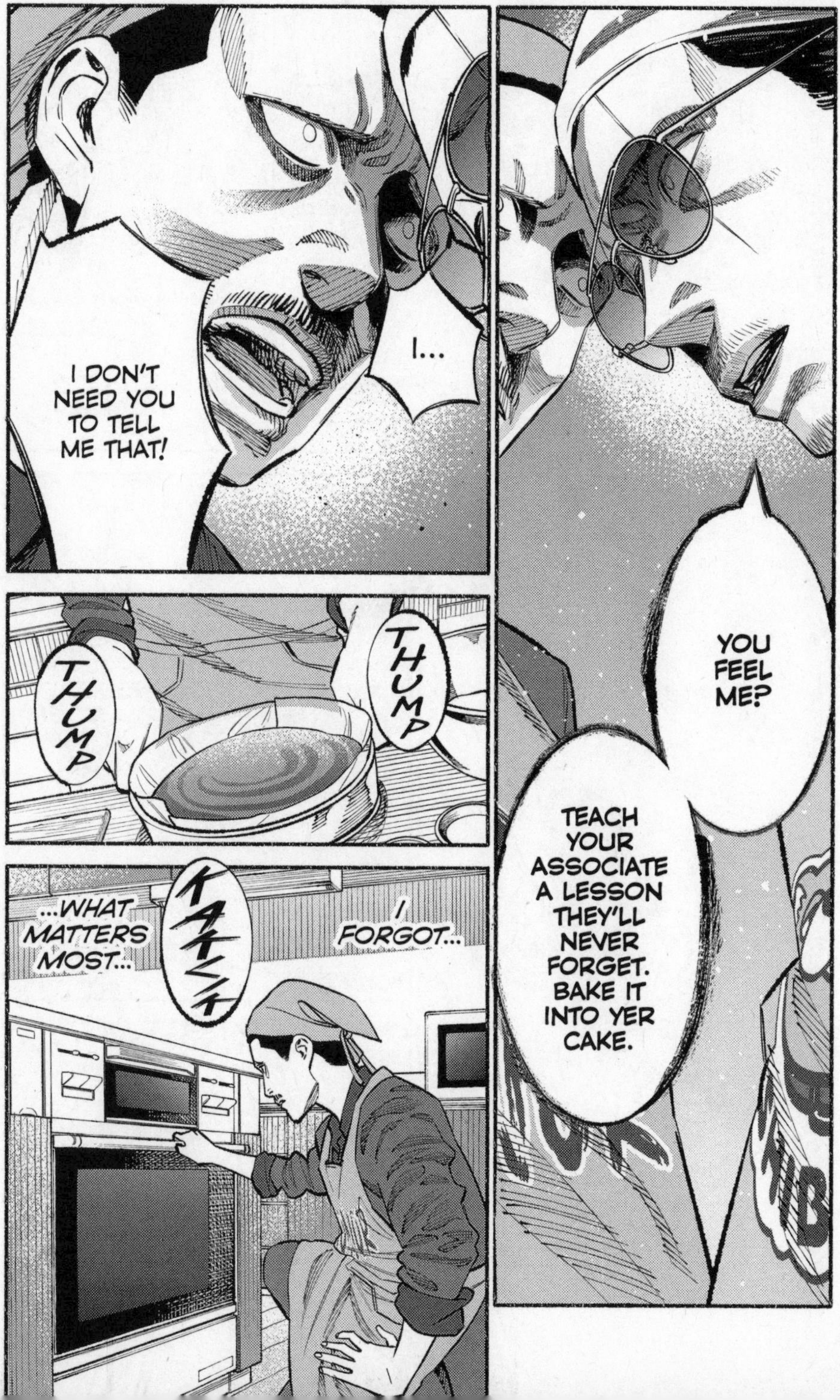
YOU FEEL ME?
TEACH YOUR ASSOCIATE A LESSON THEY'LL NEVER FORGET. BAKE IT INTO YER CAKE.
I...
I DON'T NEED YOU TO TELL ME THAT!
THUMP
THUMP
I FORGOT...
...WHAT MATTERS MOST...

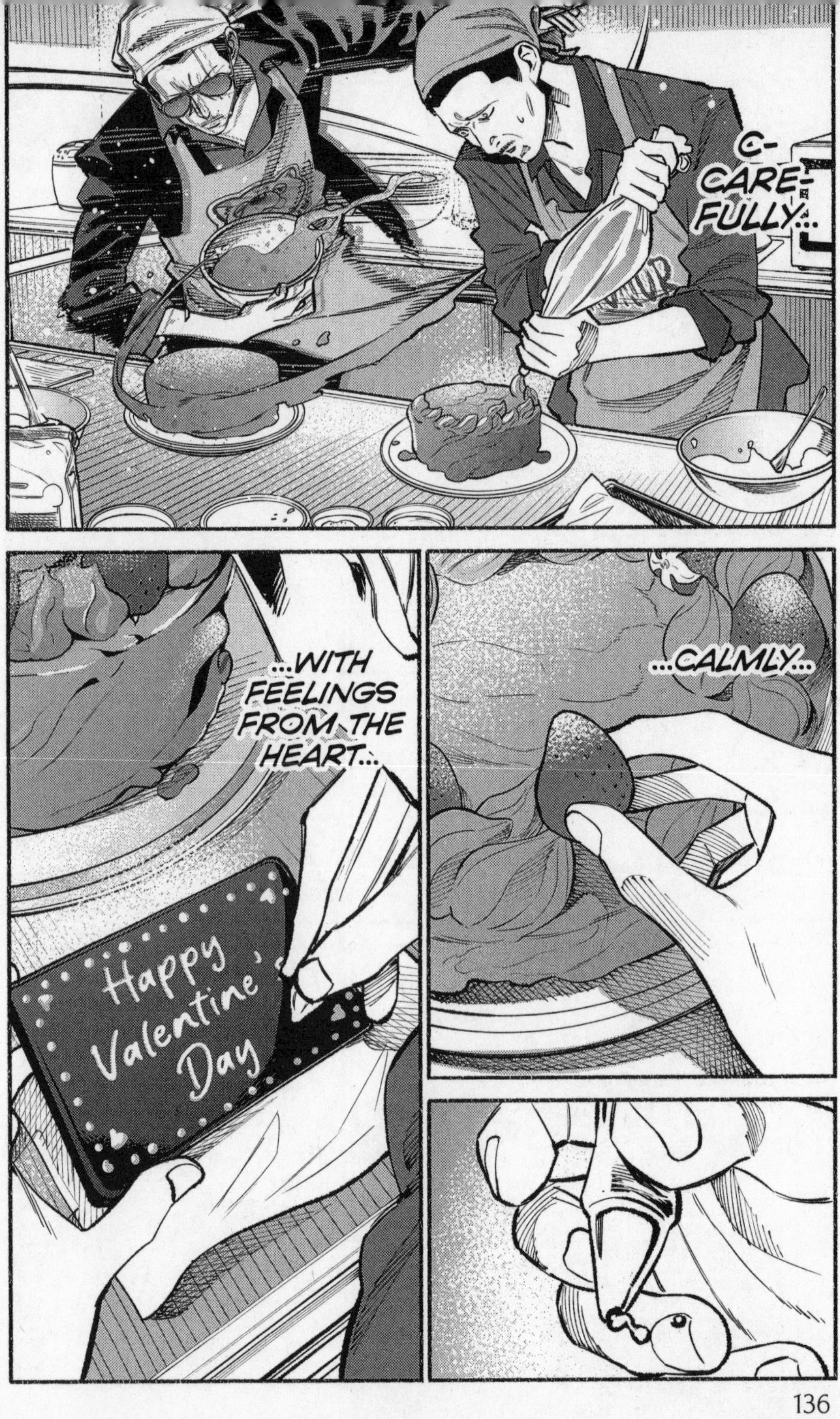
C-CAREFULLY...
...CALMLY...
...WITH FEELINGS FROM THE HEART...
Happy Valentine's Day

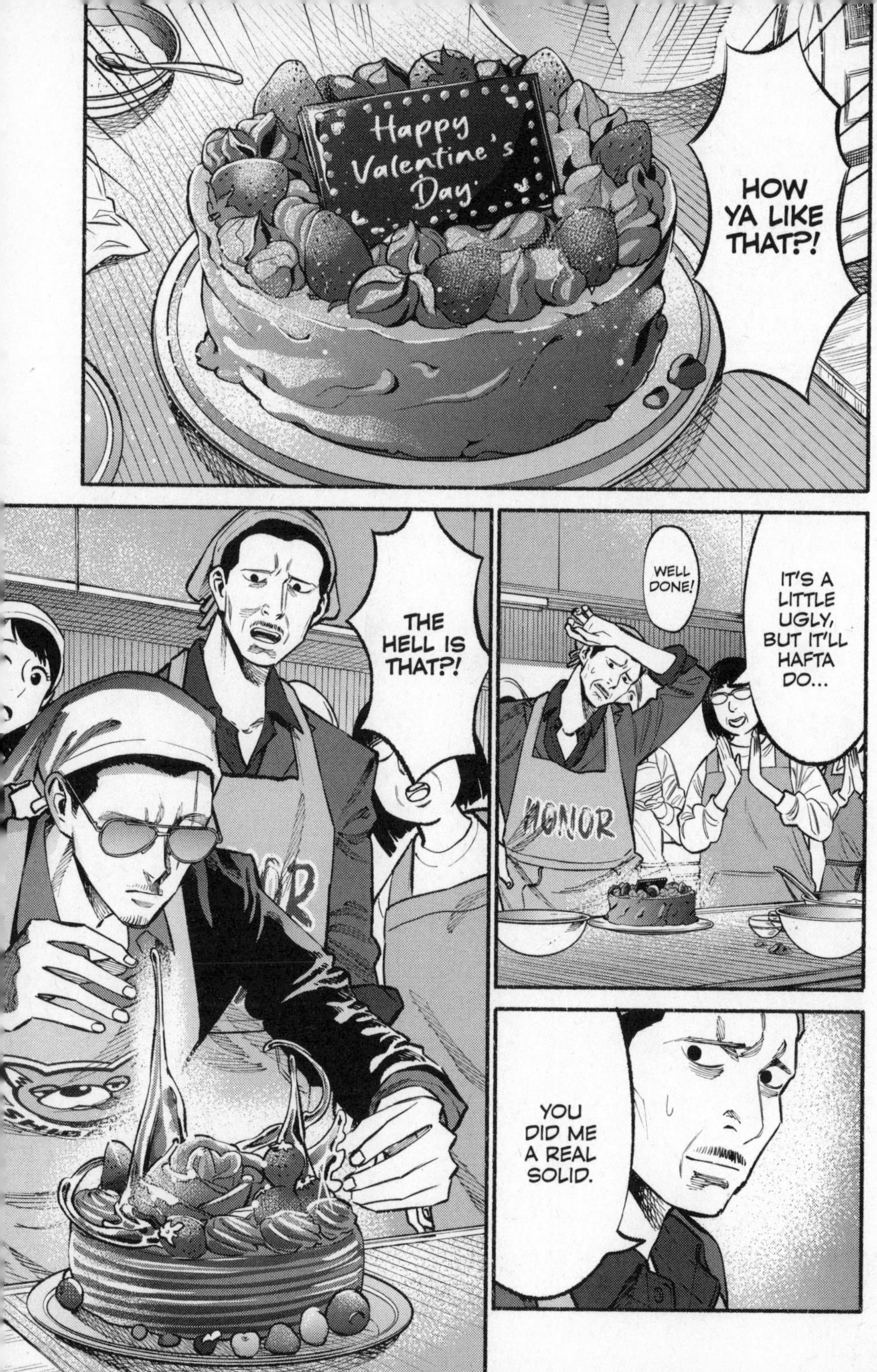
Happy Valentine's Day
HOW YA LIKE THAT?!
IT'S A LITTLE UGLY, BUT IT'LL HAFTA DO...
WELL DONE!
HONOR
YOU DID ME A REAL SOLID.
THE HELL IS THAT?!
HONOR

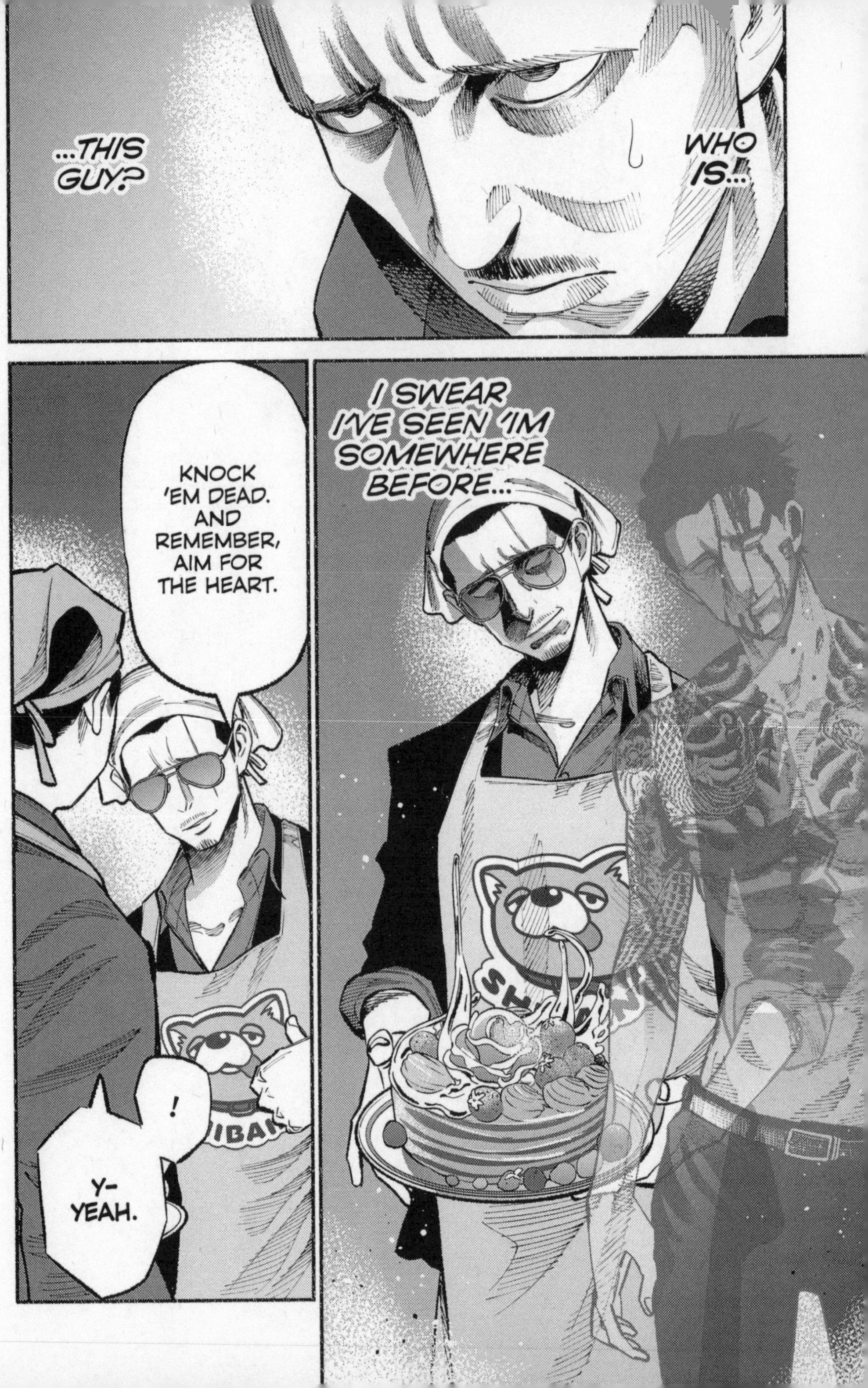
WHO IS...
...THIS GUY?
I SWEAR I'VE SEEN 'IM SOMEWHERE BEFORE...
KNOCK 'EM DEAD. AND REMEMBER, AIM FOR THE HEART.
!
Y-YEAH.

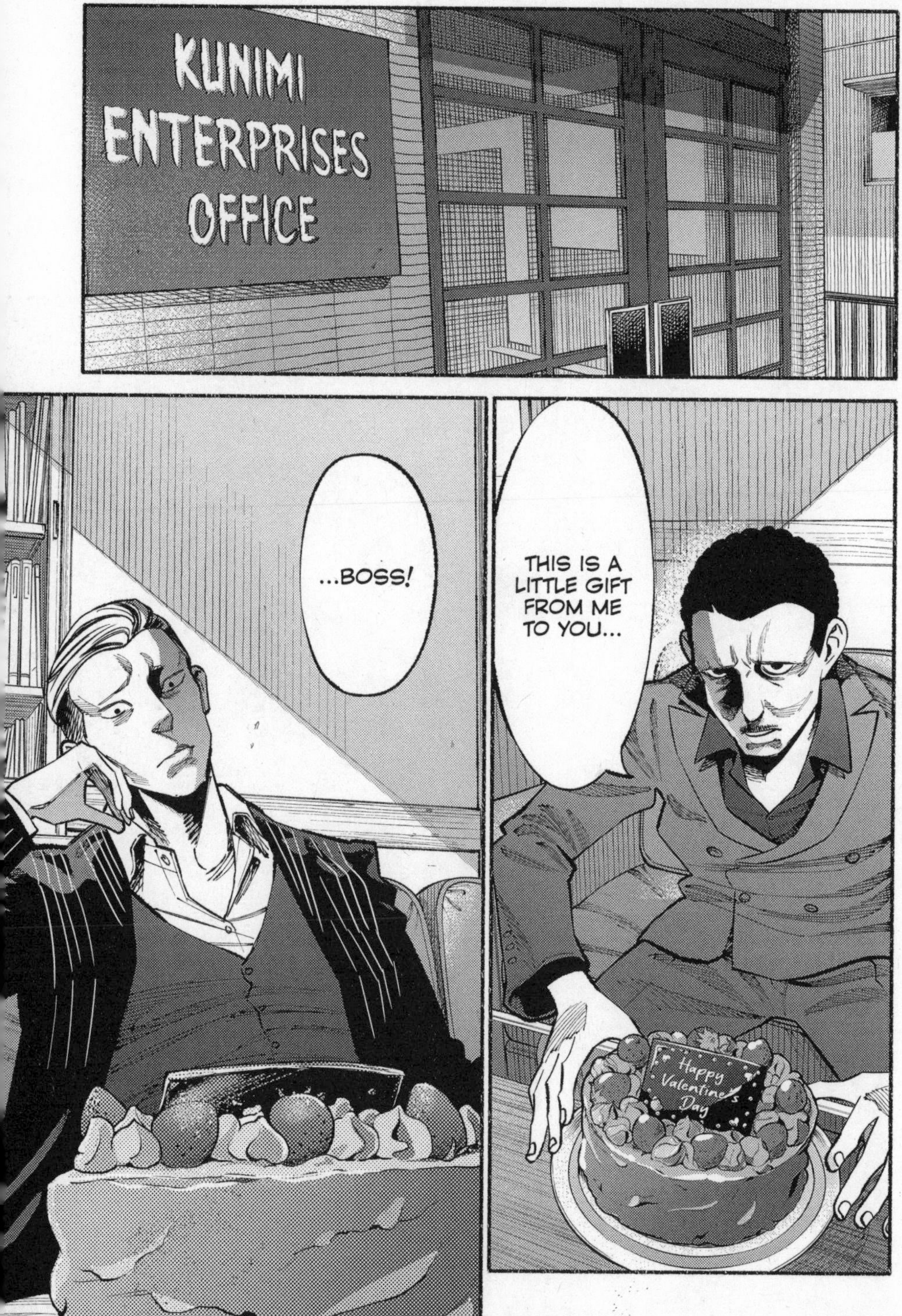
KUNIMI ENTERPRISES OFFICE
THIS IS A LITTLE GIFT FROM ME TO YOU...
Happy Valentine's Day
...BOSS!

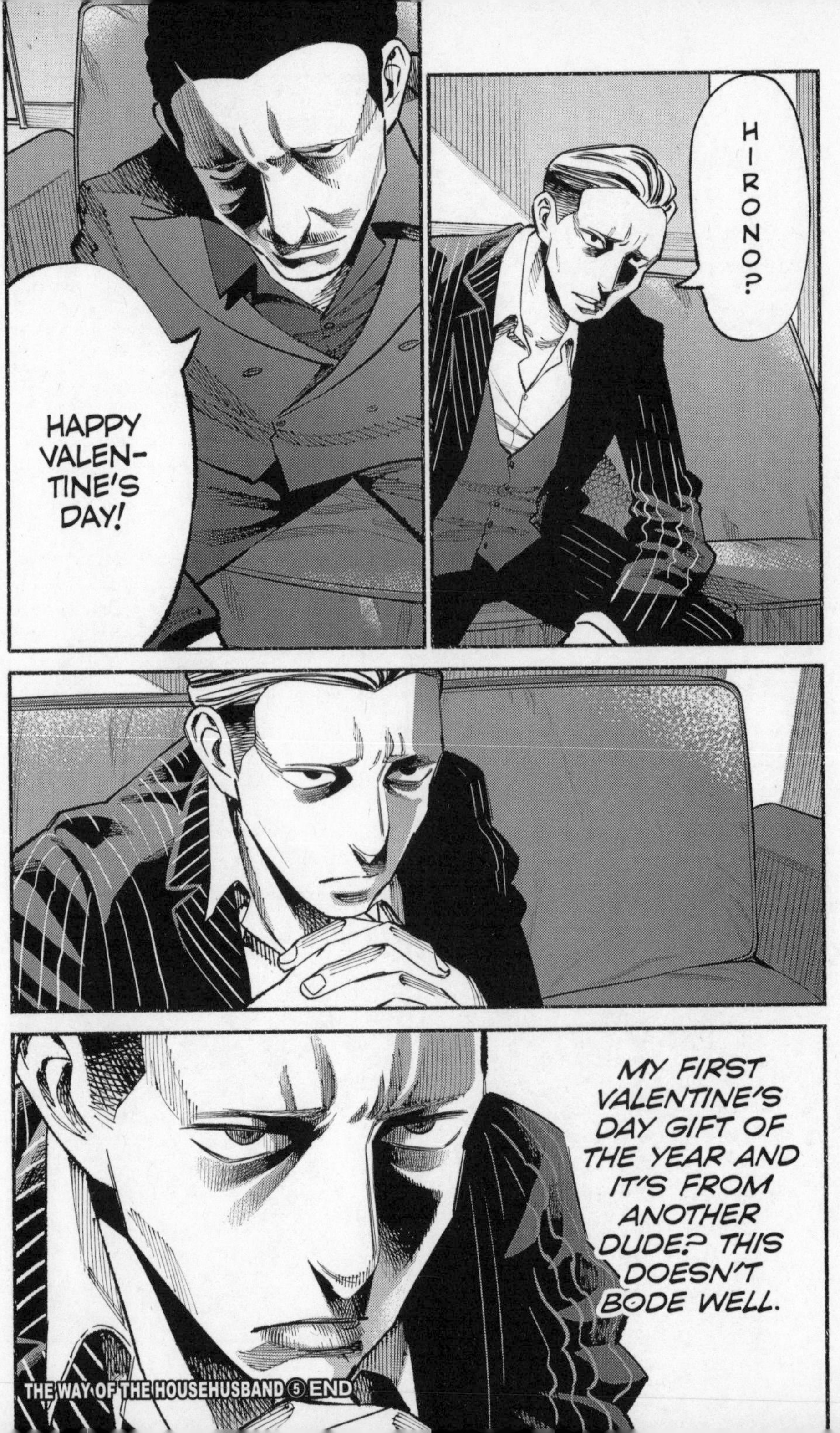
HIRONO?
HAPPY VALEN-TINE'S DAY!
MY FIRST VALENTINE'S DAY GIFT OF THE YEAR AND IT'S FROM ANOTHER DUDE? THIS DOESN'T BODE WELL.
THE WAY OF THE HOUSEHUSBAND 5 END

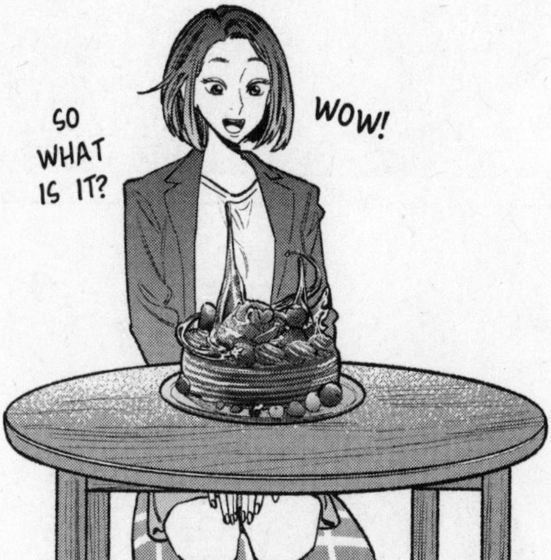
WOW!
SO WHAT IS IT?

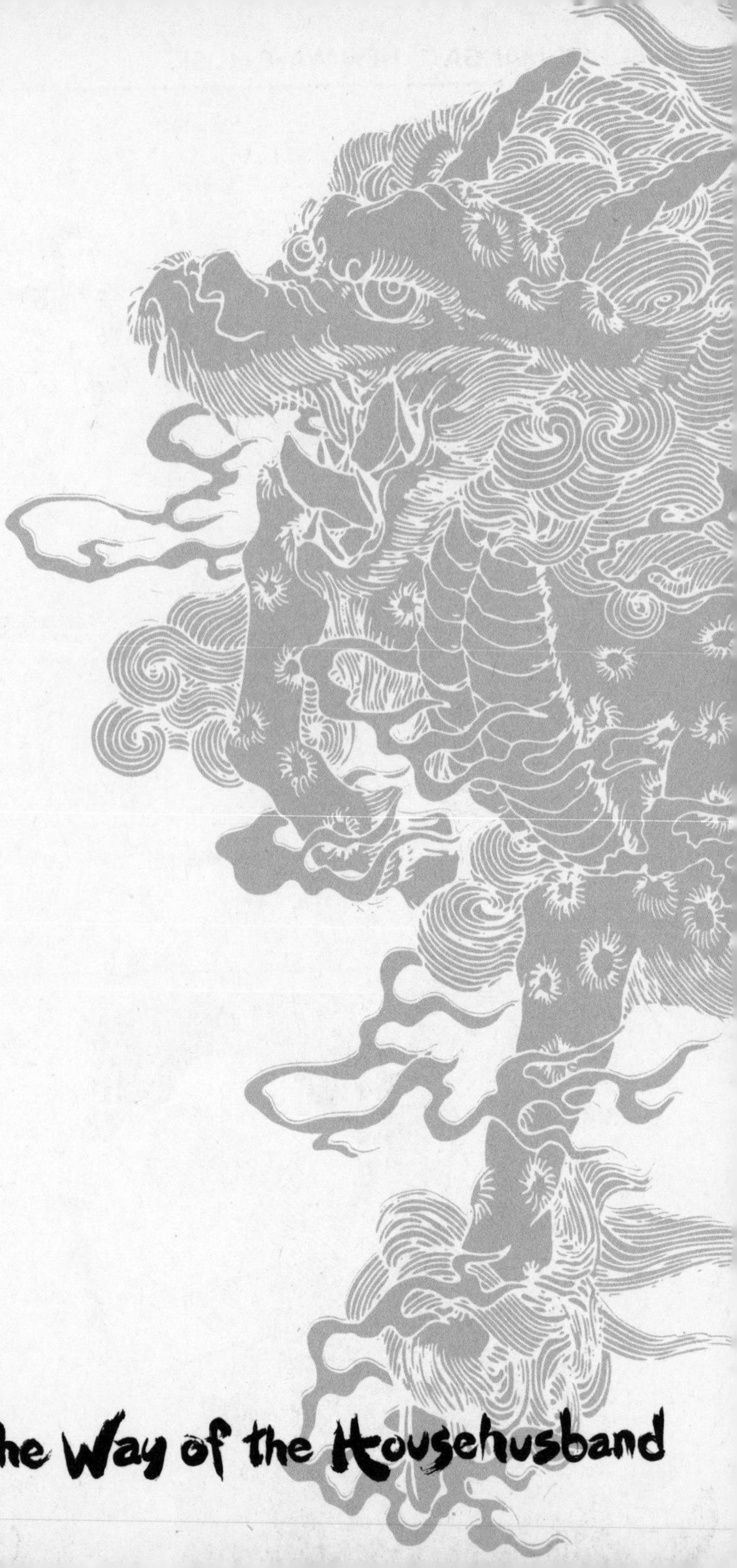

The Way of the Househusband

BONUS MANGA ① NEW WAVE MUSIC

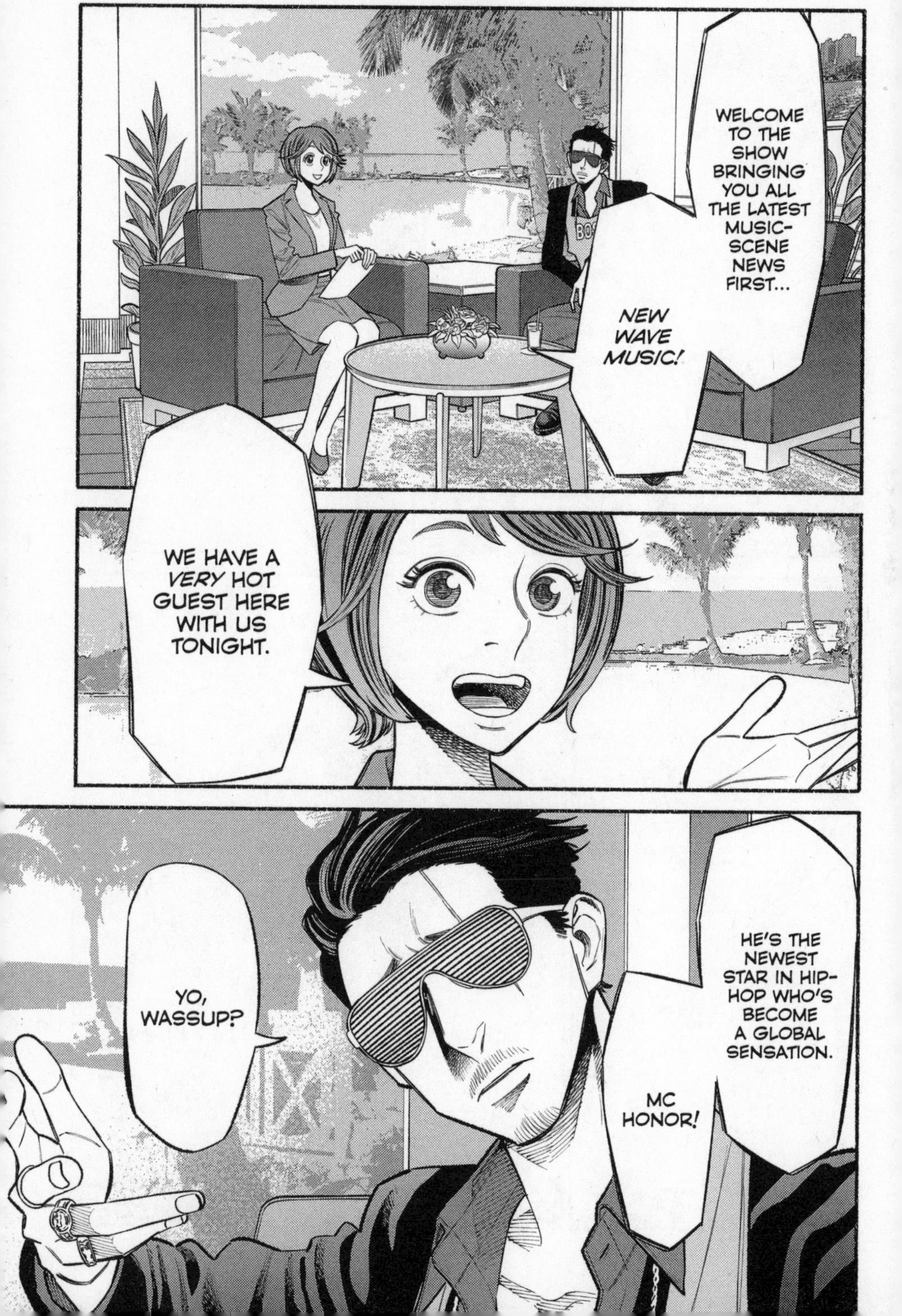
WELCOME TO THE SHOW BRINGING YOU ALL THE LATEST MUSIC-SCENE NEWS FIRST...
NEW WAVE MUSIC!
WE HAVE A VERY HOT GUEST HERE WITH US TONIGHT.
HE'S THE NEWEST STAR IN HIP-HOP WHO'S BECOME A GLOBAL SENSATION.
MC HONOR!
YO, WASSUP?

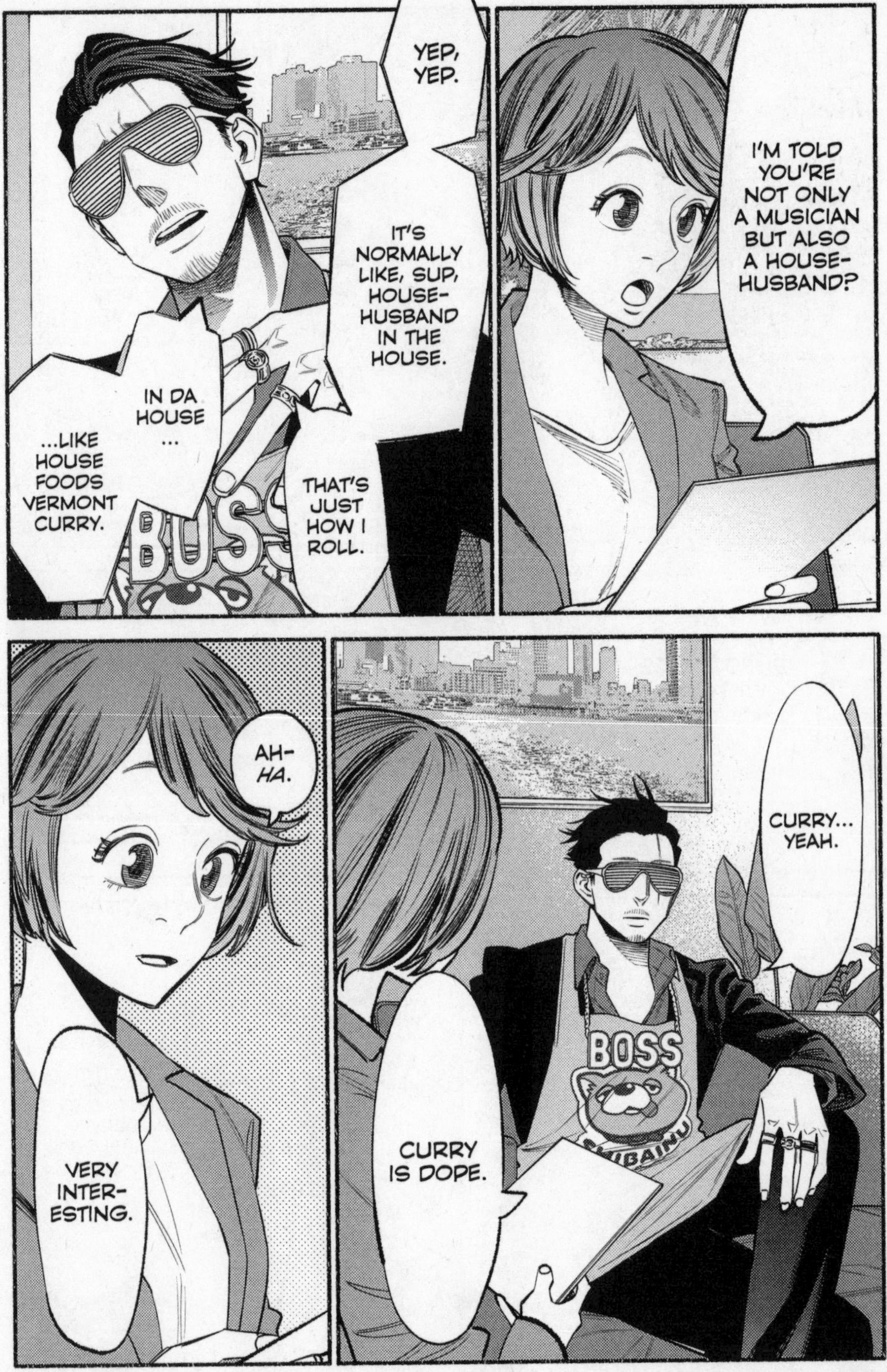
I'M TOLD YOU'RE NOT ONLY A MUSICIAN BUT ALSO A HOUSE-HUSBAND?
YEP, YEP.
IT'S NORMALLY LIKE, SUP, HOUSE-HUSBAND IN THE HOUSE.
THAT'S JUST HOW I ROLL.
IN DA HOUSE ...
...LIKE HOUSE FOODS VERMONT CURRY.
BOSS
CURRY... YEAH.
CURRY IS DOPE.
BOSS
AH-*HA*.
VERY INTER-ESTING.

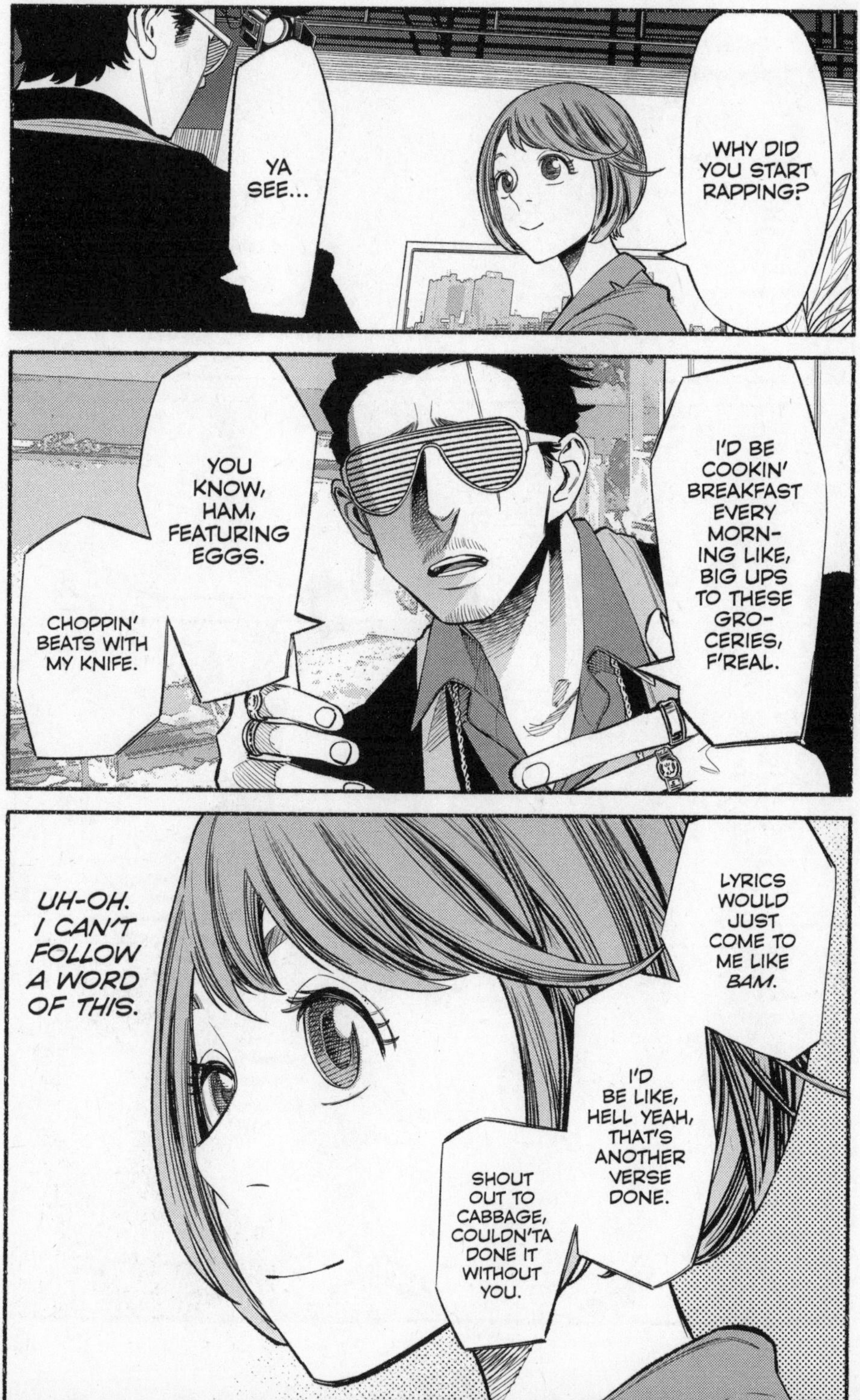
WHY DID YOU START RAPPING?
YA SEE...
I'D BE COOKIN' BREAKFAST EVERY MORNING LIKE, BIG UPS TO THESE GROCERIES, F'REAL.
YOU KNOW, HAM, FEATURING EGGS.
CHOPPIN' BEATS WITH MY KNIFE.
LYRICS WOULD JUST COME TO ME LIKE *BAM*.
I'D BE LIKE, HELL YEAH, THAT'S ANOTHER VERSE DONE.
SHOUT OUT TO CABBAGE, COULDN'TA DONE IT WITHOUT YOU.
UH-OH. I CAN'T FOLLOW A WORD OF THIS.

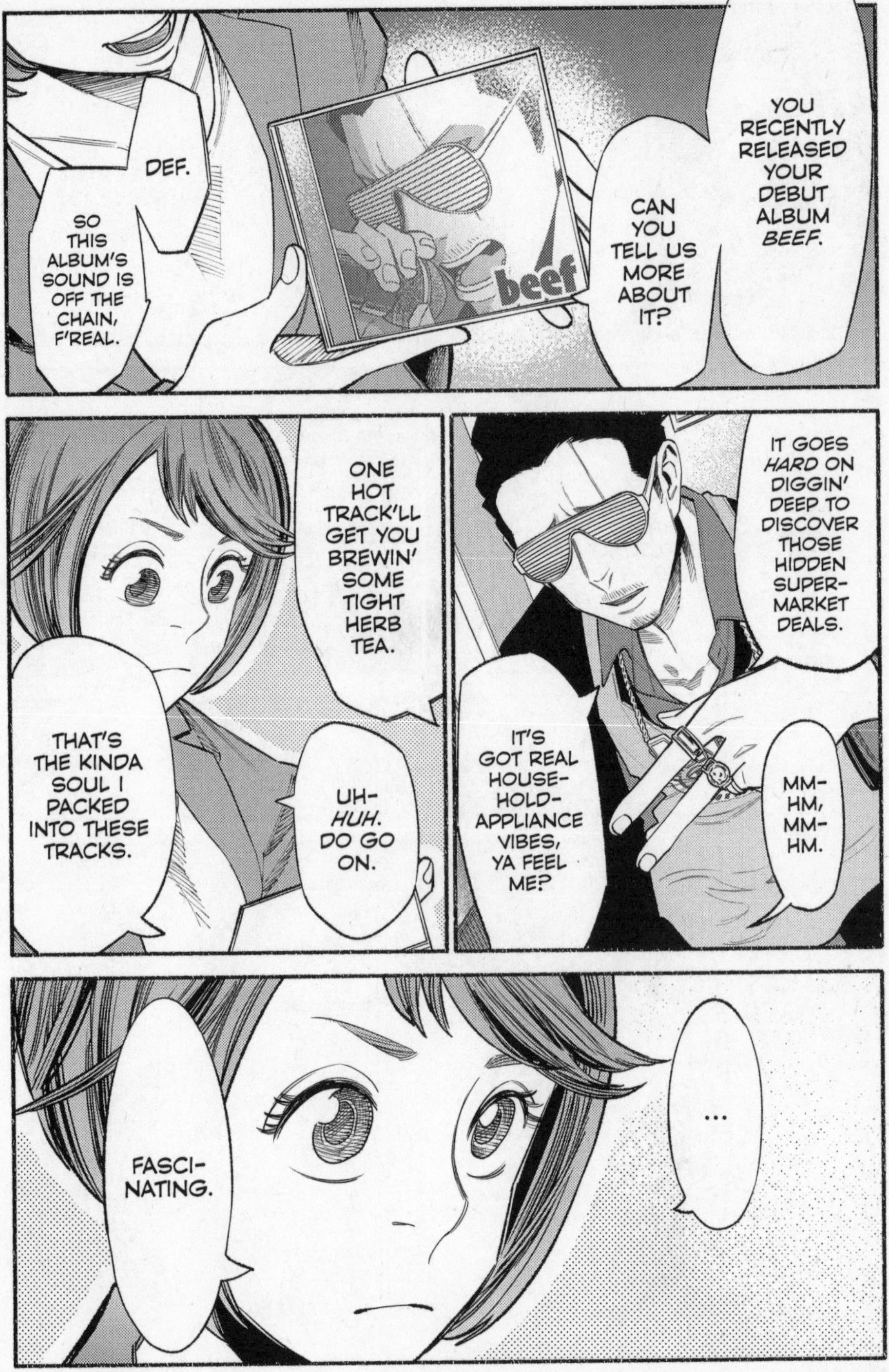
YOU RECENTLY RELEASED YOUR DEBUT ALBUM *BEEF*.
CAN YOU TELL US MORE ABOUT IT?
beef
DEF.
SO THIS ALBUM'S SOUND IS OFF THE CHAIN, F'REAL.
IT GOES *HARD* ON DIGGIN' DEEP TO DISCOVER THOSE HIDDEN SUPERMARKET DEALS.
MM-HM, MM-HM.
IT'S GOT REAL HOUSEHOLD-APPLIANCE VIBES, YA FEEL ME?
ONE HOT TRACK'LL GET YOU BREWIN' SOME TIGHT HERB TEA.
UH-*HUH*. DO GO ON.
THAT'S THE KINDA SOUL I PACKED INTO THESE TRACKS.
...
FASCINATING.

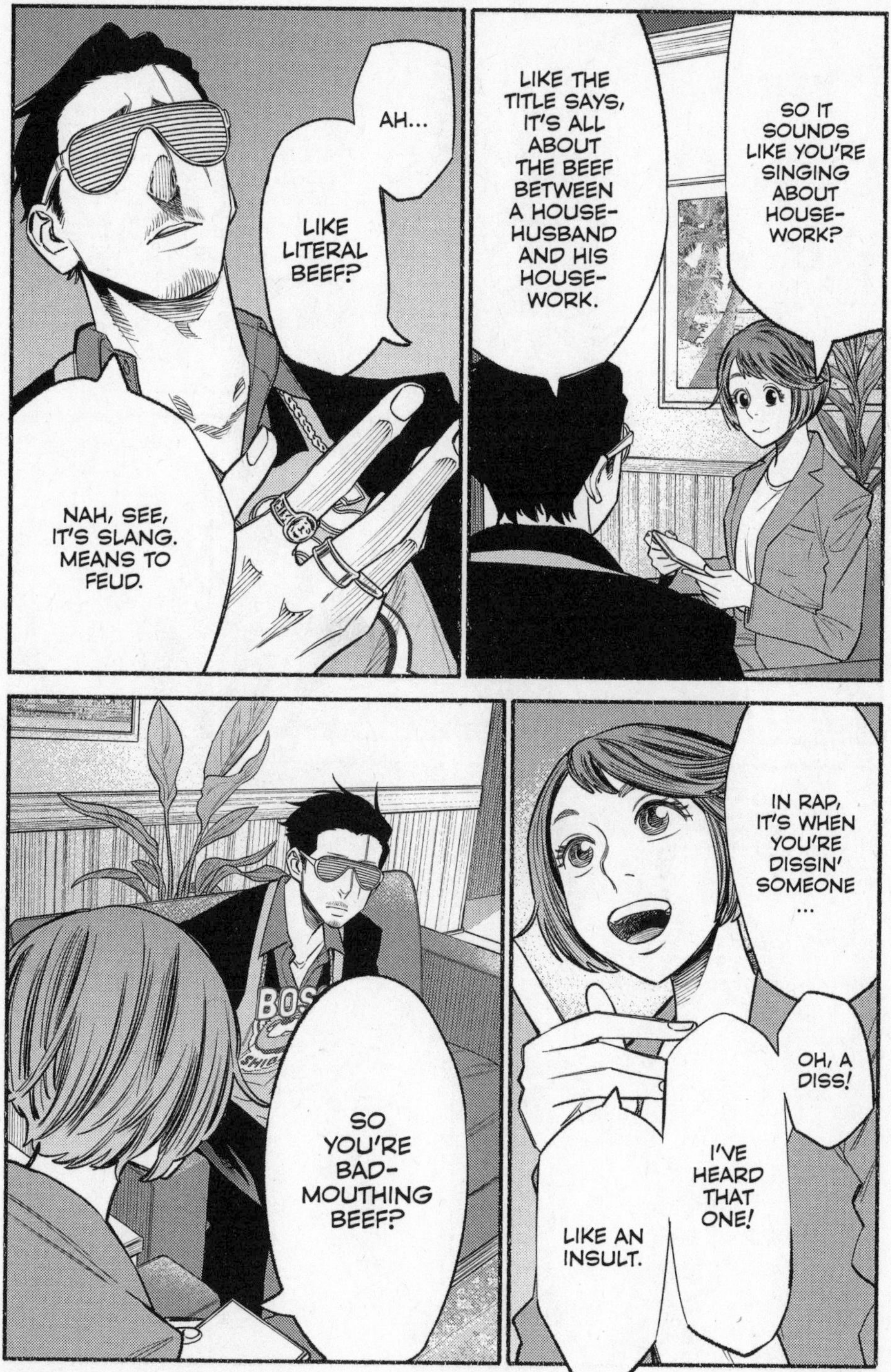
SO IT SOUNDS LIKE YOU'RE SINGING ABOUT HOUSE-WORK?
LIKE THE TITLE SAYS, IT'S ALL ABOUT THE BEEF BETWEEN A HOUSE-HUSBAND AND HIS HOUSE-WORK.
AH...
LIKE LITERAL BEEF?
NAH, SEE, IT'S SLANG. MEANS TO FEUD.
IN RAP, IT'S WHEN YOU'RE DISSIN' SOMEONE ...
OH, A DISS!
I'VE HEARD THAT ONE!
LIKE AN INSULT.
SO YOU'RE BAD-MOUTHING BEEF?

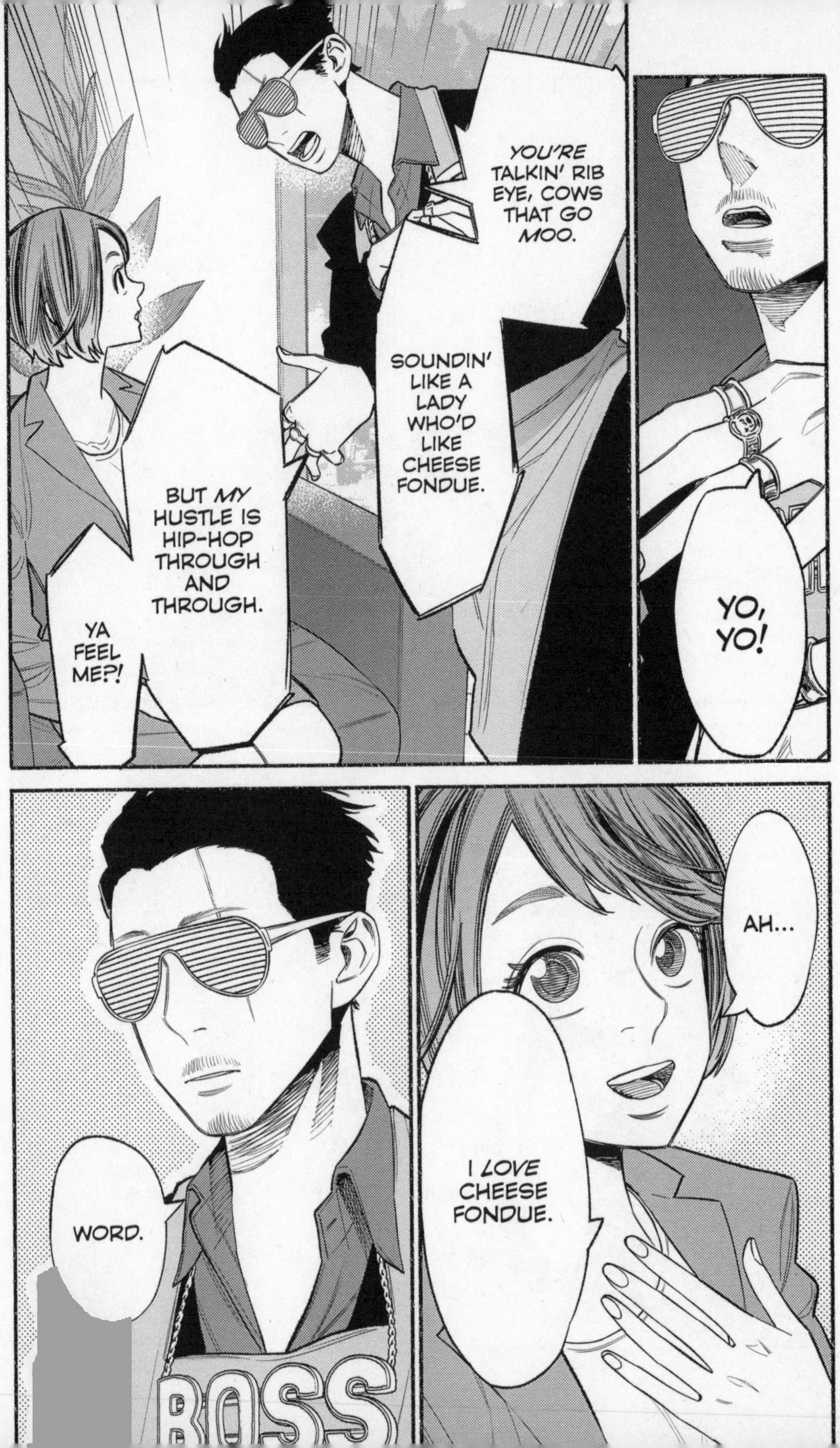
YO, YO!
YOU'RE TALKIN' RIB EYE, COWS THAT GO *MOO*.
SOUNDIN' LIKE A LADY WHO'D LIKE CHEESE FONDUE.
BUT *MY* HUSTLE IS HIP-HOP THROUGH AND THROUGH.
YA FEEL ME?!
AH...
I *LOVE* CHEESE FONDUE.
WORD.
BOSS

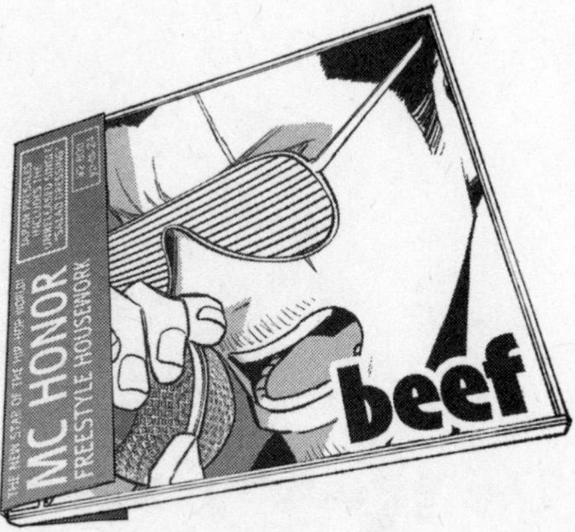
THE NEW STAR OF THE HIP HOP WORLD!
MC HONOR
FREESTYLE HOUSEWORK
beef

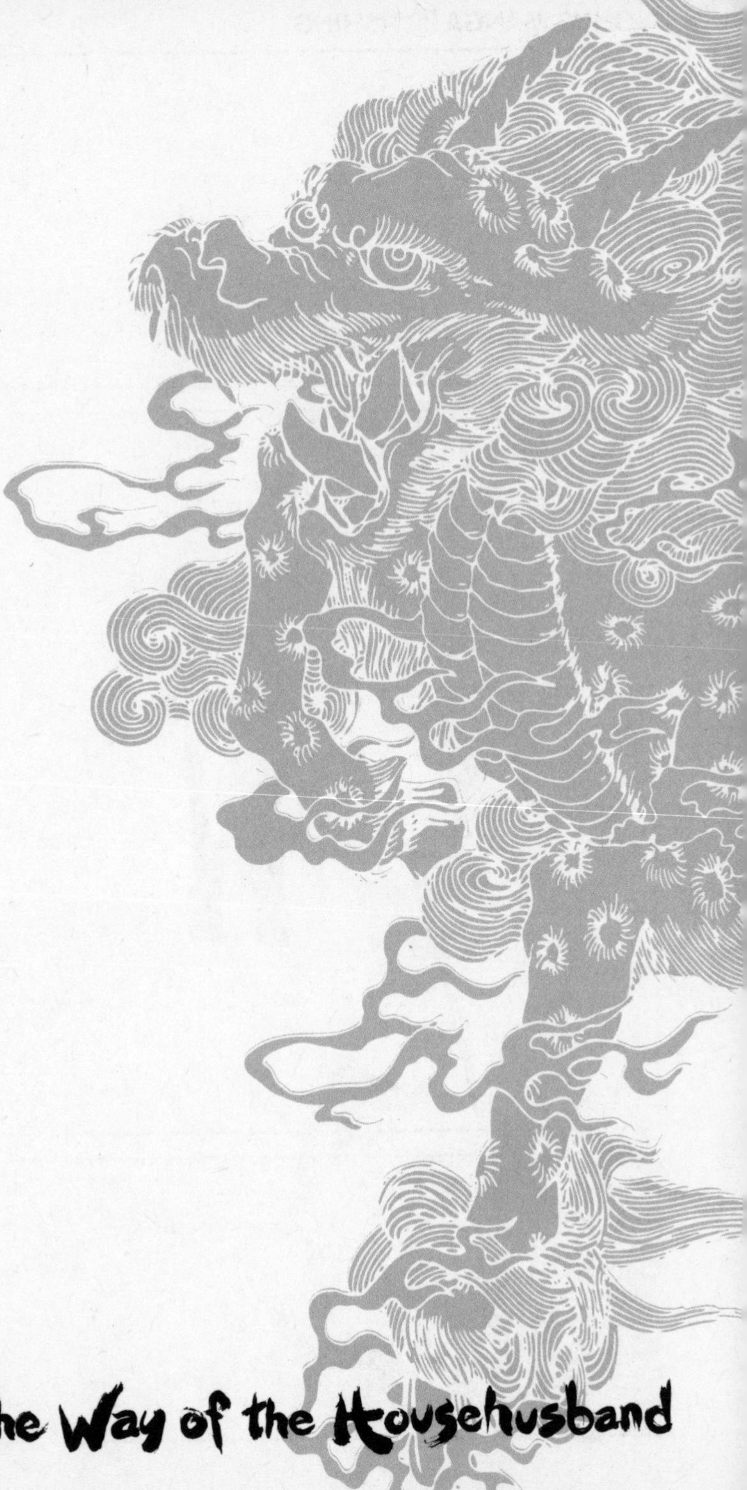

The Way of the Househusband

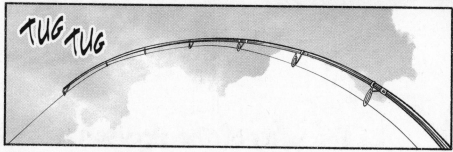

TUG TUG

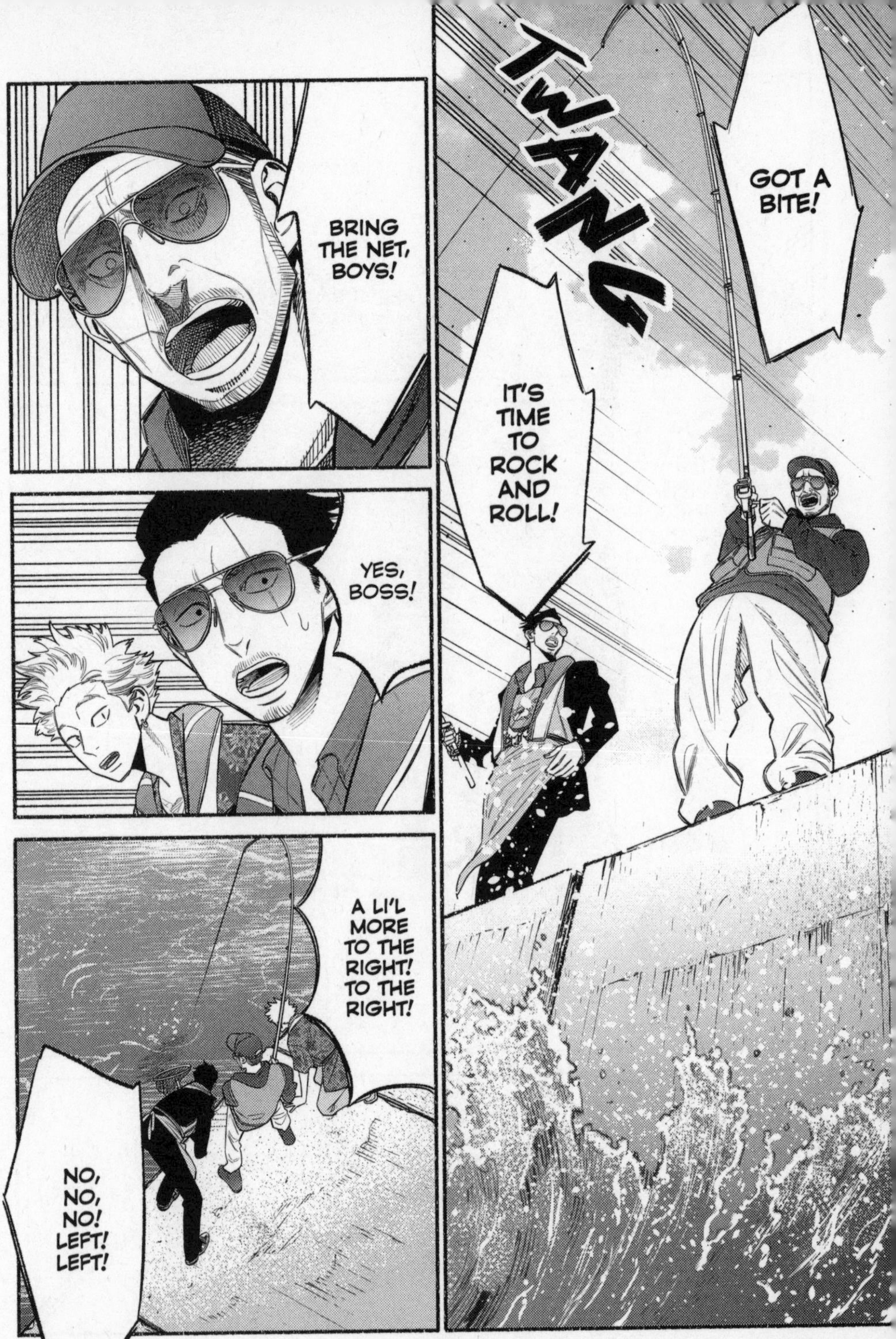
TWANG
GOT A BITE!
IT'S TIME TO ROCK AND ROLL!
BRING THE NET, BOYS!
YES, BOSS!
A LI'L MORE TO THE RIGHT! TO THE RIGHT!
NO, NO, NO! LEFT! LEFT!

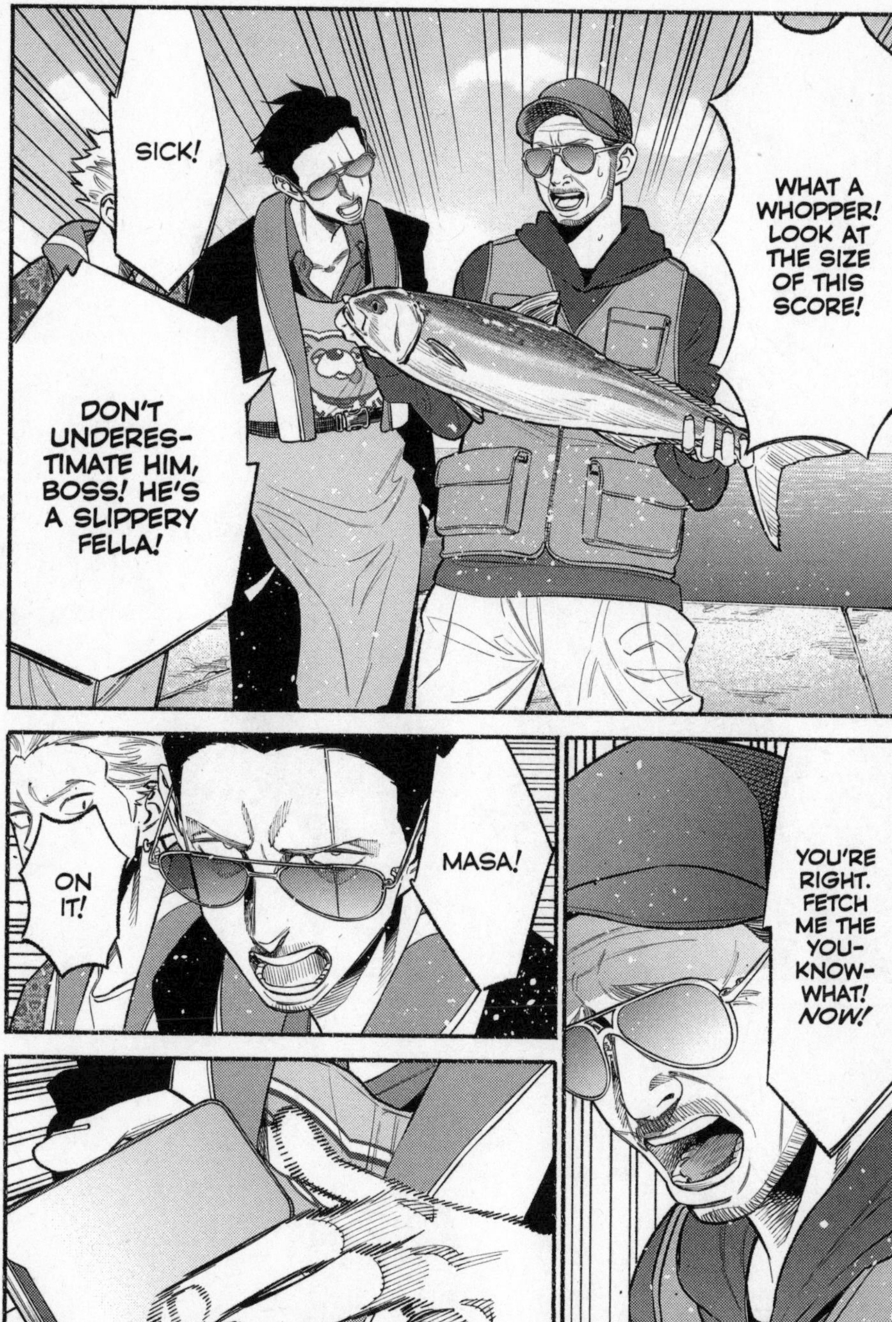
WHAT A WHOPPER! LOOK AT THE SIZE OF THIS SCORE!
SICK!
DON'T UNDERES-TIMATE HIM, BOSS! HE'S A SLIPPERY FELLA!
YOU'RE RIGHT. FETCH ME THE YOU-KNOW-WHAT! *NOW!*
MASA!
ON IT!

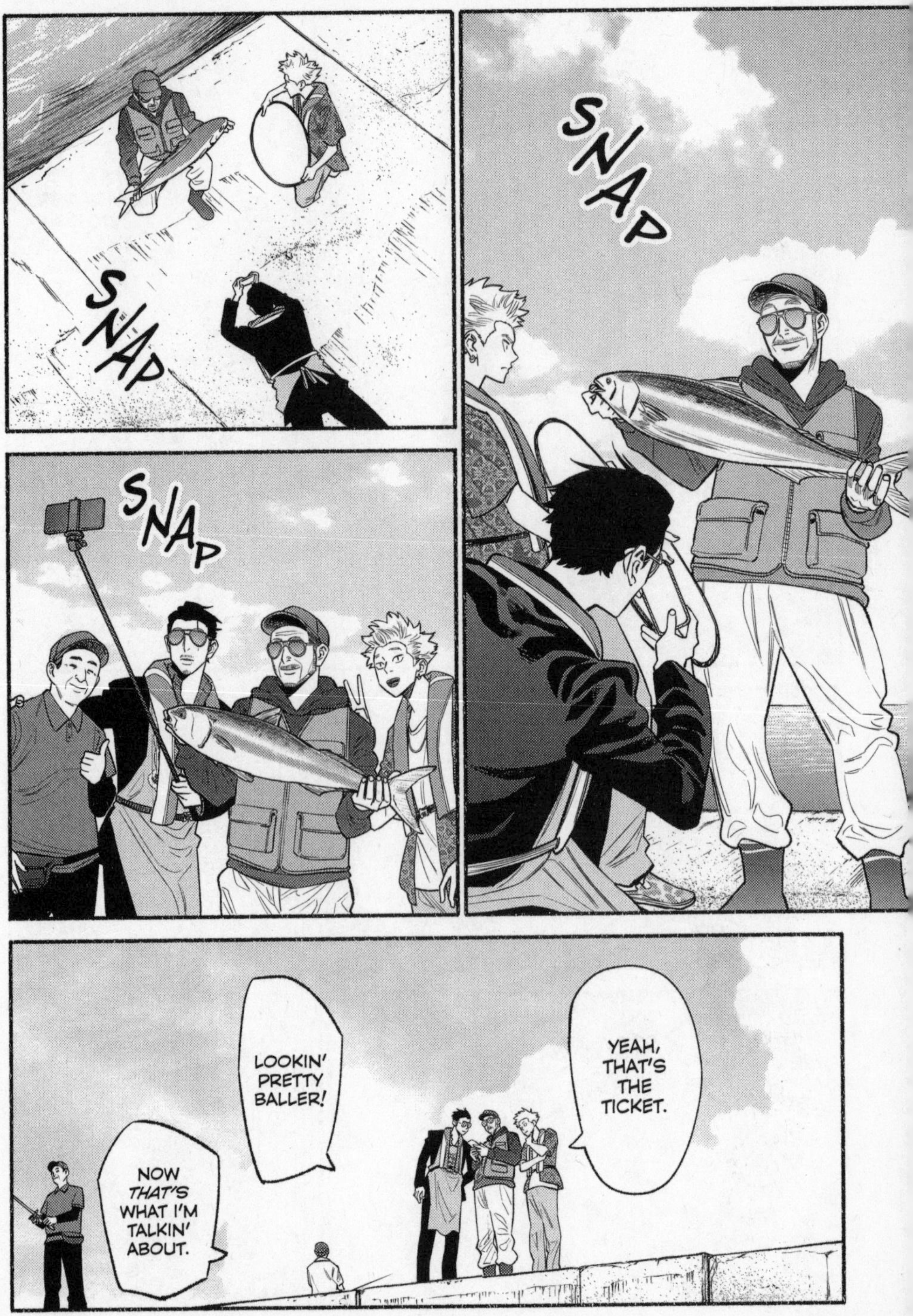
SNAP
SNAP
SNAP
YEAH, THAT'S THE TICKET.
LOOKIN' PRETTY BALLER!
NOW *THAT'S* WHAT I'M TALKIN' ABOUT.

TOTAL
STRANGER
(58)

BONUS MANGA ③ GIN'S WALK ④

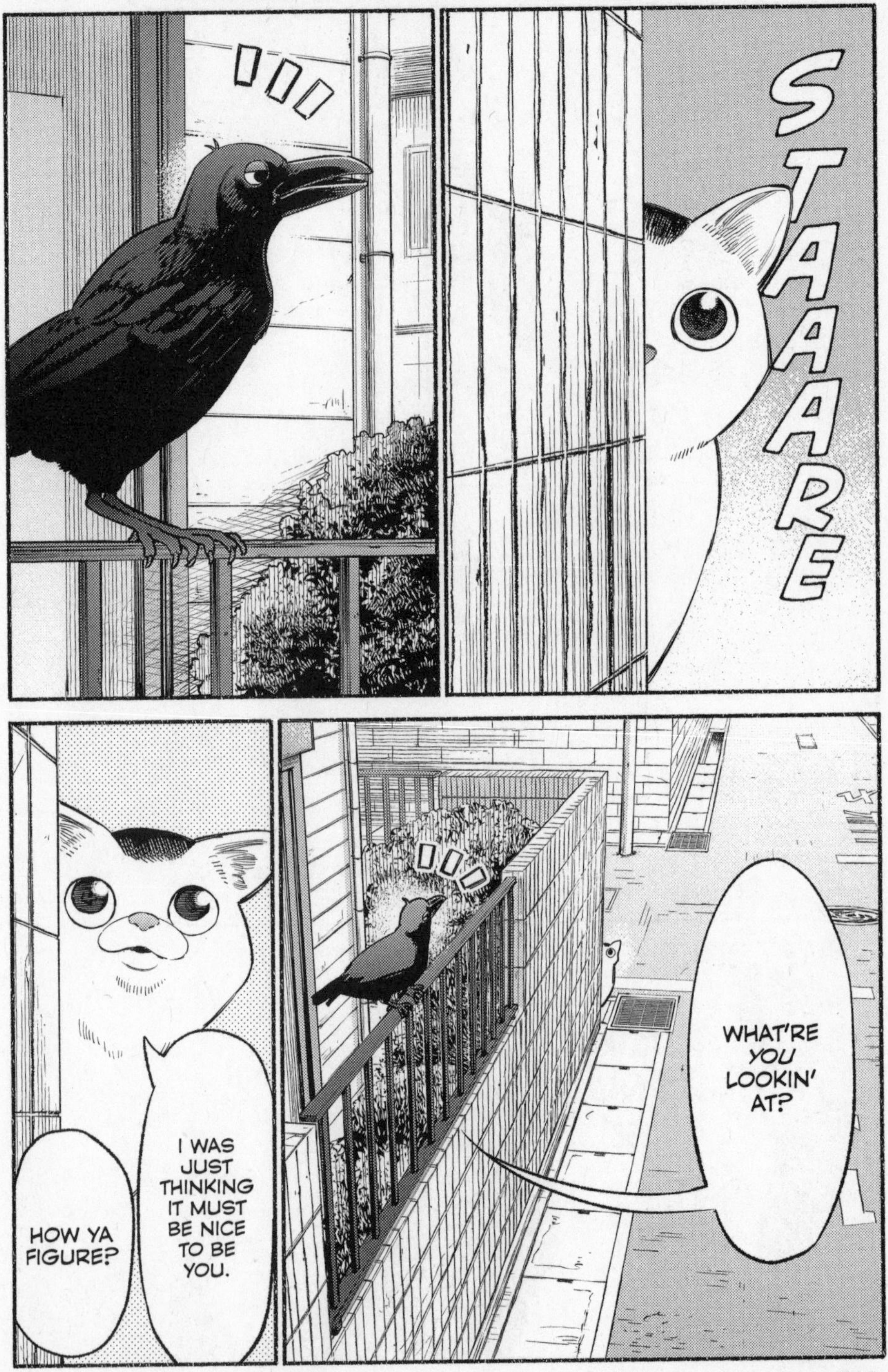
STAAARE
WHAT'RE YOU LOOKIN' AT?
I WAS JUST THINKING IT MUST BE NICE TO BE YOU.
HOW YA FIGURE?

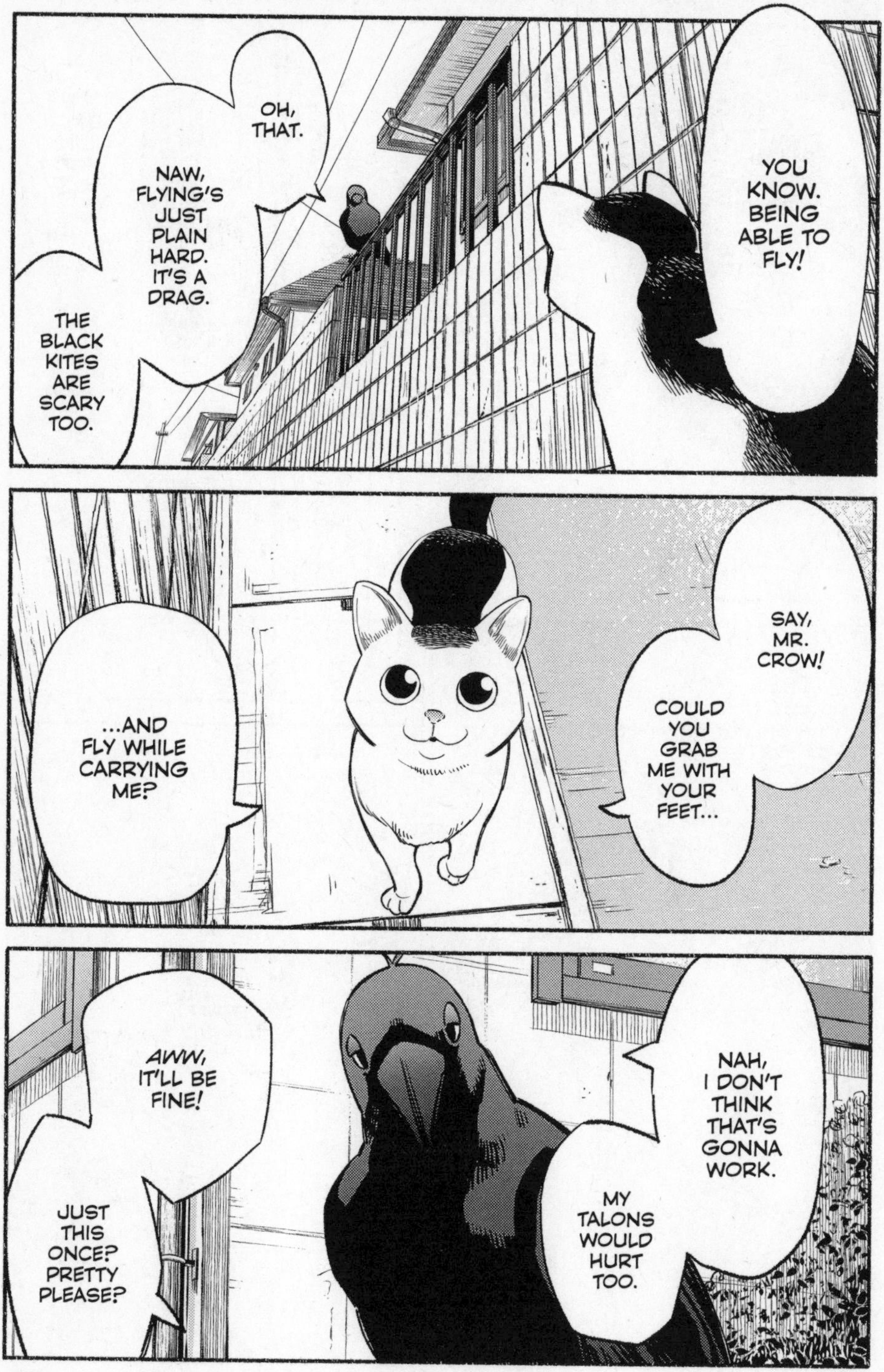
YOU KNOW. BEING ABLE TO FLY!
OH, THAT.
NAW, FLYING'S JUST PLAIN HARD. IT'S A DRAG.
THE BLACK KITES ARE SCARY TOO.
SAY, MR. CROW!
COULD YOU GRAB ME WITH YOUR FEET...
...AND FLY WHILE CARRYING ME?
NAH, I DON'T THINK THAT'S GONNA WORK.
MY TALONS WOULD HURT TOO.
AWW, IT'LL BE FINE!
JUST THIS ONCE? PRETTY PLEASE?

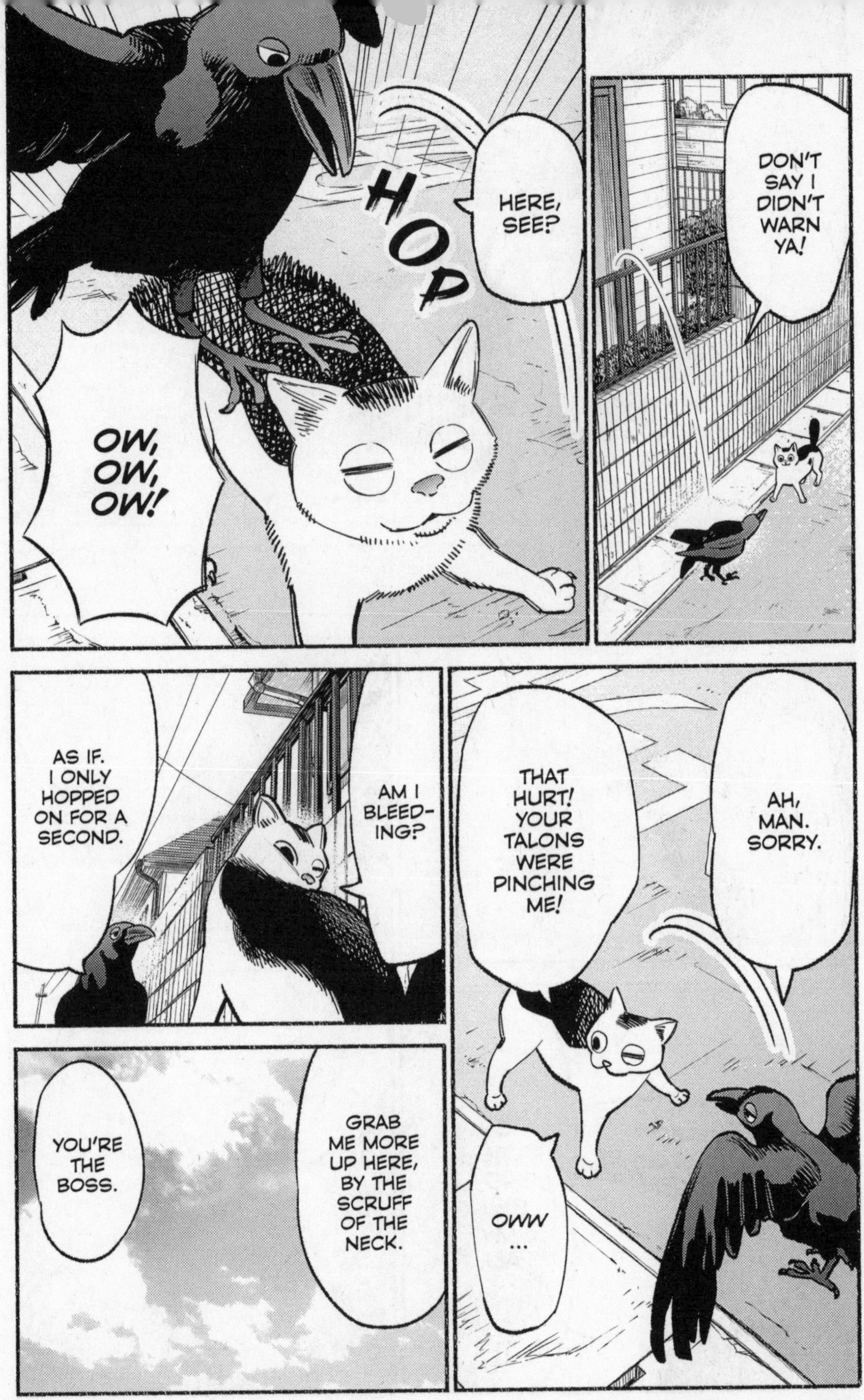
DON'T SAY I DIDN'T WARN YA!
HERE, SEE?
HOP
OW, OW, OW!
AH, MAN. SORRY.
THAT HURT! YOUR TALONS WERE PINCHING ME!
OWW ...
AM I BLEEDING?
AS IF. I ONLY HOPPED ON FOR A SECOND.
GRAB ME MORE UP HERE, BY THE SCRUFF OF THE NECK.
YOU'RE THE BOSS.

THE CROW DID NOTHING WRONG. SURELY. SEE YOU AGAIN IN VOLUME 6.

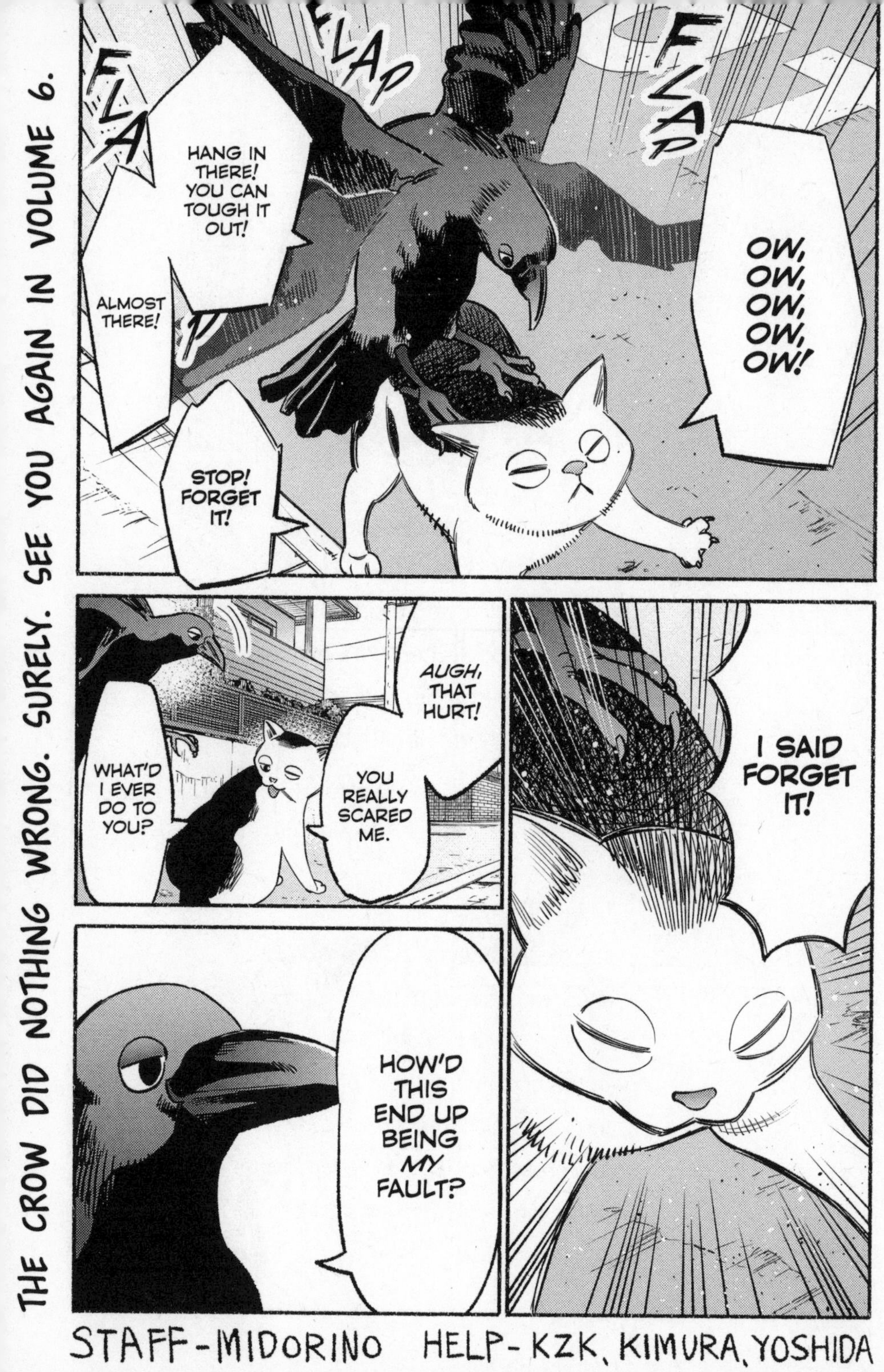
FLAP
FLAP
OW, OW, OW, OW, OW!
FLA
HANG IN THERE! YOU CAN TOUGH IT OUT!
ALMOST THERE!
STOP! FORGET IT!
I SAID FORGET IT!
AUGH, THAT HURT!
YOU REALLY SCARED ME.
WHAT'D I EVER DO TO YOU?
HOW'D THIS END UP BEING *MY* FAULT?

STAFF-MIDORINO HELP-KZK, KIMURA, YOSHIDA

The series has passed the
two-year mark and reached five
volumes. My Shiba Inu has also
passed a mark—the 30 lb. mark—
and is a plump deep-fried tofu
pocket stuffed with sushi rice.

KOUSUKE OONO

Kousuke Oono began his professional
manga career in 2016 in the manga
magazine *Monthly Comics @ Bunch*
with the one-shot "Legend of Music."
Oono's follow-up series, *The Way of
the Househusband*, is the creator's first
serialization as well as his first English-
language release.

The Way of the House Husband

VOLUME 5

VIZ SIGNATURE EDITION

STORY AND ART BY
KOUSUKE OONO

TRANSLATION: Amanda Haley
ENGLISH ADAPTATION: Jennifer LeBlanc
TOUCH-UP ART & LETTERING: Bianca Pistillo
DESIGN: Alice Lewis
EDITOR: Jennifer LeBlanc

GOKUSHUFUDO volume 5
© Kousuke Oono 2018
All Rights Reserved
English translation rights arranged
with SHINCHOSHA PUBLISHING CO.
through Tuttle-Mori Agency, Inc, Tokyo

Printed in the U.S.A.

Published by VIZ Media, LLC
P.O. Box 77010
San Francisco, CA 94107

10 9 8 7 6 5 4 3 2
First printing, May 2021
Second printing, May 2021

VIZ MEDIA   **VIZ SIGNATURE**

viz.com   vizsignature.com

Meat Your Maker Theme Song

Lyrics and Composition by: The Butcher

Fried chicken, pork tonkatsu
Getting together for a barbecue

When it comes to meat, you can count on me
Meat Your Maker

Bon bon chicken, twice-cooked pork
Pepper steak

For all your meat purchases, you can always count on me
Meat Your Maker

Chicken and zucchini steamed in white wine
Country-style pork viennoise
Beef fillet and mousseline pâté phyllo

Our meat can't be beat, you can always count on me
Meat Your Maker

YORIKIRI

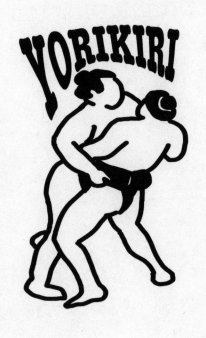

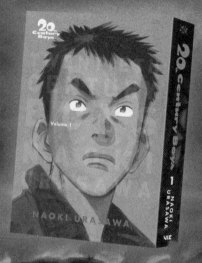